From AI to Zeitgeist

Recent Titles in
Contributions in Psychology

Personality, Power, and Authority: A View from the Behavioral Sciences
Leonard W. Doob

Interactive Counseling
B. Mark Schoenberg and Charles F. Preston, editors

Assessing Sex Bias in Testing: A Review of the Issues and Evaluations
of 74 Psychological and Educational Tests
Paula Selkow

Position and the Nature of Personhood: An Approach to the Understanding
of Persons
Larry Cochran

Ecological Beliefs and Behaviors: Assessment and Change
*David B. Gray in collaboration with Richard J. Borden and
Russell H. Weigel*

Sexuality: New Perspectives
Zira DeFries, Richard C. Friedman, and Ruth Corn, editors

Portrait and Story: Dramaturgical Approaches to the Study of Persons
Larry Cochran

The Meaning of Grief: A Dramaturgical Approach to Understanding Emotion
Larry Cochran and Emily Claspell

New Ideas in Therapy: Introduction to an Interdisciplinary Approach
Douglas H. Ruben and Dennis J. Delprato, editors

Human Consciousness and Its Evolution: A Multidimensional View
Richard W. Coan

FROM AI TO ZEITGEIST

A Philosophical Guide
for the Skeptical Psychologist

N. H. PRONKO

BF
38
,P73
1988
WEST

Contributions in Psychology, Number 11

GREENWOOD PRESS
New York • Westport, Connecticut • London

Library of Congress Cataloging-in-Publication Data

Pronko, N. H. (Nicholas Henry), 1908-
   From AI to Zeitgeist.

   (Contributions in psychology, ISSN 0736-2714 ; no. 11)
   Includes bibliographies and index.
   1. Psychology—Philosophy.   2. Philosophy.
I. Title.   II. Series.
BF38.P73   1988   150'.1   87-14921
ISBN 0-313-25888-0 (lib. bdg. : alk. paper)

British Library Cataloguing in Publication Data is available.

Library of Congress Catalog Card Number: 87-14921
ISBN: 0-313-25888-0
ISSN: 0736-2714

First published in 1988

Greenwood Press, Inc.
88 Post Road West, Westport, Connecticut 06881

Printed in the United States of America

The paper used in this book complies with the
Permanent Paper Standard issued by the National
Information Standards Organization (Z39.48-1984).

10 9 8 7 6 5 4 3 2 1

To my abiding best friend,
constant companion,
and unstinting collaborator

CONTENTS

ILLUSTRATIONS

PREFACE

It is bewildering that the world order of science is able to live comfortably for years, and sometimes centuries, with beliefs that a new generation discovers to be false.

Maclean (1970, p. 337)

What if such a dire fate as Maclean depicts were to befall psychology? Suppose that a future generation of psychologists were to find that we today have been laboring under invalid assumptions or postulates. The mere threat of such a calamity should speed us toward a zealous scrutiny of the basic assumptions that guide our inquiry into human behavior. The present work is a preliminary examination of the consequences for understanding behavior that different assumptions provide. In a nutshell, that's what this book is about, but, first, a word of explanation about the book's title.

From AI to Zeitgeist comprises a series of topics in alphabetical order designed to provide a number of bases from which to view problems, questions, and quandaries bearing on the philosophy of science for psychology. Throughout, my aim has been "to raise new problems, new possibilities, to regard old problems from a new angle. . . . The importance of seeing known facts in a new light will be stressed and new theories described" (Einstein & Infeld, 1966, p. 92).

Next, the term *philosophical*. I use that term in a modest and restricted fashion, divorced from transcendental, metaphysical philosophy, which deals with such verbally created entities as "pure being, "ultimate reality," "absolute truth," "transcendental basics," and other "a prioris" that metaphysicians talk about. Nor do I get involved in such metaphysical questions as whether objects can exist even when we're not looking at them, whether our minds create objects with or without the brain, how minds affect brains or, vice versa, how brains affect minds, and so on.

One can feign indifference to philosophy or even profess rejection of it, yet be inextricably entangled in it. How philosophical assumptions operate silently in scientific activity is revealed in the following insightful comment by Bohm and Welwood (1980, p. 25): "They [scientists] accept the philosophical notions they're accustomed to, and they're so accustomed to them they call them non-philosophical." Many psychologists accept the following propositions without question: the material body is indivisibly linked with the mind; the brain is the seat of consciousness; memory is explained as the result of traces left behind by experiences; stimuli impinge on sense organs, which carry "messages" to the brain or mind, which interprets them. These and other propositions are not recognized as based on traditional assumptions and are treated as never-to-be-questioned truths. J. H. Woodger (1929, p. 3) has recognized the role of silent assumptions that guide biological investigation, a characterization applicable at one time or another to almost any science but true of psychology as well. Woodger is impressed with the conspicuous contrast between the competence, ingenuity, and attention accorded to observation and experiment and the almost total disregard of the conceptual framework that determines the outcome and interpretation thereof.

My orientation, as reflected in the pages of this book, coincides with the statements expressed in a 1912 manifesto signed by Albert Einstein (cited in Clark, 1971, p. 154) and about three dozen other professors, the aim of which was to express indifference " 'to metaphysical speculation and so-called critical, transcendental doctrines' and opposition to 'all metaphysical undertakings.' " I concur completely with the opening statement of that manifesto, which declared, "There has long been felt the need of a philosophy which should grow in a natural manner out of the facts and problems of natural science" (Clark, 1971, p. 154). Such a *philosophy of science* for psychology derives solely from observations of living organisms in confrontation with other organisms, objects, or happenings. All initial and subsequent assumptions, presuppositions, and postulates that guide inquiry are subject to modification as determined by continued observation. Above all, one will not find here any advocacy of any general assumptions, presuppositions, or postulates imported from extraneous sources and imposed upon behavioral observations. However, one will observe an examination and analysis of such imports.

The term *guide* in the subtitle calls for particular clarification lest the reader ascribe unwarranted arrogance to the author, for who would be so bold as to presume to know the way through the confounding maze presented by contemporary psychology? Only the book's contents might serve that function in a small way.

The book is addressed to the *skeptical psychologist*, to the worker who does *not* believe that psychology has arrived at its final destination. The term *skeptical* has a variety of meanings, but the aspect of skepticism most appropriate in the present context is a *questioning attitude*. The luxury of skepticism encourages doubt, scrutiny, examination, and dissection of propositions and definitions that have enjoyed long-standing credence. The maxim that rules the present work is expressed in the following epigrammatic, Whiteheadean-flavored statement: the doctrines which best repay critical examination are those which have been accepted without question for the longest time.

THREE PSYCHOLOGICAL THEORIES

One additional point about the recurring salient theme that runs throughout the contents of this book—in examining, analyzing, and evaluating the variety of explanatory or theoretical formulations prevailing in psychology, I have found that they can all be classified under one or another of the following rubrics: self-actional, interactional, and transactional (field). Each of these is fully explained in its proper alphabetical order, and a reading of all three will serve as a useful introduction to the other entries in the book, but, for convenience, they are defined here in brief:

Self-action

Self-actional theory assumes that things and individuals act on their own as if there were some power within them that initiated action. "Urges," "instincts," "drives," "talents," and "innate IQs" are examples of self-action. Essentially, proponents of self-actional views consider their explanations largely in terms of a single factor or variable as complete and satisfactory.

Interaction

Interaction is found where one billiard ball strikes another billiard ball and action and reaction are equal and opposite. A simple stimulus-response framework that restricts itself to the two prominent variables illustrates an interactional framework.

Transaction or Field

A transactional or field view is seen when the orientation is toward the entire system or complex of interdependent and interrelated factors that constitute a psychological event viewed with "unfractured observation." Explanation is limited to the role of observable factors participating in the event, which is completely observable.

"Every age in history risks . . . a proud and fantastic infatuation with its own importance" (Hughes, 1959, p. 21). Our own age, acting as if it had reached the ultimate level of wisdom, is not immune to such conceit. But surely, as we may tend to look down on our predecessors, our successors will belittle our attainments, for there will be continued progress in the centuries to come. So it is with proper humility and skepticism that I offer the ensuing inquiries into a variety of topics in psychology as I see them at this stage in the evolution of our knowledge. I invite the reader to join in this enterprise heedful of the following cautionary comment by Alfred North Whitehead (1944, p. 70): "If you have had your attention directed to the novelties in thought in your own lifetime, you will have observed that all really new ideas have a certain aspect of foolishness when they are first produced."

USES OF THIS BOOK

In addition to being of interest to the general reader, this book may be found useful in such courses as Theoretical Psychology, Systematic Psychology, Advanced General Psychology, Philosophy of Science, or Ecological Psychology. It should elicit considerable discussion and debate among advanced students in a seminar course.

NOTE TO THE READER

The nature of the fundamental problems considered throughout this book bears little relationship to, or dependence on, the latest findings of field observation or of the prodigious laboratory experimentation such as that in cognitive or artificial intelligence areas. That's the reason for the omission of the latest literature; it simply doesn't apply. On the contrary, the reader should not be surprised at finding references to pertinent literature scattered throughout the past century. But these are intellectual gems that provide fresh, profound insights, most of them far ahead of their time. In addition to serving my purpose, they deserve to be saved from burial in the cumulative dust of history, awaiting rediscovery.

The references at the end of each article intended for further reading have been selected with the aim of elaborating the positions explored therein.

ACKNOWLEDGMENTS

I wish to thank Principia Press for its generous permission to quote from the works of J. R. Kantor and, likewise, to Rutgers University Press for its consent to use excerpts from S. Ratner, J. Altman, and J. E. Wheeler (1964), *John Dewey and Arthur Bentley: A Philosophical Correspondence.*

I owe a great intellectual debt to J. R. Kantor, who, among other things, sensitized me to the absolute necessity of scrutinizing one's assumptions, especially the hidden ones. Others whose influence will become apparent in the reading of this volume are Arthur Bentley, John Dewey, J. H. Woodger, Alfred North Whitehead, Thomas Kuhn, and B. F. Skinner.

For discussions that shaped my own thinking, I thank my colleagues David Herman and Grant Kenyon, with special thanks to the latter for directing my attention to pertinent literature. I express appreciation to Charlie Burdsal, chairman of the Department of Psychology, for his assistance as needed, and to Nancy Nairn Sobba, for her skill in transforming my arthritic chicken scratches into an elegantly typed manuscript with meticulous care far beyond the line of duty. Above all, I am deeply grateful to my all-but-collaborator Geraldine Allbritten Pronko, for her encouragement and varied forms of help.

From AI to Zeitgeist

AI (ARTIFICIAL INTELLIGENCE)

THE COMPUTER WONDERLAND

The mushrooming consequences of our entrance into the computer age overshadow, by far, the fallout of the industrial revolution of the eighteenth century. Consider the following list of remarkable computer achievements. Computers can compile arithmetical tables; play bridge, poker, and chess; read bank checks and gas and water bills; do robotic welding on assembly lines; conduct medical analyses; and classify chromosomes and identify cancer cells; and there are still greater expectations for the future.

All of the diverse functions that computers perform for humans constitute the field of AI or artificial intelligence. The activities themselves define the field. It is futile for us to seek a concise, one-sentence definition of the term. As R. C. Schank (1984, p. xi) informs us, what the field encompasses "is not agreed upon exactly by any two workers in AI." Why the lack of clarity? This is a question that demands our attention next.

THE BRAIN AS A MODEL FOR "THINKING MACHINES"

Where theory is concerned, researchers in AI have adopted the brain as their model. An age-old theory holds that the psychological processes involved in sensing, learning, remembering, thinking, and creating are located in the brain, a *biological* organ that now serves as a surrogate for the less scientifically palatable mind. This model has led to the acceptance of the bidirectional formula "the brain is a computer and the computer is a brain" (see THE BRAIN: A CLASSICAL VIEW). The formula is standard doctrine among AI workers; I have found no exceptions to it. But the same formula is standard theory in psychology. As a representative of conventional brain dogma, Ornstein (1985, p. 170) speaks the same language as do AI workers. Each aids and abets the other. What's wrong with the bidirectional formula referred to?

EXAMINATION OF THE BRAIN-COMPUTER ANALOGY

If we start with an analysis of actual events, we must acknowledge that the brain is a strategic organ in the biological economy. As part of the nervous system with its far-flung connection throughout the organism, it *makes possible* or *facilitates* an integrated, unified response. That much is clear, but to go beyond the facts by ascribing processing, storing, translating, controlling, remembering, and executive functions to the brain illustrates reliance upon pure myth. One cannot state too emphatically that none of these alleged brain functions has been demonstrated. Occasionally we need to be aware of Hanson's (1958, p. 120) stricture: "What requires explanation cannot itself figure in the explanation." How the brain processes, stores, translates, controls, remembers, and carries on executive functions must first be explained before such "explanations" can be applied to "explaining" how computers work. It follows that, in the reverse direction, it is equally invalid to ascribe computerlike characteristics to the brain.

THE ROLE OF THE NERVOUS SYSTEM

To return to a consideration of the proper role of the nervous system as a participating factor, it is possible to view it as a *necessary* but *not sufficient* condition. Granted that without an intact nervous system, the organism is handicapped in building up a behavioral repertoire, even with a "normal" nervous system or brain, wholesale stimulus deprivation can result in a severely limited psychological organism. Above all, we must not overlook the fact that, with or without an intact nervous system or brain, the organism must undergo a psychological history or reactional biography which involves a different dimension from that which yields understanding of the organism's biological growth and development.

With such a view, not only the brain but the organism itself plays a secondary role in behavioral events. Stimulus objects and the setting factors or context in which organism and stimulus objects interact must be taken into account in a field type of orientation. Present events are also understood as a function of antecedent events. Such a view is obviously a radical departure from the standard AI and mainstream-psychology approach, which sees behavior as self-actional emanations proceeding from the brain as a center. At any rate, the presentation of an alternative psychological framework brings the AI worker to a choice point in adopting a valid psychological model. Certainly, judging from an extensive literature, one is led to the conclusion that the computer-as-a-brain-and-the-brain-as-a-computer model has not advanced understanding of either the AI workers' "intelligent machine" or the psychologists' "computerlike" brain (e.g., Kagan, Havemann & Segal, 1984, p. 231). Each looks to the other for a clarification of the respective area of interest. Nevertheless, despite the lack of an adequate theory to guide their research, AI workers envision wondrous accomplishments for the future of their discipline in view of achievements already attained.

SERVANTS AND MASTERS

Such prophecies fill some people with awe. Not only the lay person but even some AI researchers think of the computer not simply as possessing some human attributes but as being the full equivalent of humans or better. For example, Simons (1983, p. 195) suggests that we had better start asking and answering the questions posed above "before they are answered for us by the infinitely superior creatures that *machina sapiens* will become!"

It is easy to be carried away with such grandiloquent praise for so-called thinking machines, but who is really the master and who the servant? Does the acronym GIGO (garbage in, garbage out) still hold? Granted that computers can perform incredibly fast calculations surpassing humans in this regard, we know that they also create bad poetry. *Whatever they do* is the result of human creativity, design, and manufacture. Computers do not come across situations that call for the design of a robot, then go ahead and manufacture it. Some AI researchers see things in proper perspective, as in Schank's (1984, p. 27) quip: "People are amazing, not computers." Andrew (1983, p. 5) refers to computers as "smartstupids" and states that "there is no getting away from the fact that a computer is a moronic program-follower." Even the "expert systems" are deflated in Amarel's (1984, p. 2) statement: "At present, expert systems acquire their expertise by 'being told' how to behave as experts." Schank (1984, p. 54) offers a specific example of a machine that humans could design to take the Scholastic Aptitude Test. "It would be a specialist at taking the SAT, a test that supposedly predicts performance in college, but if you sent the machine to college, it would be very disappointing." Dreyfus and Dreyfus (1986, p. xi) summarize their evaluation of this area as follows: "Twenty-five years of artificial intelligence research has lived up to very few of its promises and has failed to yield any evidence that it ever will." These more sober appraisals of AI seem to put things into proper perspective by reinforcing the notion that, no matter what achievements are attained with machines, humans are their masters and machines their servants and assistants. Such evaluations also assure the skeptics that they needn't dread an invasion and a takeover by a "race" of intelligent machines.

WHEREFORE THE CHAOTIC STATE OF AFFAIRS IN AI THEORY?

The trouble lies in the mechanistic theory of human behavior espoused by AI workers. Their underlying assumption of behavior as the product of a computerlike (i.e., mechanistic) brain does not do justice to the richness and creativity of humans, who devise computers among many other things, which explains why machines cannot be expected to rise above mechanical action. (See also BRAIN articles.)

For Further Reading

Dreyfus, H. L., & Dreyfus, S. E. (1986). *Mind over machine*. New York: Free Press.
Simons, G. (1983). *Are computers alive?* Boston: Birkhauser.

THE AIM OF SCIENCE

WHAT IS THE AIM OF SCIENCE?

What is science all about? For help in attempting to answer this question, we shall rely on Stephen Toulmin's (1963, p. 17) insightful little book *Foresight and Understanding*. In his attempt to define the aims of science, Toulmin discourages us from finding an answer in a nutshell. "It is . . . fruitless to look for a single, all purpose 'scientific method.' " He sees "science" as a family of varied disciplines with different goals and purposes and different aims. The sciences also change over time. Certain disciplines, such as the branch of biology known as systematics or taxonomy, are simply classificatory. The familiar arrangement into kingdoms, phyla, classes, orders, and so on is the important end result of the basic aim of systematics with scarcely any attempt at explanation. However, the ease with which the seemingly endless variety of animals and plants can be handled is achievement enough for one branch of biology. As their aim, other biological disciplines set diagnostic or therapeutic goals for themselves.

HOW ABOUT PREDICTION?

"Prediction and control" are readily associated with science. Most people consider prediction to be an especially important function of the scientist. However, Toulmin has a different conception. He reminds us that Charles Darwin made an invaluable contribution to biology with his theory of evolution. Yet, on the basis of his theory, Darwin could not have made one single prediction about the course of evolution. The great value of this theory lay in its broad explanatory possibilities. It "made sense" of the tremendous variation in the forms of plant and animal life. Apparently, then, prediction per se is not an indispensable feature of science.

Consider prediction from another perspective. As Toulmin points out, as early as 500 B.C., the Babylonians' assiduous study of the movements of celestial bodies permitted them to evolve many accurate predictions. For example, they could foretell the precise time of appearance of the new moon or of lunar eclipses. But they had no understanding or theory underlying their predictions.

As Toulmin tells the story, contemporaneous with the Babylonians, the Ionians were also zealous students of astronomy. But, by contrast with the

Babylonians, they were unable to make any astronomical predictions. However, they entertained a wealth of hunches and speculations (i.e., theory) about celestial phenomena. Thus, the Babylonians had prediction but no theory, while the Ionians had theory but no prediction. Therefore, theory per se is not a ticket of admission to the forum of the sciences. As Toulmin (1963, p. 16) sums it up, "science is not a matter of forecasting alone, since we have to discover also explanatory connections between the happenings we predict."

What a pity that the Babylonians and Ionians, each with "half a science" of astronomy, couldn't have gotten together and combined their predictive and theoretical activities. The lesson Toulmin teaches us is that the ideal of science is to strive for prediction *and* explanation. More specifically, one aim is to foretell what will happen if so and so happens. Beyond that, a second aim is to "make sense" of the prediction, to provide a statement that *accounts for* the successful prediction. The latter is at the very heart of science. As Toulmin (1963, p. 37) reminds us, even cooking recipes predict, but that doesn't endow them with a scientific status.

To recapitulate then, prediction alone, even when it works, does not a science make. The ideal of science is to achieve both, but its essence is to understand or interpret the successful prediction. Contemporary astronomers are exceedingly busy in trying to "make sense" of the origin and boundaries of the cosmos without any involvement with prediction.

For Further Reading

Toulmin, S. (1963). *Foresight and understanding: An enquiry into the aims of science*. New York: Harper & Row.

ARISTOTLE: SAINT THOMAS'S PHILOSOPHER OR MRS. ARISTOTLE'S HUSBAND?

It should come as no surprise to us to learn that medieval readers of Aristotle's *Psychology (De Anima)* did not interpret it in the same way as did Aristotle's Greek compatriots. Attempting as best we can to lift ourselves by our cultural bootstraps, we must try to insinuate ourselves into the naturalistic outlook of the Greeks of Aristotle's period. To help us set the stage for Aristotle and his way of thinking, we make use of J. R. Kantor's (1963) exhaustive analysis of Greek culture around the time of Aristotle (384-322 B.C.).

GREEK CULTURE

In a general way, we should note the tremendous heights that Greek civilization achieved. As Kantor (1963, p. 65) points out, even historians who are not very sympathetic to the Greeks acknowledge Grecian attainments in art, architecture, poetry, philosophy, politics, war, and science. The Greeks flourished in a stable society that facilitated the growth of the individual in the present. For them life was good. "They did not and could not think of themselves as subsisting in temporary misery while awaiting glory in some future state" (Kantor, 1963), a gloomy and pessimistic characteristic of people of the later Middle Ages.

More specifically, the Greeks were objective and realistic in their outlook on the world about them. They restricted their investigations to things and events that they could see, touch, hear, and smell. In other words, they were naturalistic, as evidenced in their physics, with prominent achievements in mechanics. In biology, they assembled whole catalogs of information about plants and animals. In all their pursuits, they stuck to the observable. But how about their gods? Didn't they have gods? Is this a cultural inconsistency?

As we gather from Kantor, the Greek gods were not super*natural*; they were only super*human*. "Greek gods were human or were derivations from human prototypes with greater or lesser exaggerations" (Kantor, 1963, p. 85). One is inclined to compare their gods with our mythical Santa Claus, with fairies or gremlins and other creatures of fancy. But they had an ethics. Virtue and moral and ethical action did not stem from blind obedience to the Word of God but from a knowledge of rules of conduct derived from the domain of actual human situations. According to Kantor

(1963, p. 86), it was only the imposition of later writers' own culturalization that led to the distortion of Greek civilization. Actually the Greeks were down-to-earth, rational, unromantic, realistic, and innocent of all things supernatural.

Now, fortified with a knowledge of Aristotle's cultural milieu, we are ready to tackle Aristotle's views on psychology, which we shall do under the rubric of Aristotle I. Why? Because when we next meet up with Aristotle as interpreted by Thomas Aquinas about fifteen hundred years later, it will be a radically different Aristotle deserving of the label Aristotle II.

ARISTOTLE I, MRS. ARISTOTLE'S HUSBAND

I aim to present only the broadest framework of Aristotle's psychological system. Scholars are agreed that what we have to work with are apparently only lecture notes recorded by Aristotle or his students and not a systematic and comprehensive textbook. And, as C. Shute (1941, p. 125) points out, Aristotle (see Figure 1), like many authors, experienced some difficulty in expressing himself. We must also realize the early and primitive stage of Greek science at this period. Even so, Aristotle's corpus of psychological doctrine has survived for over two thousand years, unquestionable testimony to his influence.

As our mentor, we shall rely on Shute (1941), who has written a lucid exposition of Aristotle's thinking about behavior in his excellent book *The Psychology of Aristotle*. At the heart of the matter is the frequently transformed term *psyche* or its English translation, *soul*.

Our first clue as to Aristotle I's use of *soul* comes from a statement of what it *isn't*. Says Shute (1941, p. 12), "The 'psyche' of Aristotle must not be misunderstood as something separable or apart from natural processes." Thus, we learn that soul is not an entity or object existing in its own right. The trouble stems from Aristotle's use of a noun, which usually denotes "a person, place, or thing." But we can overcome this problem through further inquiry.

We learn more about soul when we come upon three different parts or kinds of soul: the nutritive soul or function (metabolism), the sensitive soul by means of sense organs in response to the environment, and the rational soul or function, so prominently observed in humans. Shute (1941, p. 59) explains further:

When Aristotle refers to parts of the soul, he is talking about functions which can be distinguished for purposes of discussion, and not parts which have separate existence, as a leg is separate from an arm or even from a foot.

In fact, Aristotle agreed that, for purposes of discussion, one could divide the soul in an indefinite number of ways, as many as one can differentiate.

Figure 1. Bust of Aristotle (384-322 B.C.), an early philosopher and naturalistic psychologist. (Photo obtained from Ny Glyptotek, Copenhagen.)

Thus one could refer to a learning soul or functioning and so on. Such a view of multiple souls does not comport with a much later notion of a single, separate soul dwelling within the organism and leading its own detached existence even after the death of its alleged bodily counterpart.

Further evidence for the radically different view of soul by Mrs. Aristotle's husband comes from stress on the importance of the environment. For example, we learn that "the faculty of sensation is always a function of the environment, as well as of the organism" (Shute, 1941, p. 86). The same "holds for the entire field of organic activity which fits into his fundamental doctrine *of behavior as explicable only in terms of interaction between an organism and its environment*" (Shute, 1941, p. 100). The things thought about are joined in a mutual and reciprocal union with the action of the organism. As we know today, when there is thinking, there is always something thought about. You don't have one without the other. "The soul is thus a joint function of both the organism and its environment" (Shute, 1941, p. 131). Shute's statement is offered as a final refutation of the soul attributed to Aristotle II, a static entity residing within the individual that autonomously issues all manner of psychological things. In this connection, see SELF-ACTION. We are now ready to set the stage for Aristotle II's soul.

THE MEDIEVAL PERIOD

Following the decline of the Greek state, there were basic changes in civilization with radically different influences on intellectual and scientific matters. Kantor (1963, p. 155ff.), in great detail, traces the evolution of ways of viewing the world in the Middle Ages in direct contradiction to the totally naturalistic outlook of the Greeks. Turning away from an investigation of events around them, philosophers of the early centuries of the Christian era became absorbed in words and symbols. Secular learning was spurned in favor of "the real reality," the supernatural world, as revealed in the divine scriptures. "Consciousness," "mind," and "soul" crept into psychology, and the chief aim of the citizens of a troubled, wretched world was to endure this "vale of tears" in the hope of achieving salvation of the soul and its eternal existence in another, better world.

Kantor has done a fine piece of detective work for us by pinpointing the period in history at which Aristotle's term *psyche* was corrupted in meaning in line with the cultural postulates, assumptions, and models current at that time. Omitting the rich details of the early centuries of the Christian civilization provided by Kantor, we move on to the thirteenth century and to Saint Thomas, which brings us to Aristotle II, Saint Thomas's Aristotle.

ARISTOTLE II, SAINT THOMAS'S ARISTOTLE

As a Dominican student in Naples, Saint Thomas came into contact with

Aristotle's *Psychology (De Anima)*, which was introduced into European institutions by Arab scholars. Saint Thomas became an enthusiastic promoter of Aristotle's psychological views as he transformed and assimilated them to fit his theology. It is true that he used the terminology of Mrs. Aristotle's husband, but he did not use its meaning.

For Saint Thomas, *psyche* became the temporary incorporeal resident of the corporeal organism, the soul breathed by God into the organism and returning to Him at the expiration of the organism. Thus, instead of studying the observable actions of organisms as Aristotle did, Saint Thomas considered them as only surface manifestations or reflections of invisible happenings in the soul, his main concern. Eventually, *soul* (see "SOUL" entry) became transformed into *mind*, and later, *brain*.

In conclusion, the two pictures of Aristotle that have come down to us could not be more disparate. Aristotle I appears as an objective, naturalistic scientist with a broad, observational base that holds organism and environmental object in intimate union, much as the modern ecologist does his work. Aristotle II, by contrast, shrinks his observational base within the organism, which must carry the theoretical burden solo (without help from the environment). The hypothetical soul (later, mind, and still later, brain) must do all the work alone. As usual, there are choices for us to make.

For Further Reading

Shute, C. (1941). *The psychology of Aristotle: An analysis of the living being.* New York: Columbia University Press.

ASSUMPTIONS

In an article, "Assumptions in Psychology," A. Van Kaam (1970, p. 25) points out that every scientist who confronts the world of events does so laden with assumptions, either implicit or explicit. He goes on to say that physicists have become increasingly aware of the postulates that guide their observations. Not so with psychology. According to Van Kaam, some psychologists deny starting with assumptions, claiming that the viewpoints of the various schools are all relative—not realizing that an eclectic position also involves a wholesale assumption. An eclectic stance reflects a neutral acceptance or tolerance of a number of viewpoints with their respective incompatible or even contradictory assumptions.

Other psychologists argue that there are no assumptions because there is no scientific method for verifying them. They declare that the only propositions that can be confirmed are those which are submitted to the experimental method or the claim that only quantifiable data are worthwhile. Such statements reveal an unbounded faith that experimentation per se leads to "the truth." The silent assumption latent in it is that experimentation is a completely objective method—the most audacious assumption of all. Van Kaam (1970, p. 25) argues that "there is no escape from assumptions in psychology." One must agree with him.

HOW TO BECOME COGNIZANT OF ONE'S ASSUMPTIONS

As a way of encouraging a greater awareness of the role that assumptions play in psychology, Van Kaam (1970, p. 28) suggests a certain program for advanced students of psychology. When they do their research work, students should state what their guiding assumptions are and what their results mean in the light of those assumptions. Then let them interpret the same results in terms of the assumptions that underlie a behavioristic, gestalt, or psychoanalytic approach. Such an exercise would parallel the case of a prosecutor of a criminal suddenly assigned to defend the same criminal. The lawyer in both situations must show flexibility and make the best possible case in either role. So with the students, who would be forced to be flexible in handling a given set of data under incompatible or even contradictory sets of assumptions. Over a period of time, such a program would lead to a universal awareness of the role of assumptions in psychology, replacing the almost universal contemporary denial of their existence. But there are other problems with assumptions.

A BONE TO PICK

The skeptic must challenge one proposition of Van Kaam's concerning assumptions, a proposition in which he implies that there is no way of evaluating assumptions. Here are his statements. "These assumptions of psychologists are not arrived at by psychological research" (Van Kaam, 1970, p. 25). And again, "science is relatively subjective and always implies assumptions which cannot be arrived at by the scientific method itself" (Van Kaam, 1970, p. 26). If this were so, then one set of assumptions would be as good as any other. Personal preference would be the sole criterion for selecting B over A, C, or D. But there is a feature of scientific method by which assumptions may be appraised, that is, the results that any given set of assumptions yield. It has been said, "By their fruits ye shall know them"; so it is with assumptions. In line with N. R. Hanson's (1958, p. 95) stricture against theories with an overload of assumptions, that theory is to be preferred which carries the fewest assumptions. A remark of Albert Einstein's quoted by Ronald Clark (1971, p. 109) is also relevant: "A theory is the more impressive the greater the simplicity of its premises, the more different kinds of things it relates, and the more extended its area of applicability." Here, then, are some criteria for deciding among the various assumptions underlying the different schools of psychology. In sum, that theory is to be preferred which (1) is congruent with the *naturalistic* tenets of established sciences, which (2) makes the fewest naturalistic assumptions, and which (3) yields understanding or makes sense within such a framework. (See also POSTULATION.)

For Further Reading

Hanson, N. R. (1958). *Patterns of discovery*. Cambridge: At the University Press.
Van Kaam, A. (1970). Assumptions in psychology. In D. P. Schultz (Ed.), *The science of psychology: Critical reflections* (pp. 24-29). New York: Appleton-Century-Crofts.

THE BEHAVIOR SEGMENT

One problem that confronts the sciences is that of carving out a convenient unit or units of study that will permit handling the data of the science in some convenient form. The psychologist encounters the same problem, but before we get involved in its consideration, let us look into the manner in which other scientists treat this difficulty. Starting with the astronomer, we learn that our earth revolves in its orbit around the sun *continuously*, stopping for no one. And yet, despite its ceaseless motion, the astronomer can specify that a single orbit of the earth around the sun, or one solar year, takes 365 days, 5 hours, 48 minutes, 46 seconds. The year is, therefore, a practical specification of a convenient unit of study carved out of a nonstop continuum.

Coming closer to our area of interest, we next look into the study of respiration by the physiologist. Breathing, like the rotation of the earth and its revolution around the sun, goes on and on. Yet the physiologist can analyze the cyclical process into a single act of respiration, even recording its individually abstracted phases of inspiration and expiration.

The psychologist's data are also continuous. No one has grasped this fact as keenly as William James (1918, p. 230), even though he stated it in mentalistic terms as the "stream of consciousness." His catchy metaphor called attention to the succession of reactions such as seeing, talking, laughing, eating, drinking, hearing, and so on with never a dull moment. We are now ready to consider how to seize hold of an appropriate unit of that behavioral flow.

Because observation of events is the proper starting point for any science, let us set up an observation point at a busy downtown spot when people are going to work. Now let's pretend that we are inhabitants of Mars about to have a first look at earthly humans, which is another way of saying that we are divesting ourselves of such preconceptions as "controlling brains" and so on.

Here is our first observation. We see a young lady walking by, and we hear her say, "Good morning." We speculate as to "what made her do this." Is this like a knee jerk elicited by a tap on some portion of her anatomy? Or is it a "spontaneous," that is, self-actional affair? We get an answer to our question when a man comes into view. We guess that the sight of the man was somehow related to the young lady's greeting. Subsequent observations confirm our hunch. In fact, we can now predict that sight-of-man evokes the same vocal response on the part of the young lady. Incidentally, we have observed our first behavior segment.

The young lady and the man we have been observing were admittedly behaving in other ways both before and after the incident we seized hold of for analysis. Out of that continuity, we "froze" one behavioral slice for detailed analysis. It's as if we stopped a motion-picture film of the episode for examination at a single frame, an achievement comparable to that of the astronomer and physiologist referred to above.

IMPLICATIONS OF THE BEHAVIOR SEGMENT

One thing we learned from our observation of the young lady's "Good morning" utterance is that such acts are not capricious, arbitrary, or random. In fact, the situation should teach us that there is never a response without a stimulus and never a stimulus without a response. Without at least these two factors, there is no behavior segment. The two are coordinate; they are of equal rank if we expect the event to occur. Each is indispensable to the other, much as it takes two to tango.

FROM BEHAVIOR SEGMENT TO BEHAVIOR SITUATION

Our example of the young lady saying "Good morning" at sight of the man illustrates a simple, single discrete act unit. It was deliberately selected for its simplicity, but much of our behavior comes in larger connected units or "chunks." Consider a purchase at a store, hoeing a garden, splitting a log, or baking a cake. The beauty of the behavior segment notion is that any of the above *behavior situations* can be dissected into their component, sequential behavior segments. Thus, the apparent complexity of behavior has been reduced to a manageable, simple structure. We can define a behavior situation as an interrelated sequence of behavior segments.

For Further Reading

Kantor, J. R., & Smith, N. W. (1975). *The science of psychology: An interbehavioral survey*. Chicago: Principia Press.

THE BRAIN:
A CLASSICAL VIEW

Brain, N. An apparatus with which we think that we think.

Bierce (1925, p. 41)

"Let me pick your brain." "He had a brainstorm." "She's been brainwashed." "He's a brain!" "You brainless nitwit!" "X is scatterbrained." "England is suffering a brain drain." "She's a brainy one." "B's sixth book is his latest brainchild." "That puzzle is a brain teaser (or brain buster)." "C is feather-brained (or birdbrained)." "She'd like to brain him." The foregoing and still other expressions are common currency in everyday conversations; they are expressions that reflect a never-to-be-doubted and self-evident truth—in other words, a truism.

It is not only in popular psychology that we find such an exalted opinion of the brain, especially the *human* brain. Ten out of ten introductory psychology textbooks sent to me as examination copies treated the brain as a special center of power and action. According to Lichtenstein (1980, p. 453), "It would be difficult to find any proposition which would be more widely accepted by psychologists and nonpsychologists alike than this one: 'The secrets of the mind are locked up in the brain.' "

The ten textbooks referred to speak as if with one voice. The brain is said to receive information about the world, process it, and transform it into experience and action. We are told that the brain's various parts or "centers" exert a regulatory function over various activities. Some, like the association areas, evaluate incoming sensory information, other centers "monitor the internal world," and some others are involved in the "storage of memories." Then there are speech centers, taste centers, and so on. In general, the brain is what "makes you tick"; this is the essence of contemporary mainstream psychology. In this connection, see the entry under SELF-ACTION. The most astounding thing about the prevailing contemporary view of the brain is that it goes back to at least the time of Galen, physician to the Roman gladiators, who lived in the second century A.D. An important formulation about the brain was contributed by the Roman philosopher Plotinus in the next century. His views have come down to us in an unbroken continuity, generation after generation. Plotinus also states, essentially, that the brain is what "makes you tick." Doesn't the following statement of Plotinus's (quoted by Kantor, 1963, p. 264) have a modern ring (except for its use of unsophisticated terms)?

The vehicles of touch are at the ends of the nerves—which, moreover, are vehicles of the faculty by which the movements of the living being are effected . . . the nerves start from the brain. The brain therefore has been considered as the centre and seat of the principle which determines feeling and impulse and the entire act of the organism as a living thing.

Now, a theory that is seventeen hundred years old is not necessarily a false theory. Yet we need to note in passing that chemistry does not have its basis in alchemy, and astronomy has no dealings with astrology. And it is common knowledge that physics and biology have cut themselves off from their predecessors in the Middle Ages and have made great progress, which means that they have changed. Lack of change in views about the brain should alert us to examine our views. Among others, Gunnar Myrdal (1944, p. 92) urges scientists to examine their formulations for possible errors in unwitting assumptions or in hidden cultural influences on the way they view things.

Cultural influences have set up the assumptions about the mind, the body, and the universe with which we begin; pose the questions we ask; influence the facts we seek; determine the interpretation we give these facts; and direct our reaction to these interpretations and conclusions.

How can we possibly detect all the errors in our thinking about the world, errors that our culture imposes on our thinking? We can't, but we must try.

OTHER CULTURAL VIEWS

One possible insight can come from an inspection of views extant in other cultures. Z. Y. Kuo (1967, pp. 80-81), a Chinese psychologist, informs us that since ancient times the Chinese recognized the heart, and *not* the brain, as a kind of psychological center. In a five-thousand-year-long historical account of the locus of the "organ of thought," A. B. Laver (1972) points out that the Egyptians considered the dynamic heart as psychologically important, in utter disregard of the seemingly passive brain. The clear impact of such facts is that it was as natural for the Chinese and Egyptians to believe in the central importance of the heart as it is for us to fervently maintain the supremacy of the brain in the biological organization. For emphasis, we should state, contrariwise, that it is just as natural for us to hold the never-to-be-doubted belief in the ascribed powers of the brain as it was for other civilizations to hold radically different views. According to J. H. Woodger (1929, p. 68), "In order to persuade people to listen to a new point of view it is first necessary to show them that all is not well with the old."

WHAT'S WRONG WITH TRADITIONAL BRAIN DOGMA?

First of all, traditional brain dogma does violence to psychological facts by transforming them into a radically different form from that which we observe. Let us take the case of X, who has just learned a vocabulary list for his French class. If we start with observation, we note a human organism in contact with a page of a French textbook under specific conditions and with *a history* of similar interactions between the two. In addition to the organism learning a vocabulary, we must not overlook the important role of the vocabulary list that is being learned. What traditional brain dogma does is to reduce the complex observable event into an alleged occurrence within one portion or organ of the organism, that is, the brain.

We need to ask: How does it help to verbally transform what we did observe to unobservable, imaginary goings-on in the brain? In the first place, no one has ever confirmed the presence of "brain traces" or "engrams," the alleged effects of learning. And of what use would they be as an interpretation of the learning that we saw taking place? There is no way of peering inside the skull of several students in the same French class and being able to say, "This student learned the French vocabulary, and this one did not." The only check available to us is at the same level at which we made our observation, namely, in terms of the interaction between vocabulary list and student of French. But that means abandoning the hypothetical brain theory. Thomas Kuhn's (1961, p. 177) stricture against such theories is revealed in his statement "Merely conceivable theories are not among the options open to the practicing scientist." The reason is that if one merely infers brain traces, for example, from behavioral observations and then turns around and attempts to explain such behavior with the hypothetical brain states, then one is involved in circular reasoning. Only when a scientific hypothesis is confirmed can it be used to explain an event. Brain states call for verification *before* they can be used to explain behavior.

One last point needs to be made, namely, that classical brain doctrine relies on a mechanistic model. The brain is compared to the parts of an automobile engine. Alternator, spark plugs, and fuel pump have different functions, but so do the reticular formation, cerebellum, left hemisphere, right hemisphere, and so on, each with an alleged special job to do. It seems appropriate to ask: Why should explanations of mechanical things be imposed upon nonmechanical events, that is, behavioral occurrences?

WHAT DOES THE BRAIN DO?

Should one ignore the brain completely in understanding behavior? Not at all! Since psychological events consist of many factors, the variables localized in the biological organism must certainly play a role in the total event. A starved, sick, or drugged organism can surely change the outcome of an event. Blindness, deafness, and brain injuries have their effects. In all such cases, we have a changed organism, which makes it a different event from one in which the organism has lost more than one-third of the body's normal blood supply. That organism may act confused, even "pathological," but surely we wouldn't be justified in attributing the abnormal behavior to the drained blood. No more should we attribute abnormal behavior to an injured brain.

As to the normal brain, it is a necessary but not a sufficient condition for nonpathological behavior. Woodbridge (1965, p. 183) puts it this way: "We may be convinced that without brains we could not think, but to expect a brain to think seems to be about as unreasonable an expectation as one can entertain." When it comes to thinking, there is no such thing as "pure thought" emanating from inside an organism. Where there is thinking, there is always something (or somebody) thought about. Also, thinking demands whole or minimally intact organisms, never brains in isolation. Setting factors and a history are also required; for example, infants cannot engage in sexual fantasies. By the time we have taken into account the variables enumerated above, we are involved in complex field or interbehavioral or transactional theory (see FIELD THEORY; INTERBEHAVIORAL PSYCHOLOGY; TRANSACTION).

In conclusion, we need to give serious consideration to a development in recent physics. The older physics had to invent ether, the medium through which light waves traveled. Relativity physics dispensed with the hypothetical ether, which stimulated Arthur Bentley (Ratner, Altman & Wheeler, 1964, p. 524) to come up with the following ingenious epigram: "A brain is no more needed as a carrier through which thinking is conveyed than ether is needed to carry the light waves."

For Further Reading

McConnell, J. V. (1977). *Understanding human behavior* (2nd Ed.). New York: Holt, Rinehart and Winston.

THE BRAIN: A MODERN VIEW

Over a half-century ago, in a daring paper entitled "The Nervous System: Psychological Fact or Fiction?," J. R. Kantor (1922) contrasted the scientifically verifiable account of the nervous system's biological functions of connecting, coordinating, and integrating the biological organism and its improper, imputed role as an initiator and controller of psychological action. He objected to assigning the nervous system, particularly the brain, dual functions, that is, (1) a biological role and (2) a psychological job of thinking, remembering, and all the rest. Both in the aforementioned article and in his *Problems of Physiological Psychology*, Kantor (1947) argued that the traditional theory has prevented us from comprehending the actual function of the nervous system and caused us to look in the wrong place for a proper understanding of behavior.

SKINNER'S VIEW OF THE NERVOUS SYSTEM

In 1938, B. F. Skinner wrote a book, *The Behavior of Organisms*, in which he developed a system of behavior without recourse to any such mystical entities as mind, ego, will, and intellect dwelling within the person. Skinner maintained that behavior could be studied *in its own right* and *at its own level of organization*. He also insisted that no amount of information about the nervous system would explain or make sense of behavior. To take an example, total knowledge of the brain would never by itself permit us to understand why one person spoke Persian and another French. Yet the classical view of the nervous system (or brain) treated behavior as basically disordered behavior which had to be reduced to an order that was somehow guaranteed by the nervous system. Skinner labeled such a nervous system or "CNS" (central nervous system) a "conceptual nervous system." In sum, Skinner argued strongly for the establishment of psychology as an independent science without *explanatory* ties to neurology. Both Kantor's and Skinner's views of the nervous system are still considered bold and unpopular and represent minority viewpoints.

Why do popular conceptions of the central nervous system thrive and survive over the centuries? The answer appears to lie in the pervasive broadcast and dissemination of such themes through the television, radio, and print media and by *vox populi*. And why do they have such a strong hold in psychology, biology, technology, and medicine? Where else do we recruit psychologists, biologists, technologists, and physicians but from among lay persons, who bring their indoctrination with them? For are we not all children of our culture? John Dewey (Ratner, Altman & Wheeler, 1964, p. 121) understood this point clearly, as evidenced by his revealing statement "People have got their 'philosophies' in the nursery."

SOME RECENT RESEARCH FINDINGS

We round out our discussion of modern views of the brain with a consideration of some recent research and its implications. Our job has really been done for us by S. Finger and D. G. Stein (1982). Their book *Brain Damage and Recovery: Research and Clinical Perspectives*, our source, is unquestionably a compendium of brain inquiry into laboratory and clinical, animal and human, subjects, offering current as well as historical perspectives on all. Right off, we learn "how current models of brain evolved" and that "some of the same concepts that are debated today were proposed and argued decades, if not centuries, ago" (p. x). This long continuity of viewpoint needs to be emphasized.

There are a multitude of intellectual goodies in Finger and Stein's book, but we shall limit our survey to those aspects which pertain to the role of the brain in psychological events. In conformity with the traditional view, Finger and Stein *began* their career by creating lesions in various parts of the brain in animals in order to localize various alleged functions in those parts. Presently, they refer to their reductionistic views of that time as "the new phrenology" (p. 1). When they scrutinized their data, they found exceptions to the "accepted ways of thinking about lesion data and localization of function—exceptions that seemed to be largely ignored or treated as interesting curiosities by our colleagues working in research settings and by professionals treating patients in hospitals and clinics" (p. 2). But the greatest impact on their thinking came from the results of a study by one of their colleagues. Briefly, that study showed that a one-stage operation on the reticular formation of cats had a devastating effect, as evidenced by the cats' slipping into a deep coma. However, when the same amount of damage was inflicted on the reticular formation in discrete surgical stages three weeks apart, the cats showed sleep-wakefulness cycles that "closely resembled those of normal cats" (p. 2). These results appeared to challenge traditional conceptions and called for a reexamination of "some well-accepted views about how structure-function relationships could be derived for given brain areas, and the issue of just what was being localized in brain lesion experiments" (p. 3).

One can hardly argue for an arousal-attention center in the reticular formation when one gets such different results with the same damage inflicted in staged versus single operation. The results of this study and of clinical findings in which massive brain damage was not necessarily followed by psychological deficit argued for the plasticity of the brain. Together, such results also called into question the rigid localization of function implicit in traditional brain dogma.

Still more basic to our purpose are Finger and Stein's further reflections on the tremendous output of research in an attempt to connect specific brain areas with specific behaviors. When we ask what is the upshot of all of this industry, the answer is perplexity, contradiction, and inability to replicate results. Here is Finger and Stein's (1982, p. 6) distressing assessment.

After almost 200 years of making lesions to specify the "organs of the mind," one might ask why there is so much confusion, so little agreement, and why such limited progress has been made. Could this suggest that perhaps our interpretations extend well beyond our data, that our logic is faulty, and that possibly a "paradigm shift" might be helpful?

In my opinion, Finger and Stein reveal the sharp difference between the classical and emerging views of the role of the nervous system in psychological events. The former sees the nervous system mechanistically as a machine consisting of different parts, each presumably correlated with a specific psychological function after the analogy of a machine and its parts. The emerging view considers the brain as a holistic system serving only one function, that is, to connect the diverse parts of the organism, thus *facilitating*, or *making possible*, the organism's unified, integrated action. As such, the nervous system is, at best, a participating factor in psychological events.

PARTICIPATING FACTOR DEFINED

Because *participating factor* may be easily misunderstood, we must take special pains to make clear what the term really means. As an aid, let us consider the skeleton or bony framework of the organism. As skillfully as possible, by means of a graduated series of surgical operations on one of the world's piano virtuosos, suppose we should skillfully remove the entire skeletal system of such a concert performer. Now, here it is the night of the anticipated concert and we wheel in our hypothetical virtuoso to the piano. Clearly, the recital can't even begin with a boneless human blob. Thus, the skeletal system is a necessary, but not sufficient, condition in staging a piano recital. A similar case could be made for the circulatory and hormonal systems. No more, and no less, then, is the brain a participating factor in psychological events. The emerging views assign it a single (i.e., biological) function, not the dual (i.e., biological and psychological) function of traditional theory.

In conclusion, the importance of guiding assumptions in psychological investigation shows up clearly in our examination of two contrasting paradigms of the nervous system, the widespread classical one and an emerging, minority notion.

For Further Reading

Finger, S., & Stein, D. G. (1982). *Brain damage and recovery: Research and clinical perspectives*. New York: Academic Press.

CAUSE AND EFFECT

Everything in nature is a cause from which there flows some effect.
Benedictus de Spinoza (1632-1677)

This couple, as inseparable as Tweedledum and Tweedledee, constitute the basis of both common sense and some scientific ways of thinking. There is no question about the general acceptability of a cause-effect formulation by psychologists, a fact reflected even in the most recent textbooks of introductory psychology. One prominent example is the widely approved formula of the independent variable (cause) and dependent variable (effect), with grudging acknowledgment of other, controlled and uncontrolled, variables playing a secondary role. According to one prominent textbook, a disordered brain (cause) produces disordered behavior such as violence (effect). Incidentally, one can't help noticing the similarity in this explanation and Shakespeare's delineation of Macbeth's hallucination of the dagger (with which he had killed Duncan) as "proceeding from a heat-oppressed brain." This particular model, which focuses on the brain, has an enduring history. And as for cause-effect thinking in general, the quotation from Spinoza at the beginning of this article proves that it was in use at least three hundred years ago.

Stimulus as cause and response as effect, a popular method for analyzing behavior, also fits the Newtonian interactional framework in which one body exerts a force (i.e., cause) upon another body, which feels the impact (i.e., effect). Cause-effect thinking is so common and seems so "natural," right, and proper that one begins to question it. Can it be that we have simply learned to see certain events in this way and in no other way? Immediately one recalls the following statement of N. R. Hanson's (1958, p. 36): "Perhaps facts are somehow moulded by the logical forms of the fact-stating language. Perhaps these provide a 'mould' in terms of which the world coagulates for us in definite ways." Has our language coagulated the world for us into causes and effects? Let us analyze these terms to see what sense we can make of them.

Ask almost any person to explain cause and effect and you will probably get the answer, "It's a case in which every event regularly follows, and is regularly preceded by, some antecedent." But, surely, if I sneeze three times in succession after the clock strikes three, the situation doesn't demonstrate cause and effect. This would be a case of a "post hoc, ergo propter hoc," or an "after this, therefore because of this" error. Superstitions such as the case of a person who claims to have experienced a piece of bad luck after a black cat crosses his or her path illustrate this fallacy.

Obviously, there has to be more of a connection between cause and effect than a certain temporal sequence. Let us analyze the following causal chain with the help of Hanson. "For want of a nail a shoe was lost; for want of a shoe a horse was lost; for want of a horse a rider was lost; for want of a rider a battalion was lost; for want of a battalion a battle was lost; for want of a victory a kingdom was lost—all for want of a horseshoe nail." The series of sequences in the preceding causal chain seem almost to explain themselves. Yet Hanson (1958, p. 53) warns that "reference to one link of a chain . . . explains nothing about any other link—why, how, or from what it was made, and so on. *It does not even entail the existence of any other link*" (emphasis added).

To get the full significance of Hanson's statement, consider what the foregoing chronicle of one tragedy after another, beginning with the horseshoe nail, would mean to a person living the simple, Stone Age life of an Australian aborigine with no access to nails, horses, riders, and so on. Such an example also shows how much we know about horses' hooves, horseshoe nails that can work loose from metal horseshoes, battalions, wars, kingdoms, and so on. Unwittingly, we impose all such knowledge upon the pegs provided by the recital beginning with "For want of a nail." As Hanson (1958, p. 54) puts it, "What we refer to as 'causes' are theory-loaded from beginning to end. They are not simple, tangible links in the chain of sense experience, but rather details in an intricate pattern of experience. . . . only its simplicity and familiarity makes this background knowledge fade before the spectacular linkage of the attention-getting events."

We get a similar insight into the problem of cause and effect from John Dewey. Dewey (1938, pp. 445-446) argues that these terms serve to call attention to two events that are commonly seen as separate and independent but which are a "means of instituting, in connection with determination of other similar linkages, a single unique *continuous* history." Once one has attained a description of a temporally and coexistentially continuous situation, "the conception of causation has served its purpose and drops out." Dewey seems to be saying that cause and effect are a shorthand way of referring to the most attention-getting aspects of a situation or a history.

Another way to avoid the problems created by a cause-effect approach is by way of a field type of procedure. The modern physicist and the inter-behavioral psychologist have no use for cause-effect explanations. Instead of cause and effect, both of them depend on a broader approach in terms of FIELD THEORY. Also, both cause and effect and field ways of thinking are theory-laden. Both are ways in which *we* structure the world. Stated otherwise, both are constructs that invite choices.

For Further Reading

Hanson, N. R. (1958). *Patterns of discovery*. Cambridge: At the University Press.

COGNITIVE PSYCHOLOGY

> The field of cognitive psychology is increasing in complexity, diversity, and sheer size at a dizzying rate.
>
> Wessells (1982, p. ix)

M. G. Wessells' book *Cognitive Psychology* lists over 450 references! Acquaintance with the journal literature and inspection of any university library's shelves of books in the area of cognitive psychology will convince any doubting Thomas of the truthfulness of Wessells' statement at the head of this article. There has been a tremendous resurgence of interest in topics that classical behaviorism has long neglected. Because of its preference for so-called overt behavior, or movements-in-space, of the organism, the behavioristic program avoided the more subtle interbehaviors such as perceiving, imaging, memorizing, learning, discovering, judging, and thinking. But, for a cognitivist's definition, we rely on the following statement of U. Neisser's (1967, p. 4):

Cognition refers to all the processes by which the sensory input is transformed, reduced, elaborated, stored, recovered, and used. It is concerned with these processes even when they operate in the absence of relevant stimulation, as in images and hallucinations. Such terms as *sensation, perception, imagery, retention, recall, problem-solving,* and *thinking,* among many others, refer to hypothetical stages or aspects of cognition.

AN EVALUATION OF NEISSER'S FORMULATION

What have we here? A long train of unwarranted assumptions that predestine the outcome of Neisser's procedure as well as that of those cognitivists who follow in his footsteps.

1. According to Neisser, the world of objects is only an illusion, because "out there" are only light rays, sound waves, and so on. These are translated into a neural language that the brain processes into the various aspects of consciousness. We are not told how consciousness or the mind transforms these internal goings-on back to the objects "out there" where we see and hear them.

2. Thus, Neisser's approach is a mentalistic or dualistic one. It follows

the age-old paradigm of matter and spirit or body and mind, a paradigm derived not from scientific observation but from our cultural heritage, a paradigm that he imposes upon the data. According to Neisser, we do not *directly* perceive the world of objects. Whatever we come to know about "reality" has to be *mediated* by the sense organs but even more so by the brain. As Neisser (1967, p. 3) puts it, "the brain and not the eye is surely the most important organ involved." Why? Because, says he, "we have no immediate access to the world, nor to any of its properties" (Neisser, 1967, p. 3). Neisser believes that the light rays that impinge upon the retina in no way resemble the objects in the world that are their source. But from their inauspicious beginning as retinal patterns, they are metamorphosed into perceptions, memories, and so on by the brain.

3. According to some psychologists, perceivings are events in which, for example, a hunter discriminates or recognizes a deer, or a deer discriminates or recognizes a hunter and "tears off." These are the so-called crude data (although not so crude, at that); they set the stage for the psychologist's analysis. They are what one starts with. Contrast this view of behavioral data with Neisser's view as set forth in his definition of cognition.

According to Neisser (1967, p. 4), the "raw data" are *not* the interaction of hunter with deer or deer with hunter but "all the processes by which the sensory input is transformed, reduced, elaborated, stored, recovered, and used." It is impossible to overemphasize the radical difference between the two viewpoints. Instead of organism–stimulus object interaction, if Neisser were to conform to his definition of cognition, he would say that his data are "processes" transpiring within the hunter's and the deer's brains. The alleged "processes" are his starting point.

And how about these "processes"? What evidence are we offered to sub-stantiate such entities or functions? None whatsoever, for Neisser (1967, p. 4) admits that they "refer to *hypothetical* stages or aspects of cognition" (emphasis added). This is a frank acknowledgment that such processes are speculative, or "merely conceivable." Then shouldn't we heed Kuhn's (1961, p. 177) warning that "merely conceivable theories are not among the options open to the practicing scientist"? "Processes" themselves require explanation. As Hanson (1958, p. 120) counsels us, "What requires explanation cannot itself figure in the explanation." And now for a dissenting voice from the noncognitive camp.

SKINNER: "WHY I AM NOT A COGNITIVE PSYCHOLOGIST"

B. F. Skinner starts with a statement of his basic orientation: that behavior is a function of variables that are localizable in the environment. According to him, this is the starting point for all investigators, including cognitive psychologists, but he criticizes cognitivists because "they invent internal surrogates which become the subject matter of their science"

(Skinner, 1978, p. 97). In other words, they ignore observables in favor of imagined unobservables.

Skinner continues with an example from Ivan Pavlov's familiar conditioning experiment. A bell is sounded, and the dog is fed. Over and over the two are repeated. Eventually, the dog salivates at the sound of the bell. According to the cognitivists, as one variety of mentalists, "the dog 'associates' the bell with the food. But it was Pavlov who associated them! 'Associate' means to join or unite. The dog merely begins to salivate upon hearing the bell. We have no evidence that it does so because of an internal surrogate of the contingencies" (Skinner, 1978, p. 97).

Skinner continues in similar vein with many other behavioral specimens, which he explains in terms of contingencies of reinforcement. He rejects all notions of "storage." For him, acquired behaviors occur when their appropriate stimuli elicit them. There is no need to ask, "Where is the behavioral response when it isn't being performed?" any more than one should ask, "Where is the lightning when it isn't lightning?" For Skinner, all behaviors are organism–stimulus object interactions, not self-actional agents encapsulated within the organism, which statement sums up the radical difference between competing theories of psychology's subtle behaviors.

For Further Reading

Skinner, B. F. (1978). *Reflections on behaviorism and society*. Englewood Cliffs, N.J.: Prentice-Hall.

Wessells, M. G. (1982). *Cognitive psychology*. New York: Harper & Row.

CULTURAL OR
SHARED REACTIONS

Man is custom made, tailored according to the pattern prevailing in each culture.

Montagu (1956, p. 14)

An Arab Muslim can, legally and morally, marry as many as four wives at one time if he can afford them. In another culture, men who marry more than one woman *at a time*, even though they can afford them, are punished with prison sentences. The religious holy day of the week is Friday among Muslims, Saturday among Jews, and Sunday among Christians.

Dietary practices show the same variability among different social groups. Among Hindus, the sacred cow must not be eaten, but its milk may be consumed. For Muslims, pork is forbidden. Dogs and snakes approved by certain Oriental groups are anathema to others. Some Europeans eat horsemeat knowingly; we may have consumed the same unknowingly, but we would rebel if horsemeat were identified as such. Although Americans might consume fish eggs labeled as caviar, they would gag at the Eskimo diet J. L. Briggs (1970, p. 229) tried to assimilate during her seventeen-month stay with an Eskimo family. In describing the capricious food supply Briggs (1970, p. 164) writes:

On some days there is nothing to eat except rotting whitefish from the dog food caches, not bad for a change but still a less desirable food than the boiled heads of salmon trout and char trout that usually provide the evening meal in summer and early winter.

CULTURALIZATION

Culture, in the sense of behaving organisms such as family, peer groups, school, church, neighborhood, print and TV media, clubs, and so on, does its work so thoroughly that it stamps an individual as the product of a particular group. The process involved is culturalization, which means that the individual takes on the behaviors of the members in his or her group. Thus language, even the dialect, customs, habits, economic and political attitudes, religion, skills, and professions, are shaped via residence in, and interaction with, the individual's group members. This is how we recognize whether people learned German, French, or Russian in their infancy and childhood. Their accent gives them away when they speak English (or any other second language that they acquired in later years). Figure 2 also makes a cogent point for the power of culturalization. It shows a feature of Indian culture, which, although it proscribes the eating of beef, nevertheless exploits the cow's products: milk and cheese for their food value, and its excrement, that is, cow dung, as a cheap fuel. The Indian girl in the photo is shown casually shaping cow dung bare-handed as she smiles at her photographers. Her work will add to the income of her family or provide fuel for its cooking. One might be hard pressed to induce a child from another culture to engage in such activity. But is there any reason to doubt that the proper culturalization would produce the same results in children from other cultures? Certainly there is no reason for assuming that Indian children are inherently more susceptible to molding cow dung into standardized fuel chips.

HOW TO MAKE A CHINESE

Experimentation with humans isn't as feasible as it is with infrahumans. If it were, we could demonstrate the efficacy of culturalization by taking an infant in one culture, rearing it in a very different one, and observing the product. Sometimes "nature's experiment" gives us the results ready-made. The following case from Kluckhohn speaks eloquently in behalf of the power of culturalization. It concerns a young, white American who visited New York but found himself a stranger in his native country. Here is Kluckhohn's (1960, pp. 21-22) account of the incident:

Some years ago I met in New York City a young man who did not speak a word of English and was obviously bewildered by American ways. By "blood" he was as American as you or I, for his parents had gone from Indiana to China as missionaries. Orphaned in infancy, he was reared by a Chinese family in a remote village. All who met him found him more Chinese than American. The facts of his blue eyes and light hair were less impressive than a Chinese style of gait, Chinese arm and hand movements, Chinese facial expression, and Chinese modes of thought. The biological heritage was American, but the cultural training had been Chinese. He returned to China.

In a psychological sense, the young man was thoroughly a Chinese. His language, dress, diet, religion, politics, customs, manners, and gestures identified him as a member of the group in which he had been reared. It's obvious that yellow skin and "slant eyes" are not essential for creating a Chinese in any psychological sense. Rearing by Chinese alone will get the job done, after which the individual shares the reactions of those Chinese.

CONCLUSION

What I have tried to do in this piece is to identify and analyze a significant form of behavior, the cultural or shared response and culturalization, the

Figure 2. A beautiful Indian girl with a smile for the visitors who are taking her photo, while she, bare-handed, shapes fresh cow dung. Her activity, which would be revolting to a child in our culture, brings her satisfaction deriving from an activity that adds to her family's cooking fuel and/or income in a culture where handmade dung cakes are readily marketable as a fuel supplement. (Photo courtesy of Professor Carrol Izard.)

process which brings that response into being. These are valuable forms of behavior similar to the way in which index fossils serve the geologist. Such fossils, widely distributed but with a narrow time range, serve to identify geological formations. Similarly, cultural reactions specify the various culturalizations that an individual has passed through. On the other hand, if we know the culturalizations that individuals have undergone, we can predict their cultural reactions. This is an area that permits prediction and control. Who would want more?

A final word about social psychology as usually conceptualized. This branch of psychology stresses the interaction between an individual and other individuals or a group. Accordingly, shared reactions don't show up as clearly as I have described them above. The notion of cultural or shared reactions brings out another difference between the traditional construct and the one I have developed here. Once shared reactions have been built up by an individual, they can be performed in total isolation from other individuals. For example, a lone hermit can engage in flag-raising ceremonies with a pledge to the flag and can pray and sing as others do (as groups), without the presence of a single other human being. For a contrasting type of response see IDIOSYNCRATIC ACTION; for a fuller discussion of both cultural and idiosyncratic action see Pronko (1980) and Kantor and Smith (1975).

For Further Reading

Kluckhohn, C. (1960). *Mirror for man*. New York: Fawcett.

DATA

Datum (singular) and *data* (plural) refer to the events that are available for scientific observation and analysis. These terms derive from the Latin verb *do, dare, dedi, datus,* meaning "to give." Webster's *Ninth New Collegiate Dictionary* defines *datum* as "something given or admitted especially as a basis for reasoning or inference." The English and English *A Comprehensive Dictionary of Psychological and Psychoanalytic Terms* defines these terms as "that which is given in sensing; the perceived; loosely, a fact." Warren's *Dictionary of Psychology* offers the following characterization: "the group of known or 'given' facts on which a scientific discussion is based."

Are the facts really "givens" in the sense of raw sense data? A partial answer to the question comes from Hanson's commentary on observation (see OBSERVATION: WHAT IS OBSERVABLE?) to the effect that observations are theory-laden. Dewey (1929, p. 178) sees this clearly, as the following statement of his bears out:

The history of the theory of knowledge or epistemology would have been very different if instead of the word "data" or "givens," it had happened to start with calling the qualities in question "takens."

Scientists, as well as butchers, bakers, and candlestick makers, are children of their age and approach things and occurrences about them loaded with presuppositions and superstitions. We have all lost our perceptual virginity and see "things" through our cultural spectacles, unaware of the accretions of imposed attributes. How else are we to understand that three psychologists engaged in observing the same laboratory experiment can differ so radically in stating what they see there? One claims that mental images or representations are taking place in the subject's mind. Another asserts that "information processing" is occurring in the subject's computerlike brain. The third one sees only an interaction taking place *between* an organism and a stimulus object within a complex behavioral field.

Is the situation hopeless, then? No, not at all. But the only hope is a rigorous self-examination for the purpose of flushing out unwitting postulates and assumptions that we carry around with us as excess baggage. Such "baggage" constitutes a heavy intellectual burden that hampers our seeing things free of the many alleged invisibles that our cultural heritage has imposed upon us. But if we are once relieved of that onerous scientific handicap, we are then free to see nothing but what's observable.

For Further Reading

Dewey, J. (1929). *The quest for certainty.* New York: Minton, Balch & Co.

DISEASE, BODILY AND "MENTAL"

The term *disease* has had a variable history. For a start, let us consider its dictionary definition. *Webster's New International Unabridged Dictionary,* second edition, defines *disease* as "a condition in which bodily health is seriously attacked, deranged, or impaired; sickness; illness; as mortality from *disease*; a particular instance or cause of this; any departure from the state of health presenting marked symptoms; also a particular ailment having special symptoms or causes; as Addison's disease, Bright's disease, and so on." Further help comes from an inspection of the contrary term *ease,* which is defined as "a state of being comfortable; freedom from pain, trouble, or annoyance." We should also note the significance of the prefix *dis,* which signifies "the opposite of" or "absence of," as in *appear, disappear; own, disown; satisfied, dissatisfied.* Thus, *ease, dis-ease.*

The dis-ease aspect of the term *disease* is easily overlooked. Its prevailing contemporary meaning is in the direction of disease as an entity, a specific illness, "effect," produced by a specific "cause" (see also CAUSE AND EFFECT), for example, parasites, filtrable viruses, and nutritional, environmental, or genetic deficiencies. This has not always been the way to understand disease.

King (1963, p. 3) has documented the radical notions of disease that have prevailed over the ages, notions that appear bizarre to us. Ours may appear so to our successors. In the past, conceptions of disease have been influenced by demonology, magic, voodoo, and even theology. In the Middle Ages, the Black Death killed off hundreds of thousands in Europe. The church attributed the pestilence to punishment by God "for man's sins" (Walker, 1955, p. 99). Aspects of these notions still linger on in certain populations, but a microorganism theory of disease dominates current theorists.

MENNINGER'S ANTI-"MENTAL DISEASE" STAND

How about "mental disease"? Karl Menninger (1964), for one, has seen through the fallacy of applying this medical model to people who are upset, tense, in conflict, depressed, and so on. Why? Because "schizophrenia is no more a clear-cut disease than 'the falling sickness' or 'biliousness' " (p. 2). Menninger considers words such as *schizophrenia, neurotic, psychopathic,* and many others "dangerous words." But Menninger's position represents only "half a loaf," because, while he rejects the enduring "mental disease" conception, he still adheres to the notion of "mental illness." We now consider the validity of the latter notion by Thomas Szasz (1957, 1961), who dropped an intellectual bombshell in his effort to explode the myth of mental illness.

THE MYTH OF MENTAL ILLNESS

From the traditional standpoint, it was a courageous stand that Menninger took in abandoning the disease paradigm in dealing with troubled people; even today some practitioners (Siegler & Osmond, 1974) believe in the disease model. But imagine the outrage of psychiatrists and some psychologists to be told that there is no such thing as "mental illness."

Here is how Szasz develops his argument. He finds a contradiction between the ways "therapists" *communicate with* their patients in discussing their problems and the way they talk *about* their procedures in the language of physicians, physiologists, and even physicists. Why is this so? Because, from the start, psychiatry was identified with medicine. Therefore, when psychiatrists dealt with people's conflicts, worries, depressions, fears, and confusions, they adopted the medical model and attempted to treat such people as if they were sick. Obviously, malaria, diabetes, syphilis, herpes, and AIDS are illnesses, but how could anyone identify these conditions with anxiety reactions, delusions, and hallucinations? According to Szasz, this could happen only by miscasting the latter in the same traditional framework that treats broken bones, measles, and pneumonia.

One is tempted to ask, "So what? What difference does it really make?" According to Szasz, it makes a great deal of difference because you will be treating a phobic or a hysteric as a "patient." Patients are labeled as "sick" and are sent to a hospital to be "treated" with "bed rest" and "medication." When, in a past era, hysterical reactions were considered evidence of witchcraft, they were "treated" either by exorcism or by burning at the stake, according to the prevailing theological notions. The witchcraft model turned out to be a myth. According to Szasz, the medical model is also a myth.

As an alternative, Szasz would treat "problems of living" as learned behaviors that have a development of their own. As such, they must be studied in their own distinctive, biographical dimension, not in the framework in which meningitis and cancer are understood. Because "problems of living" are developed in relation to other people, Szasz (1966, p. 230) "eschews biological considerations as explanations and instead attempts to construct a consistently psychosocial explanatory scheme in which . . . not only is so-called psychological growth learned but so are childishness, immaturity, and mental illnesses."

At this phaseout of our discussion, the skeptical psychologist is faced with the problem of evaluating (1) the mental disease model, (2) the mental illness model, and (3) the problems-of-living model, in understanding unusual, unadaptable, and socially disapproved forms of behavior. Again, different consequences stem from different starting assumptions.

For Further Reading

Menninger, K. (1964). Psychiatrists use dangerous words. *Saturday Evening Post,* April 25.
Szasz, T. S. (1966). Mental illness is a myth. *The New York Times Magazine,* June 12, 30, 90-92.
Szasz, T. S. (1984). *The therapeutic state.* Buffalo, N.Y.: Prometheus Books.

DYNAMIC VERSUS STATIC VIEWS

> You cannot step twice into the same river, for fresh waters are ever flowing in upon you.
>
> Heraclitus

"All things are in a state of flux" is another saying attributed to Heraclitus, a Greek philosopher who lived and worked about the turn of the sixth century B.C. Take such a homely example as the flame of an oil lamp. It looks fixed and solid, like an object. Yet, Heraclitus would say, if you study it more carefully, you will note that the oil is being constantly drawn up by the wick, where it is continuously being translated into flame; the resulting gases evaporate into the air, and soot is formed and falls down as a by-product. As long as the supply of oil lasts, the *process* goes on and on. Implicit in Heraclitus's view is the notion of *dynamic action*; the only constancy in the ongoing flow of events is change. Heraclitus's conception is by no means obsolete. There are contemporary scientific views that are very much in harmony with this early approach to the study of nature. But before we leave Heraclitus, we should emphasize that where one person senses a ceaseless chain of ongoing activity, another person sees only a lamp or a flame.

THE TRADITIONAL STATIC VIEW

The Heraclitean view as presented above is the opposite of the prevalent "commonsense" view, a view that we must consider because it has insinuated itself even into scientific activity. According to the conventional, static conception of nature, the world consists of bodies at rest, which stay put until some other body pushes or pulls them. If nothing disturbs the peace, everything remains in a quiet, stationary state. Under this view, the fundamental reality is *substance* or *things* having a discrete and more or less permanent existence. The *solid* is the model for this kind of approach simply because of its greater familiarity and wide acceptance.

According to J. H. Woodger (1929), "the commonsense" view stresses things or stuff above all else. It confers "thinghood" (p. 182) upon objects such as wood, stone, water, lightning, and organisms. These are then thought of as independently existing entities with certain properties. It should be obvious that such conceptions are contrary to the injunction "To be is to be related." But there are more serious criticisms to be made of the "commonsense" view. Woodger's concept of "event" as "something going on" will help to make objections to them clear. For him, "an object" such as "an organism" is *not* an object but a property or character of an event. To keep the flaming-lamp analogy, where one person sees only a lump of stuff when he or she views an organism, Woodger sees a highly dynamic series of "goings-on" instead of a static thing. For him, stress is on *action*, with the organism playing a subordinate role as a perseverative aspect of a series of events in which the organism is seen as a continuing or enduring aspect of those events.

WHAT IS A HEART?

Perhaps an example from Woodger can help illuminate the view he espouses. Take the heart. How is it commonly thought of? Some think of it as a *thing*, in appearance somewhat as it looks on a Valentine card. As for anatomy itself, most people think of this branch of biology as a very concrete science. Yet, when one thinks about it, the anatomist studies the heart as a *visual* object after it has quit its biological existence and becomes a mummy. From this standpoint, he is a "geographer" of the pickled heart. Far from being concrete, his procedure is, in fact, quite abstract. Should the anatomist dissect out pieces of the heart for microscopic analysis, he has gotten even more abstract, with the heart still further removed by comparison with the concrete, living, pulsating heart.

If we consider the heart in the living organism, we come out with a totally different picture, seen as an aspect of the organism. The ever-changing contours of the heart as it rhythmically pumps blood throughout the organism make it impossible to pick out any particular configuration as *the* shape. Furthermore, the heart is not an independently existing object.

Now, Woodger (1929, p. 329) admits that abstraction is essential in any scientific study, and anatomy represents one way of abstracting and simplifying. Physiology does the same thing when it focuses on the *functioning* heart. The trouble arises when, in forgetting the abstract nature of such analyses, "we fall into the fallacy of misplaced concreteness" and treat the dead, pickled heart as "the real thing." We don't need to debate which heart is *really* real as long as we also realize the existence of the concrete four-dimensional event, which we refer to as the beating heart in the living organism. "Heart" and "organism" are only the most easily observed and therefore the most stable and enduring phases of the series of occurrences in which they are involved. Their easy visibility makes them convenient anchoring points for lazy thinking.

The fundamental question here is: Is there any lesson for us in Woodger's study of the living heart? I think there is. We can either learn to see nature in its fullest, richest, and most dynamic aspect or view it with all the life squeezed out of it, reduced to a static, embalmed state. Some see the living cell as a bit of life struggling for a foothold on its substrate, changing in shape from moment to moment, involving "space" as well as "time." In fact, we can understand a cell only if we expand our observation to a dimension known as history. Study of the fixed cell under microscopic view at an instant of time omits the historical dimension. It is comparable to the mortuary specimen of the aborted fetus or the pickled heart.

In our inquiry of what we might refer to as "human nature," we have the option of viewing our data as passive, mysterious "mental states" that happen *to* us in a mental theater said to transpire inside us somewhere "inside" our head. On the other hand, we may view our data as lively, dynamic occurrences or events localizable in a field involving not only the organism but also the objects, people, and situations in the organism's sur- roundings, for to be is to be related. Similarly, as in understanding the cell, we find the need for including a historical dimension in psychological inquiry. As in any form of study, one may go about it in different ways. We have the choice of a static view or of a dynamic, process view, the latter demanding a temporal dimension in order to achieve understanding.

For Further Reading

Woodger, J. H. (1929). *Biological principles: A critical study*. London: Kegan Paul, Trench, Trubner & Co.

ECOLOGY AND ECOLOGICAL PSYCHOLOGY

ECOLOGY

No science exists in a vacuum any more than do plants, people, or planets. The fairly recent emergence of ecology from the science of biology is already influencing other disciplines. However, before proceeding further, we must first define the field.

As a branch of biology, ecology deals with the totality of interrelationships among organisms and their environments. Why are pine trees stunted when they grow at eight thousand feet of altitude by comparison with others of the same species that grow at fifteen hundred feet of altitude, or why, at the same altitude, do we see such a differential in height between plants grown on the north side of a mountain versus those on the south side of the same mountain? The answer is to be found in a study of their ecologies. The uniqueness of an ecological approach is its stress on viewing all the relevant factors in their interrelationship. Because Roger Barker attempts to broaden his approach to behavioral investigation beyond the traditional organism-centered view, we now examine his ecological formulation as reported in his (Barker, 1968) *Ecological Psychology: Concepts and Methods for Studying the Environment of Human Behavior.*

BARKER'S ECOLOGICAL PSYCHOLOGY

Barker's stress on the environment of human behavior appears as a compensation for the centuries-long stress on the organism as the (self-actional) source of behavior. As such, it is an aborted field approach. However, his move in the direction of a field view deserves recognition. Among other praiseworthy insights, Barker (1968, p. 4) found that he "could predict aspects of children's behavior more adequately from knowledge of the behavior characteristics of the drug stores, arithmetic classes, and basketball games they inhabited than from knowledge of the behavior tendencies of particular children." Barker found that people behaved in certain ways depending on whether they were in church, at the post office, or in a tavern or bar. Therefore, behavior settings had to be taken into account in order to understand behavior.

Barker might have gone on to a larger field approach, but his cause-effect thinking limited him to treating behavior settings as independent variables and the resulting behaviors as dependent variables (Barker, 1968, p. 28.) His formulation pits the organism and environment against each other and therefore achieves, at best, an interactional status.

BRONFENBRENNER'S *THE ECOLOGY OF HUMAN DEVELOPMENT*

Urie Bronfenbrenner (1979) starts out by criticizing mainstream psychology's asymmetrical treatment of organism and environment. He objects to its hypertrophy of theory and research focusing on the properties of the person and only the most rudimentary conception and characterization of the environment in which the person is found (p. 16). It is a noble attempt to enlarge the traditional, observational base for the investigation of behavior, but his whole enterprise comes to naught because of his dualistic framework. Here is how Bronfenbrenner's enterprise breaks down. He does not take "the environment" as factually presented. Because Bronfenbrenner espouses Lewin's dualistic framework, the symmetry that he had aimed for is transformed into an asymmetry. For Bronfenbrenner, behavior turns out to be "a phenomenological world," "intrapsychic processes" (p. 12), and so on. According to him, there is an "external world" and an "internal world." The way to the "internal world" and "of greatest relevance for the scientific understanding of behavior and development is reality, not as it exists in the so-called objective world, but as it appears in the mind of the person" (p. 23). By this time, the asymmetry in Bronfenbrenner's formulation should be apparent. The role of the environment is acknowledged, but the whole enterprise becomes unbalanced once more on account of his phenomenological framework. According to it, the environment can never be known directly but only indirectly, by studying the manner in which it is "experienced" by the individual. The following statement of Bronfenbrenner's (1979, p. 23) confirms and concludes my appraisal of his approach as an attempted restoration of the traditional asymmetrical type of interaction, one that assigns the bulk of "psychological work" to the organism's mind: "the environment of greatest relevance for the scientific understanding of behavior and development is reality not as it is in *the so-called objective world but as it appears in the mind of the person*" (emphasis added). Here is another example of how our philosophies predestine our enterprises.

What is the outlook for an ecological psychology? Outside of the ecologists mentioned in this article and SETTING FACTORS, one finds very few others. Inspection of the *Annual Review of Psychology* for 1982, 1983, and 1984 reveals little hope for the development of an ecological perspective on behavioral events, a perspective that might attain a full, integrated field orientation. Tradition dies hard; progress comes at a snail's pace.

For Further Reading

Barker, R. G. (1968). *Ecological psychology*. Stanford, Calif.: Stanford University Press.

Bronfenbrenner, U. (1979). *The ecology of human development: Experiments by nature and design*. Cambridge, Mass.: Harvard University Press.

EMBRYOLOGICAL DEVELOPMENT: PSYCHOLOGICAL ASPECTS

In his book *An Introduction to Embryology*, Balinsky (1975, p. 3) defines embryology as the study of the "ontogenetic development of organisms" (i.e., *individual* organisms) by contrast with the longer-spanned phylogenetic development or evolution of the species. The topics that confront one in embryology are fertilization, organ formation, growth, and histological differentiation. Other recent publications in embryology (Ebert, 1965; Wolstenholme & O'Connor, 1969; Tanner, 1978) follow the same pattern, with a focus on the anatomy and physiology of development. With such a limited interest in intrauterine events, the possibility of observing any occurrence resembling behavior is precluded. Consequently, according to the prevailing view, the fetus is an inert passenger in the womb of the mother. Outside of some random kicking in the fifth month of pregnancy, the psychological zero point of the infant is generally placed at birth. This is when learning is said to begin. But there is more to embryo and fetus than anatomical and physiological investigation reveals. Recent studies disclose how erroneous earlier views have been.

LILEY'S OBSERVATIONS

A. W. Liley's (1972) fresh slant on life in the uterus has yielded unprecedented observations of the hitherto hidden drama. Formerly, fetal movements were reported only at about sixteen to twenty-two weeks of gestation. But Liley reports shifts in fetal posture as early as the eighth week. Maternal movement and maternal change of position induce shifts in the posture of the fetus as if to regain what Liley (p. 100) calls comfort. The variety of such postural changes prepare the developing organism for the postuterine encounter with gravity, when extrauterine standing and walking begin. Gesell (1945, p. 32), an early student of fetal behavior, reminds us that "man begins his life-long contest with gravity even before he is born . . . most of the basic organization of this distinctly human posture is laid down during the fetal period." There is much more drama occurring in the uterine theater. Swallowing, hiccups, and sucking originate as the result of the close proximity to toes, fingers, and thumbs to the fetus's mouth, a feature illustrated in Figure 10 (see PERSONALITY). Liley (p. 103) tells us that "thumb-sucking has been photographed in the 9-week abortus." With such developmental facts at hand, why do we need the ancient notion of the thumb-sucking instinct? Apparently, sucking can be learned in the uterus.

Through all the changing uterine events, conditions of the organism and its surroundings provide opportunities for learning to occur. Indeed, DeCasper and Fifer (1980) determined experimentally that infants younger than three days of age preferred the maternal voice over the voice of another female, even after only 12 hours of contact with the mother's voice. But mothers talk during their pregnancy. Therefore, the researchers couldn't be certain that their results weren't influenced by their subjects' uterine experiences with their mothers' attenuated voices. This uncertainty led to the next interesting study by Spence and DeCasper (1982). These investigators had pregnant mothers read the same story aloud daily for five to six weeks prior to their delivery. Tested within 48 hours of birth, ten of the 12 test babies preferred listening to the story read aloud to them in utero over a story they had not heard while they were in the womb.

In the next experiment, DeCasper and Sigafoos (1983) discovered that the maternal heartbeat was the only nonspeech auditory stimulus that was able to reinforce sucking behavior in the newborn infant. These findings strongly suggest (1) that prenatal experience is positively related to postnatal behavior and (2) that the zero point of an individual's reactional biography starts earlier than the moment of birth. Here is another instance of events, in this case uterine occurrences, that were overlooked as long as certain assumptions held sway.

For Further Reading

Liley, A. W. (1972). The foetus as a personality. *Australian and New Zealand Journal of Psychiatry, 6*, 99-105.

EMERGENCY OR CONTINGENTIAL BEHAVIOR

A truck was stuck at an underpass. The driver underestimated the height of his vehicle and jammed the truck against the top of the underpass just barely into the entrance; another two or three inches and the truck would have made it. What to do? The usual crowd soon gathered around, and all stood speechless, watching, until a twelve-year-old boy piped up and asked, "Why don't you let some air out of the tires?" The driver did, and the problem was solved. The truck got through. The boy's contingential behavior turned the trick.

A robber handed a bank teller a note demanding money from her cash drawer. The young woman pretended to faint and crashed to the floor. The robber was so dumbfounded that he ran out of the bank without the money or his note.

A woman driving along a California freeway found that her accelerator pedal was stuck at a car speed of sixty miles an hour. She stepped on her brakes, but that soon burned out the brakes and set the tires on fire. Finally, in desperation, she decided to abandon the car and jumped out. The driver-less car crashed, a total wreck. When asked, "Why didn't you turn off the ignition key?" she replied, "I never dreamed of doing that."

ANALYSIS OF THE PRECEDING CONTINGENCIES

Let's start with the twelve-year-old's behavior in the jammed-truck situation. Everyone who stood around staring at the occurrence knew how to let air out of a tire. We may assume that such a reaction may have occurred in the experience of many observers as when, on past occasions, a tire was overinflated. Here we meet up with the specificity with which behavior must be considered. Letting air out of a tire because it is under too great pressure is not necessarily equivalent to carrying out the same act in the case of a truck jammed in an underpass. The two situations are radically different, and different situations make a great difference in psychological events.

Next, let's look at the bank teller's unprecedented behavior when she was confronted by the robber. Let's assume that she had never *actually* fainted in her life before. But almost any adult knows how to simulate fainting, and this is what she did; she carried out a quite ordinary act. What makes her behavior stand out so prominently is the circumstance that elicited it.

Now, let's analyze the case of the jammed accelerator pedal. The freeway driver had never before experienced the situation in which she found herself. The contingential behavior evoked was to bear down on the brake, a response surely called out previously when her car required slowing down. But this situation was very different, and that reaction didn't help. An alternative, inefficient response, jumping out of the car, came next. It, too, was contingential under the assumption that she had not acted that way in any previous, similar situation. Why didn't she turn off the ignition key and save car and personal injury? How many times does anyone carry out that act in a stream of traffic? Such acts normally occur when one comes to a complete stop. Once more we note the specificity of conditions that influence behavior. Suppose now that our bruised and battered driver experiences the same incident again at a later time, recalls the possibility of turning off the ignition key in such a situation, and actually does so. Will her behavior qualify as a contingential response? Not at all. Why? Because it was a specific reaction that was now a part of her acquired behavioral repertoire ready for usage *in such situations*.

WIT AND REPARTEE

Wit and repartee also illustrate contingential behavior. For example, A answers the phone. The unfamiliar voice at the other end asks, "Is Joe Doakes there?" A answers, "No; he isn't." The stranger's voice at the other end persists: "Are you sure?" A responds by asking, "Have I ever lied to you before?" A's response meets the criterion of contingential behavior because of the situation in which it occurs. Many of us have often asked, "Have I ever lied to you before?" It is the unexpected situation in which A asks a perfect stranger this question that gives it the fresh and unstudied feature of contingential behavior.

FURTHER SPECIFICATION OF CONTINGENTIAL ACTION

Examination of the behavior that occurs in emergencies or contingencies reveals no *new* behavioral acquisition. What happens depends only in a general way upon one's past behavior acquisition. The apparent freshness and spontaneity is granted by the context in which it appears. Each of the preceding illustrations reveals mundane action. What surprises us is the setting in which the respective behaviors arise. Thus, the setting or context stands out prominently in contingential or emergency behavioral fields, once again emphasizing the importance of a field construct in psychology. One looks in vain for a construct of contingential action in mainstream psychology, demonstrating the consequences that follow from the guiding assumptions that one starts with.

For Further Reading

Kantor, J. R., & Smith, N. W. (1975). *The science of psychology: An interbehavioral survey*. Chicago: Principia Press.

Pronko, N. H. (1980). *Psychology from the standpoint of an interbehaviorist*. Monterey, Calif.: Brooks/Cole.

EVENT

The term *event* is usually defined as an occurrence, happening, or episode, not something static or inert. Tornadoes, snowstorms, and earthquakes provide unambiguous illustrations of the dynamic nature of events. The question is: Can the term *event* be usefully applied to behavior analysis? John Dewey and Arthur Bentley (1949, p. 75) seriously considered incorporating the term into psychological terminology for a number of reasons. *Event* appealed to them because a behavioral occurrence "takes place" just as a storm or earthquake occurs in a definite *place*. Also, an event takes time; it has a history, a duration or time span. Recalling something always involves a past and a present time. Another phase of an event that Dewey and Bentley emphasized was its wholeness or totality. While admitting stimulus and response as phases of an event, they urged that we train ourselves to see the single, total event so and to work with it as such. Otherwise, we are likely to overemphasize the role of the organism with a danger of localizing behavior *within* the organism. For that reason, they avoided the term *behavior*, preferring instead the comprehensive term *event*. A final point about *events*: events don't come separately packaged; they are always connected with other events and should be studied contextually.

WHITEHEAD'S CONTRIBUTION

A philosopher, Alfred North Whitehead, who preceded Dewey and Bentley also had something to say about *event*. It seems reasonable to suppose that Whitehead's writings must have had some influence on Dewey and Bentley. At any rate, Whitehead's thoughts on the topic provide additional insights into the meaning of the term. For Whitehead (1957, pp. 14-15), "the immediate fact before us is the whole occurrence of nature. There is no way of holding nature still and looking at it" because the complex of passing events flows by us. The dynamic character of events is implied in Whitehead's (1957, p. 53) statement that "nature is a process," something going on. Implicit in the term *process* is the sense of duration, not instantaneity.

Whitehead (1957, pp. 165-167) offers an unforgettable illustration of *event*, one that, at first glance, appears to be a homely example. Let us start with his statement about a certain red, granite monolithic pillar, known as

Cleopatra's Needle, that stands in London. He writes, "Cleopatra's Needle is on the Charing Cross Embankment" (p. 165). With our habitual thing orientation, we are ready to argue, "Well, there is nothing eventlike about a chunk of stone that just sits there year after year."

I can almost hear Whitehead's expostulation: "But Cleopatra's Needle hasn't *always* sat on the bank of the Thames River." In fact, we learn from the *Columbia Encyclopedia* (1975, p. 577) that the obelisk was first erected near Heliopolis, Egypt, about 1475 B.C., its birth date. In 14 B.C., it was moved to Alexandria. In 1878, it was presented as a gift to England, but it was not there yet when Whitehead was a small boy. And if London smog and acid rain continue to dissolve it unimpeded, it will some day cease to exist. Thus, we see that Cleopatra's Needle has a long history, albeit an unexciting one, with gradual changes over time.

Some events have slow and uninteresting histories, while others, such as tornadoes, earthquakes, and explosions, have rapid and dramatic careers. Broad's (1952, p. 54) definition of *event* embraces both kinds. He defines an event as follows: "By an *event* I am going to mean anything that endures at all, no matter how long it lasts or whether it be qualitatively alike or qualitatively different at adjacent stages in its history." In addition to duration, we must take into account the phases of an event that follow in a certain order. We don't first hear the thunder and then see the lightning. The order is important. Running the motion-picture projector in reverse illustrates the point. In a scientific framework, events make sense only when we can know their various parts in relation to subsequent as well as earlier phases of the cycle. An economical characterization of *event* furnishes a suitable conclusion to our consideration of *event* in the following epigrammatic statement by Goodman (1951, p. 185): "A thing is a monotonous event; an event is an unstable thing."

For Further Reading

Dewey, J., & Bentley, A. F. (1949). *Knowing and the known*. Boston: Beacon Press.
Whitehead, A. N. (1957). *The concept of nature*. Ann Arbor: University of Michigan Press. (Original work published 1920)

EXPERIMENTAL DESIGN

Experiments that test the adequacy of mathematical models and other types of deductive theory currently carry great prestige, and their importance is taken for granted.

Sidman (1960, p. 6)

Sidman's statement is still on the mark today. Kagan, Havemann, and Segal (1984, p. 18), who espouse the prevailing cause-effect postulate for behavior analysis, consider experimentation as "the ultimate method," one in which "the psychologist makes a careful and rigidly controlled examination of cause and effect." It is this cause-effect thinking as an aspect of psychological experimentation that we pursue first.

CAUSE-EFFECT THINKING

In their book *Research Methods and Analysis*, Walizer and Wienir (1978, p. 12) agree that "scientists do not believe that things just happen. They confront the observable world with the idea that one thing causes another." Figure 3 offers a diagrammatic representation or framework of an experiment according to the prevailing causal view. *I* is the independent variable or *cause*. It can be varied in a measurable way. *D* is the dependent variable, that is, the subject's response or *effect* produced by *I*. The converging arrows, labeled *C*, are other variables or conditions that might affect the response and that must, therefore, be held constant in order to produce a "pure cause-effect" result.

CRITICISM OF CAUSE-EFFECT THINKING

What's wrong with the cause-effect paradigm that dominates the prevailing view of psychological experimentation? The answer is that the conventional view is based on an obsolete, Newtonian, mechanistic paradigm. According to Hanson (1958, p. 65), causal explanations have been modeled after the mechanical notion of pushes and pulls as causes and the results of their impacts as effects. The simplistic, behavioristic stimulus-response theory reveals this pattern; stimulus is *cause* and response becomes *effect*. The immediate question is: Do cause-effect assumptions do justice to the

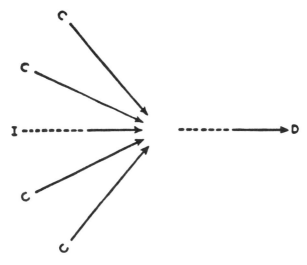

Figure 3. Schema of an experiment to illustrate its underlying paradigm of cause-effect. *I* is the independent variable, the stimulus, or *cause*. It is varied in a predetermined way in order to ascertain its outcome on *D*, the organism's response or the *effect*. The converging arrows *C* represent the controlled variables, which, because they might affect the outcome, are held constant throughout the experiment.

richness of behavioral events? Also, many experimentalists deal with behavior in the laboratory as if in isolated fragments, in violation of the principle "Present events are a function of antecedent events."

THE MATTER OF STATISTICAL MODELS

Another criticism of traditional experimentation concerns its forcing behavior data into a procrustean bed in its adherence to a rigid, statistical design. Inspection of such texts as those by Kimmel (1970), Keppel and Saufley (1980), and Gravetter and Wallnau (1985) reveals a bewildering array of group comparison designs, designs often uncritically adopted from the statistical mathematician.

However, there are dissenting voices here and there. Kimmel (1970, p. 149), for one, considers statistics as playing an ancillary role, arguing that experimentalists who understand and are in control of relevant factors can interpret their findings "with little or no statistical analysis at all." Bergin and Strupp (1972, p. 440) also criticize those who start an investigation by choosing a factorial design or behavior that will allow dealing with it by means of "statistical and mathematical niceties." Skinner (1959, pp. 77-78) joins the dissenters in his criticism of the traditional training of young psychologists whose education is loaded in the direction of "model building," "theory construction," and "experimental design." Sidman (1960, p. 214) takes a position close to that of Skinner, arguing that "there are no rules of experimental design." While Sidman's statement suggests experimental anarchy, what comes out of it is the principle that may be stated in the form of a question: Should not scientific method proceed from the requirements of behavioral observations and not from the imposition of arbitrary and rigid models borrowed from extraneous sources? The same question needs to be addressed to reliance on statistical usage.

CONCLUSION

An overemphasis on experimentation in an effort to be "scientific" encourages us to overlook the progress achieved by some largely nonexperimental sciences such as astronomy, geology, and comparative anatomy, which are mostly satisfied with simply observing, rather than manipulating, their data. Like astronomers, we need to realize that, in nature, we have an inexhaustible source of raw materials awaiting observational analysis. As Sidman (1960, p. 9) reminds us, "Behavior is a rich subject matter, and thus far we have observed only a small sample in the laboratory."

For Further Reading

Sidman, M. (1960). *Tactics of scientific research*. New York: Basic Books.
Skinner, B. F. (1959). *Cumulative record*. New York: Appleton-Century-Crofts.

EXPLANATION OR
DESCRIPTION?

It is difficult to separate explanation and description. . . . to *describe*
what goes on in a chemical reaction is to explain what goes on there.
Theobald (1968)

According to their dictionary definitions, *to describe* means to represent or
give an account of in words and *to explain* means to make plain or
understandable. Even the dictionary definitions of the terms would permit
their use as synonyms of each other.

SCIENTIFIC USAGE

A student asks his psychology professor to explain "memory." Let's
pretend that the professor states that memory is to be explained by "neural
traces" laid down in the frontal lobes of the cerebral cortex at the time of
learning, although of course such traces have never been observed. Let's
assume that the student is well satisfied with his professor's "explanation."
Here is an instance of an "explanation" which is really no "explanation" at
all in the sense of advancing understanding or prediction. For would anyone
claim that one could see whether a poem had been learned by looking into
the poem learner's brain? Nevertheless, the term *explanation* is sometimes
used this way. What seems to be demanded is a statement in terms of some
esoteric, behind-the-scenes, mystical entity that is believed to be "causing"
or "producing" the phenomenon in question, an answer to the question
why. Obviously, the explanation referred to above is a reductionistic
explanation. It translates the language of observation (e.g., a person's recit-
ing a childhood nursery poem) to language in terms of a hypothetical
anatomy and physiology. It is this type of explanation that the physicist
Feyerabend (1975, pp. 246-247) inveighs against in the following statement:

Knowledge . . . is not obtained by trying to grasp an essence behind the reports of
the senses but by (1) putting the observer in the right position relative to the object
(process, aggregate), by inserting him into the appropriate place in the complex
pattern that constitutes the world, and (2) by adding up the elements which are
noted under these circumstances.

Among psychologists, Kantor (1933, p. 34) makes "no ultimate division between description and explanation" because for him explanations are only "elaborate descriptions" (p. 34). Once one has adequately described the relevant factors in an event and has related events to one another, explanation or understanding follows.

Skinner (Wann, 1964, p. 102) appears to follow suit when he defines explanation as "the demonstration of a functional relationship between behavior and manipulable or controllable variables."

The intimate connection between description, explanation, understanding, and prediction is manifested in the following statements. First, Scriven (1970, p. 102) on explanation: he defines it as a "topically unified communication, the content of which imparts understanding of some scientific phenomenon." Kemeny and Oppenheim (1970) make no distinction between explanation and prediction. Caws (1965) agrees that you can show how events fit into the universe, but the universe at "rock bottom" cannot be explained. But if you can predict the outcome of an event by applying a formerly derived explanatory scheme, you have achieved an explanation.

All of the foregoing statements from various sources may be summed up for our purpose as follows. If, as psychologists, with postulates clearly stated, we restrict ourselves to direct observation of events, and if we achieve a proper assessment of the participating factors in those events and can discern an order, regularity, or patterning in a series of related events, then we may be sure that we have achieved a satisfactory description or explanation of our observations. If we know the particular cluster of factors that are involved in the occurrence of an event, then we should be able to bring that event about. With the attainment of such a goal, we may say that we can fully describe or explain the given event.

For Further Reading

Caws, P. (1965). *The philosophy of science*. Princeton, N.J.: Van Nostrand.
Wann, T. W. (Ed.). (1964). *Behaviorism and phenomenology*. Chicago: University of Chicago Press.

FACT

It now seems to me that the firm opposite of "fact" is "fiction." "Fact," something made *out*; "fiction," something made *up*.

Dewey, in a letter to Bentley (Ratner, Altman & Wheeler, 1964, p. 173)

In elaboration of Dewey's epigrammatic statement, such occurrences as a child reading a story, or two people conversing with one another, can be made *out*, that is, they can be discriminated out of a matrix of ongoing events. However, "mind," "consciousness," "will," and "superego" have never been made *out* because they are, by definition, nonobservable. Therefore, they belong under the made-*up* or fiction category. The distinction between fact and fiction can be secured through observation. That which is observable can be nailed down as fact because it can be made *out*. That which is not observable has to be made *up* or invented. Such hypothetical entities as learning centers in the brain, memory traces, and executive powers of the brain are "merely conceivable" and therefore must be classified as made-*up* entities. It is an astounding fact (because it is observable) that fictions are often treated with the same respect as facts. Much depends on the assumptions that one starts with.

For Further Reading

Bentley, A. F. (1935). *Behavior, knowledge, fact*. Chicago: Principia Press.

Ratner, S., Altman, J., & Wheeler, J. E. (1964). *John Dewey and Arthur Bentley: A philosophical correspondence*. New Brunswick, N.J.: Rutgers University Press.

THE "FALLACY OF DOGMATIC FINALITY," OR THE COLLAPSE OF CERTITUDE

It is an easily overlooked fact that every age suffers from a kind of superiority complex. Being on the frontiers of civilization, we can convince ourselves that we are the most knowledgeable, the most advanced of all who preceded us. In science, such an attitude can easily slip over into what Alfred North Whitehead has labeled the fallacy of dogmatic finality. A fallacy is a false or mistaken notion.

Lucien Price, a follower of Whitehead's, explains the fallacy with a memorable example from the science of physics. He points out that, for five hundred years following Isaac Newton's brilliant formulations, physicists mistakenly believed firmly that the laws of the physical universe would hold for all time. They acknowledged that there were a few obscure areas, such as radiation, that would be cleared up shortly. But, except for that minor gap in knowledge, they "supposed that nearly everthing of importance about physics was known" (Price, 1954, pp. 6-7). Then came the Einsteinian revolution, and Newtonian physics, as the ultimate description/ explanation of nature for all time, collapsed.

However, according to Price (1954, p. 7), scientists haven't learned from what should have been a powerful lesson. As they continue to make progress, they easily convince themselves that this time they have arrived at the truth. The clear implication is for all investigators to heed Whitehead's admonition as quoted by Price (1954, p. 7):

Nothing is more curious than the self-satisfied dogmatism with which mankind at each period of its history cherishes the delusion of the finality of its existing modes of knowledge. . . . This dogmatic common sense is the death of philosophic adventure.

Whitehead's charge should impel us to seek out the hidden assumptions that guide our inquiry, to check how well they advance our inquiry, and to be willing to give them up for other possibly more advantageous assumptions.

For Further Reading

Price, L. (1954). *Dialogues of Alfred North Whitehead as recorded by Lucien Price*. Boston: Little, Brown & Co.

THE "FALLACY OF MISPLACED CONCRETENESS"

Science is always abstractive, and that's as it should be. As discussed in the entry SPACE-TIME IN BIOLOGY, the heart in the cadaver is studied for its structure, that is, its spatial configuration or shape. Some would see that pickled specimen of the heart as somehow fundamental. Our cultural preference for matter or the material favors the anatomical specimen. But J. H. Woodger (1929, p. 328) has cautioned us not to adopt the dead heart as the starting point for inquiry, because, if you look to the living organism, you will find that the heart has a highly dynamic and exciting history within that context. Thus, by stressing the preserved, dead organ, you are missing a highly dramatic sequence of events involving the heart as only one aspect of the living organism. Woodger might add that, by emphasizing the dead, preserved specimen in the museum jar, you have furnished us with an instance of misplaced concreteness. The less concrete or more abstract, incompletely representational, anatomical specimen is given priority over the dramatic, pulsating, throbbing heart in the living organism.

Does the "fallacy of misplaced concreteness" (Whitehead, 1944) have anything to do with psychology? Let us examine the facts. First, we need to call attention to the data that set the stage for our inquiry. Are there not people loving, hating, fearing, rejoicing, quarreling, working, creating, warring, driving, swimming, praying, marrying, divorcing, and so on? This crude specification implies, of course, that marrying involves someone marrying someone under certain circumstances. The same goes for divorcing and all the preceding action terms, which are shorthand ways of pointing to complex events or happenings involving a number of variables.

Now, we move on to an inspection of a contemporary textbook's formulation of psychology. In the fourth paragraph of their preface, Kagan, Havemann, and Segal (1984, p. v) list as their "top priority to foster an appreciation of such momentous findings as the brain's marvelous complexity and versatility" and so on. The following revealing quotation is included as a psychological illustration of the fallacy of misplaced concreteness.

The brain and the wondrous ways it processes and stores information are the very core of modern psychology, and it is impossible to grasp the thrust of the science without a basic knowledge of what the brain does and how it operates. (Kagan, Havemann & Segal, 1984, p. vi)

What have we here? We started with people involved in the many activities listed above, but according to Kagan et al., "the brain and the wondrous ways it processes and stores information are the very core of modern psychology." Thus, the highly speculative functions of the brain become *the* subject matter as the means for understanding human loving, fearing, hating, and so on. We have a reversal here of what psychologists study, of what they consider concrete, or a fallacy of misplaced concreteness. The hypothetical takes priority over the observable.

We must not overlook another important point. If we acknowledge that the activities of humans, and not the alleged functions of the brain, are the fundamental data of psychology, then we must admit that the notion of the imputed psychological functions of the brain was not derived from observing humans in action; it was actually derived from centuries-long traditions about brain functioning. It is this notion that has been *imposed upon* the data that we start with. The end result is a set of constructed data instead of "crude" data uncontaminated by unwarranted preconceptions, that is, organism-object interactions. In short, then, when we find psychologists stressing the importance of brains, memory or processing "centers," glands, drives, mind, consciousness, and so on, there will we find an instance of the fallacy of misplaced concreteness.

For Further Reading

Woodger, J. H. (1929). *Biological principles: A critical study*. London: Kegan Paul, Trench, Trubner & Co.

FASHIONS IN SCIENCE
AND ELSEWHERE

The fashions of science? They exist but they seem to come from nowhere and they disappear again, and nobody can say why or even when.

Chargaff (1976, p. 329)

Chargaff continues, "As for scientific fashions, I should think that they last longer than women's fashions but less long than men's. . . . At one time, you could get money only for work on animal organs; bacteria were out. Then, suddenly, bacteria were in, everything else was taboo" (Chargaff, 1976, p. 330). Today AIDS and cancer are "in." Chargaff's comments on biological research serve to launch us on a probe of the role of fashion in a number of areas beginning with music.

FASHIONS IN MUSIC

The composers whom we currently consider "classic," in the sense of traditional, standard, exemplary, and established, were anything but that in the composers' own time. It has been said that the classical composers are "dead radicals" whose music was eventually accepted into the typical concert repertoire. When Tchaikowsky's music was first played in Berlin, it was considered barbaric noise. Acceptable now, it was not acceptable then. According to Harold C. Schonberg (1970), the same was true of the classicists in their own times.

The critics of Bach's time considered him an extremist for tinkering with the musical forms considered standard or *in fashion* then. Handel, so popular in his day, was long ignored until a recent resurgence of interest in his work. Gluck and Haydn were also considered revolutionary composers. Mozart and Beethoven, international favorites ranking among the top composers of all time, were not universally admired in their time. Now they are; fashions in music change.

FASHIONS IN GEOLOGY

Until comparatively recently, geologists believed that the continental landmasses were stable throughout the earth's history. According to Holmes (1965), some naturalists had speculated that the continents had at one time been united, but the idea was so preposterous that it was soon forgotten. Then, in 1908, a German and an American geologist set forth the theory of continental drift, that is, that the continental landmasses, united during earlier geologic ages, had drifted apart into their present configurations. Was this notion accepted at once? Not at all. And even today, not all geologists, especially older ones, subscribe to the theory of continental drift. As with clothes, some are followers of the designer-created fashions and some are not.

FASHIONS IN MEDICINE

An egregious example of resistance to change in traditional medical practice is provided by the lamentable career of Ignaz Semmelweis. Célestine (1979) details the story of the young surgeon's determination to teach obstetricians of his day to scrub before attending their patients in the delivery room. His attempt to change this medical fashion of his day cost him his career and his sanity and led to his early death. Today no surgeon would dare to violate that inflexible preoperative procedure. Lister's germ theory of disease (Walker, 1955, p. 220) and Jenner's use of cowpox to vaccinate against smallpox (Beveridge, 1951, p. 39) are other examples of resistance to changing fashions in medicine.

OTHER FASHION REVOLUTIONARIES

We have seen how thorough indoctrination in the prevailing vogue increases one's resistance to a new and different fashion. How, then, do new ways originate? We get some hints from Feuer (1974), who indicates that such towering scientists of our century as Albert Einstein, Niels Bohr, Werner Heisenberg, Louis de Broglie, and others developed in an intergenerational conflict with their tradition-bound fathers and with a rigid, scientific establishment.

Concerning Einstein, we learn about his rebelliousness from his earliest grades through his graduate years. At the university level, he was surrounded by social, philosophical, and political radicals in a revolt against the science of the establishment. His thesis on relativity "was more or less rejected by most of the contemporary physicists. The professor of experimental physics returned Einstein's study saying: 'I can't understand a word of what you've written here' " (Feuer, 1974, p. 54). One more particular about Einstein needs to be set down here: that he was not burdened by too much traditional learning about the past of physics. Feuer (1974, p. 62) quotes the great mathematician David Hilbert as stating, "Do you know why Einstein said the most original and profound things about space and time that have been said in our generation? Because he had learned nothing about all the philosophy and mathematics of time and space." Therefore, it was easier for him to strike out in a direction away from the prevailing fashion and to start a new fashion.

B. F. Skinner has made a rich contribution to psychology. Yet he entered graduate school at Harvard to study psychology lacking the usual indoctrination of the traditional psychology major. Indeed, Skinner had "had no psychology as an undergraduate." He, too, had not read the literature. Was it Skinner's escape from orthodox indoctrination into the prevailing ways of construing behavior that permitted him to develop operant conditioning? A remark by Einstein and Infeld (1966, pp. 47-48) seems apropos at this point: "It is a strange coincidence that nearly all the fundamental work concerned with the nature of heat was done by non-professional physicists who regarded physics merely as their hobby." They also note that Brownian movement "was first observed by the botanist Brown" (Einstein and Infeld, 1966, p. 59). Along similar lines, Wohlsetter (1964, p. 12) quotes the British geneticist C. D. Darlington as stating that

bacteria were first seen under the microscope by a draper, that stratigraphy was first understood by a canal engineer, that oxygen was first isolated by a Unitarian minister, that the theory of infection was first established by a chemist, the theory of heredity by a monastic schoolteacher, and the theory of evolution by a man who was unfitted to be a university instructor in either botany or zoology.

It appears that, by escaping the conventional indoctrination of their colleagues in the establishment, Einstein, Skinner, and the rest were able to see things fresh. As Hanson (1958, p. 36) would put it, the world had not "coagulated" for them the way it had for their traditional associates. Why not? Because they had not been subjected to the language of the establishment, language that provided a "mold" in terms of which the world had jelled for their associates in very definite ways, ways hard to depart from.

CONCLUSION

One would think that when new insights, slants, assumptions, or ways of viewing events are proposed they would be received with open arms and investigated forthwith. Yet the several examples of theories or procedures in our survey have suffered resistance, neglect, or instant rejection. It seems that, particularly in science, original views should find a ready haven, yet the history of science shows just the opposite. That the prevailing fashion dominates even physics, the most advanced science, is no exception. The following quotation by the discoverer of the electron, J. J. Thomson, echoes the opening statement of this article, but in a more cogent fashion: "The really deeply penetrating theories of physics, those that deal with fundamentals, are curiously a matter of fashion" (G. P. Thomson, 1966, p. 181).

For Further Reading

Chargaff, E. (1976). Triviality in science: A brief meditation on fashions. *Perspectives in Biology and Medicine, 19*(3), 323-329.

Feuer, L. S. (1974). *Einstein and the generations of science.* New York: Basic Books.

FIELD THEORY

FIELD IN PHYSICS

Newton's thinking dominated physics for two centuries. The paradigm that guided understanding all of nature could be stated as follows: the universe is made up of independently existing objects or bodies possessing certain attributes. The two entities matter and force were considered the basic building blocks of the universe. But as Einstein and Infeld (1966) narrate the story of physics, certain observations failed to fit Newton's postulates. Challenges to the prevailing mechanistic view of the universe came from research on electromagnetic phenomena by Michael Faraday, James Clerk Maxwell, and Heinrich R. Hertz.

The deviation from a strict, Newtonian physics came with Faraday's investigation based on the lines of force that appeared to leave and return to a magnet at its poles. The finding led him to the assumption of a field surrounding respectively masses, electric charges, and magnets. The field or region throughout which a force manifested itself called for a broader approach than the older one. Thus, fields of force began to take priority over matter. However, it was Maxwell whose work broadened still more the notion of continuous fields not explained mechanically. Then Hertz proved the actual existence of electromagnetic waves spreading with the speed of light. Today the field concept takes priority over the notion of substances stressed in the older mechanical view, and the old distinction between matter and energy is blurred. Matter takes on the property of radiation, and radiation, of matter. The universe in the newer view becomes a more dynamic process. Einstein and Infeld (1966, p. 244) sum up the notion of field and its significance in the following passage.

A new concept appears in physics, the most important invention since Newton's time: the field. It needed great scientific imagination to realize that it is not the charges nor the particles but the field in the space between the charges and the particles which is essential for the description of physical phenomena.

Einstein and Infeld seemed to be groping for a comprehensive field physics, but they never succeeded in unifying field and matter into a merged, integrated system.

FIELD IN PSYCHOLOGY

Constructs that prove to be successful in one science often find uses or echoes in some other field. Recognizing the fact that all the sciences can advance together, J. R. Kantor considered Einstein's formulation of field but found it too restrictive. By expanding it, he achieved a satisfactory analytic tool for psychological inquiry.

J. R. Kantor's definition of field derives from his basic unit of behavior, the *behavior segment*, which he isolates out of the connected series of events in which it is embedded. In his *The Scientific Evolution of Psychology*, volume 2, Kantor (1969, pp. 370-371) considers that

For a science such as psychology, it is advisable to look upon the field as the entire system of things and conditions operating in any event taken in its available totality. It is only the entire system of factors which will provide proper descriptive and explanatory materials for the handling of events.

Kantor seems to be saying, "Don't be in too big a rush lest a myopic view prevent you from taking in the entire territory before you. Make sure that you don't omit any discoverable factor in the matrix that constitutes the event. If you should make that error, it is bound to have an effect on your theoretical outcome."

Having specified his locus of operations, Kantor proceeds to an analysis of the distinguishable (but integral) aspects of the psychological field under observation. Out of a number of factors in the situation, the organism and stimulus object loom prominent. However, they do not hold center stage as in traditional psychological theory. In his formulation of field, Kantor has demoted the organism as positively as Copernicus did the earth when he formulated his heliocentric theory. Henceforth, the organism, which has been the center of attention comparable to the earth in the geocentric theory, holds a less exalted position, one parallel with that of the stimulus object. The two factors are held together jointly in a relationship mutual or reciprocal to each other. That does not mean that they are coequal, because each functions differently in the observed event.

But there is more to field than the two nuclear factors of organism and stimulus object. If one is to perceive something visually, there must be light as a medium of contact to bring organism and stimulus object into a proper relationship. Setting factors or the surrounding conditions must be considered. Physical and chemical experiments and muscle-nerve preparations are immune to the experimenters' exchange of banter or off-color jokes, a setting factor that could devastate a psychological experiment. In addition to the preceding factors, one must not overlook the principle "Present events are a function of antecedent events."

A field theory seems reasonable enough. Why? Because the factors specified are not inferential or imaginary. They are all open to inspection and therefore verifiable. But to put a field theory to work is another matter, because it demands a radical "intellectual retooling." A powerful or organism-centered stance that has localized psychological events within the organism's head or mind (as a reified entity) constitutes the greatest barrier. The same holds for a simplistic, fragmented stimulus-response viewpoint that restricts itself to stimulus as cause and response as effect. Only a complete rejection of the geocentric parallel of the traditional organism-centered approach as well as the simplistic cause-effect thinking of stimulus-response psychology stands in the way of a genuine field theory as developed by Kantor. Thus, if one asks Kantor, "Where is the locus of behavior? Where is behavior located?" the answer is, "Not in the organism, not in the organism's mind or brain, but in the entire situation or field."

For Further Reading

Einstein, A., & Infeld, L. (1966). *The evolution of physics*. New York: Simon and Schuster.

Kantor, J. R. (1969). *The scientific evolution of psychology*. Vol. 2. Chicago: Principia Press.

FORCE

" 'Force' was looked upon as an *actor* even down to 50-75 years ago. Today 'energy' is treated by all the old-timers and many of the solemn younger ones as a *performer*; they speak of it as though you catch and cage a quantity of it all by yourself."

Bentley, in a letter to Dewey (Ratner, Altman & Wheeler, 1964, p. 309)

In his statement, Bentley is deriding the reification of *force* and *energy* because the terms encourage us to think of them as *things* rather than as aspects of events. Such thing-ification was common under Newtonian auspices. In their very philosophical book *The Evolution of Physics*, Einstein and Infeld (1966) state that, for the past two hundred years, physicists dealt with their subject matter as (a) force and (b) matter. All of nature was explained in terms of simple forces of attraction and repulsion between unalterable objects. In short, there were said to be only bodies which have certain properties, that is, forces which acted only on other bodies. In passing, we must note a parallel model prevalent in psychology, that is, that behavior is a property of a body, namely, a person's brain or mind. Both models are self-actional. Mainstream psychology still espouses the Newtonian paradigm of bodies with certain attributes. Fortunately, after a revolution, physics moved on to a radically different paradigm, namely, FIELD THEORY. A few psychologists are moving in the direction of a field paradigm for behavioral inquiry, but most of psychology adheres to the Newtonian paradigm.

For Further Reading

Ratner, S., Altman, J., & Wheeler, J. E. (Eds.). (1964). *John Dewey and Arthur Bentley: A philosophical correspondence.* New Brunswick, N.J.: Rutgers University Press.

FREE WILL
VERSUS DETERMINISM

> The plain man . . . has no objections to determinism as applied by
> physicists to atoms, by himself to machines, or by his doctor to his
> body. He has an emphatic objection to determinism as applied by
> anyone to his reflection and his will, for this seems to make him a
> gigantic mechanical toy, or worse, a sort of Frankenstein monster.
>
> Blanchard (1958, p. 10)

Do humans have free will, or do they behave in certain ways because they
can't do otherwise, that is, because their actions are strictly determined? The
riddle originated in theology going back in history to Saint Augustine
(354-430) and Saint Thomas (1225-1274).

Both theologians believed in predestination, according to which, from
eternity, God predestines the salvation of certain souls. The contrary notion
of free will was held by some Christian groups, but other sects could
reconcile the two seemingly contradictory views by arguing that it is "the
self that determines."

Were these notions only historical curios, it would be a waste of time to
consider them at all, but because they have baffled humans throughout
history down to the present time, they deserve our attention. Furthermore,
psychology itself has been saddled with the free-will-versus-determinism
problem. As evidence, we point to discussions in Grünbaum (1952) and in B.
F. Skinner's notorious book *Beyond Freedom and Dignity* (1971).

The free will–determinism conundrum can be analyzed from a number of
perspectives. First, as previously mentioned, we pursue the point about the
origin of these polar terms. They did not arise as the result of behavioral
investigation. A person from another planet, that is, one uncontaminated
by earthly indoctrination, could not possibly raise this question from observing people at work, play, prayer, dining, cooking, dancing, and all the
rest. Only we earthlings have imposed a purely verbal construction upon behavioral data, forcing them, unsuccessfully, into that linguistic straitjacket.

Second, the notion of free will is antagonistic to scientific procedures and
assumptions that the world makes sense. As a definition of the term *free
will*, let us accept that found in *Webster's Ninth New Collegiate Dictionary*:
"freedom of humans to make choices that are not determined by prior
causes or by divine intervention." The statement amounts to saying, in

cause-effect terms, that free will is an effect without a cause. How would an *indetermined* or *undetermined* act come about? Such a statement implies that behavior is chaotic—that it just happens without rhyme or reason. Here is another example of SELF-ACTION, an assumption that behavior somehow springs from within the person on its own power. The damage to proper understanding of behavior comes from a failure to recognize that the notion of free will is only an assumption that can be abandoned for a more serviceable assumption or assumptions.

How about determinism? This concept usually implies a strict cause-effect type of thinking, which is treated adequately in the article CAUSE AND EFFECT. Therefore, we now move on to a consideration of a solution to the ancient dilemma.

TOWARD A RESOLUTION OF THE FREE WILL-DETERMINISM DILEMMA

As I indicated above, the attribution of free will to the individual derives from a self-actional view that localizes the prime mover inside the person. According to the free will conception, the following elementalistic entities residing within the person are supposed to start the psychological ball rolling: "motives," "genius," "IQ," and "will." Of course, you get *out* what you put *in*. The outcome is inevitable under the given set of assumptions. On the other hand, determinism, in the strict sense, relies upon a rigid *cause* considered to be external to the organism producing an *effect* in the organism. How is one to choose between them? But *why* choose between them?

An alternative to this unhappy perplexity is offered by a field or inter-behavioral type of approach that views psychological occurrences as field events. While, admittedly, organism and stimulus object are the chief focus of the event, as are the participating anatomical and physiological factors, the surrounding conditions as well as the past history of the interrelated events must also be taken into account. Because *all* the factors involved in the particular occurrence are essential, no single factor (such as the organism or stimulus object) is glorified above another. Let us take, as an example, a man in the act of chopping. The indeterminist would focus on the man and state that the man "wills" to chop. But, as Dewey and Bentley (Ratner, Altman & Wheeler, 1964, p. 366) point out, "When chopping occurs, something is being chopped and when seeing takes place, something is seen." The determinist focuses on the "something" and transforms it into a cause. The transactionist or interbehaviorist would feel a need to coin such "double-barreled" words as "choppingness" or "seeingness" to span the ongoing action and to shift the focus away from the two nuclear variables to the entire field event with its component variables. The relationship of the complex of variables and the interrelationship of the flow of events constitute the scientific job of trying to achieve foresight and understanding.

Thus, in the field or event approach suggested above, with its even-handed treatment of the relevant factors involved, there is no need for *either* free will or determinism. As a colleague of mine, G. Y. Kenyon, quipped, "We don't need 'will,' so why do we need 'free'?" The age-old two-valued controversy is really an artifact of a self-actional procedure. Should the self-actional and cause-effect type of theory become extinct some day and come to be replaced by a field theory, it is my conjecture that the question "Do people have free will, or is behavior strictly determined?" will be a philosophical and linguistic fossil. Instead, concern will center on trying to understand the patterning or orderliness of the flow of behavioral events. The fundamental point is that we may adopt that set of assumptions to guide our study that yields the greatest degree of understanding.

For Further Reading

Blanchard, B. (1958). The case for determinism. In S. Hook (Ed.), *Determinism and freedom in the age of modern science* (pp. 3-15). New York: New York University Press.
Skinner, B. F. (1971). *Beyond freedom and dignity*. New York: Alfred A. Knopf.

GENIUS, GIFT, TALENT, BENT, FACULTY, ABILITY, CAPACITY, APTITUDE, KNACK

The first thing to note about all of the above terms is that they are closely synonymous. They can be used interchangeably because they all refer to an imaginary innate power, X, somehow implanted in a given individual to give him or her an edge over another individual lacking X. No one has ever specified what X is, the principle or principles by which it is distributed or apportioned among individuals, or how it facilitates musical, mathematical, or other acquisitions. Second, the entire list of these terms has a centuries-long existence and pervasive usage in our culture. According to *Webster's Ninth New Collegiate Dictionary,* some of these terms originated in the fourteenth and fifteenth centuries and some even in the twelfth and thirteenth. Certain ones, such as *gift,* have a theological derivation. We read in the same dictionary that *"gift* often implies special favor by God or nature."

In television interviews, one frequently hears victorious athletes express appreciation for their special giftedness. In one such interview, a prominent boxer stated that God had "given" him the special gift of boxing and he felt obligated to use it for the entertainment of the public.

We should note about all the terms in the heading of this article that they are not, by any means, scientific terms to be equated with H_2SO_4, *adrenaline,* and such others. They are ancient locutions handed down to us through the ages, terms that have been incorporated into popular psychology and, sad to say, into some areas of mainstream psychology as well.

When we search for a sharper specification of the hypothetical entities underlying genius, giftedness, and the rest, we find only speculation. Some think in terms of unobservable psychic powers. Others prefer a more concrete but hypothetical "physical energy" or sensitivity of sense organs. In his psychoanalytic biography of Leonardo da Vinci, K. R. Eissler (1961, p. 205) argues that Leonardo must have had "a hypertrophy of the visual function." Eissler (p. 205) also argues that Mozart's auditory system was singularly endowed. Is it necessary to point out that such superior organs are merely assumed and then used to explain the exceptional performances of their possessors? A student of logic should recognize the circular reasoning involved in assuming an entity and then using it to explain something else. In explaining superior performance in humans, it is more conservative methodologically to offer explanations in terms of a gradual buildup of reaction sensitivity instead of a hypothetical receptor sensitivity (Cameron, 1947, p. 65).

People who follow the paradigm of the genius's possession of some unobservable native power or alleged superior sense organs are often blind to plain-to-see brute facts. Manuel (1968, p. 4), a biographer of Isaac Newton's, relates how Newton, a bachelor and a recluse, spurned rest and relaxation and food as well, working until two or five o'clock in the morning. We learn that Newton's father was a ne'er-do-well. His mother as well as his ancestors for three generations past were undistinguished from their farm neighbors. The genealogical record revealed no clue to Newton's outstanding accomplishments. When, in his old age, Newton was praised for his contribution to our knowledge of the universe, he remarked humbly, "I had no special sagacity, only the power of patient thought" (Strother, 1955, p. 25). And yet Manuel (1968, p. 4) himself sees Newton's excellence as "a grand sport of nature," in other words, a freak. Thoughtful reader, what kind of "explanation" is that? What if physicists and astronomers had been similarly overwhelmed prior to the investigation of physical and astronomical phenomena? Where would these sciences be if they had declared their data "sports of nature," in other words, unnatural or supernatural?

Let us try to understand the geniuses and the rest as *a part of nature, not apart from nature.* Can we find evidence for excellence as a function of opportunity for behavior acquisition without reliance on imaginary, alleged innate intraorganismic powers? Let us turn to a report by Paul Engle on some creators of literary masterpieces. Writing about Gustave Flaubert, the author of the first really modern novel, *Madame Bovary,* Engle (1964, p. 12) writes that Flaubert would isolate himself from society for a week to whip two pages into the perfect prose he demanded of himself. Sometimes fifteen or twenty pages would be reduced to four that had passed his final approval.

In a penetrating analysis of Beethoven's many notebooks and sketches, Leonard Bernstein offers compelling evidence toward the notion of genius as acquired behavior. Commenting on Beethoven's discarded materials, Bernstein (1959, p. 78) states that this supreme composer "rejected, rewrote, scratched out, tore up and altered a passage as many as twenty times." This is a far cry from the myth that compositions just pour out of the genius in one steady gush.

Elsewhere (Pronko, 1980, p. 59) I have described how Margaret Mitchell agonized for a whole month over a single chapter of *Gone with the Wind.* She rewrote some chapters thirty times, and one in particular she rewrote seventy times. And is it not pertinent to note that Alex Haley's research and writing of *Roots* consumed twelve years of his life and that Truman Capote worked five years on his book *In Cold Blood?* There are many other such examples of superior achievements, but they will be completely ignored as long as the self-actional assumption of an innate, indwelling power within the "gifted" individual holds sway.

Michelangelo, the man who knew so well the agony and ecstasy of creativity, adds the finishing touch to this piece with a remark attributed to him: "If people knew how hard I have had to work to gain my mastery, it wouldn't seem wonderful at all." Michelangelo seems to be saying that if people had observed him over the span of his career developing his skill as a sculptor, they would find law and order in it, and it would make sense. The alternative is to impose on the facts the traditional, unobservable, imaginary power-in-a-spot label such as "genius," "talent," and so on leading only to mystification and serving as a barrier to the proper understanding of excellence in human achievement. There is always a choice of assumptions to guide our thinking.

For Further Reading

Bernstein, L. (1959). *The joy of music.* New York: Simon and Schuster.
Pronko, N. H. (1980). *Psychology from the standpoint of an interbehaviorist.* Monterey, Calif.: Brooks/Cole.

HEREDITY VERSUS ENVIRONMENT

"Do you believe in heredity or environment, in nature or nurture?" This is a question that beginning students are likely to toss at their psychology instructor at the beginning of the semester. For a common answer to such a question, the instructor need only refer the inquiring student to one of the popular textbooks.

To learn what our hypothetical student would find in the way of enlightenment on the topic of heredity and environment, I probed the following textbooks made available to me: McConnell (1977), Weiner et al. (1977), Zimbardo (1979), Kretch et al. (1982), Gleitman (1983), Carlson (1984), and Hassett (1984). Note that the publication dates of my specimen texts span seven years; all are recent issues and therefore representative of current thinking.

To our hypothetical student's question, the clear answer is that contemporary psychologists do not believe in heredity alone or in environment alone, but in both. They assume an *interaction* or a *confounding effect* (Zimbardo, 1979, p. 21) between the two. Nowhere do we find a definition of heredity or environment. Apparently, the terms are used in the same loose way in which lay people use them, and, as such, they hardly qualify as technical, scientific terms. It is most important, though, to note that they fit the Newtonian mechanistic model of two "forces" *interacting* upon each other. One textbook (Carlson, 1984, p. A48) shows the following item in the index: "heredity vs. environment"—the "vs." emphasizing the notion of two opposed entities contending with each other. Observer (1970, p. 123) has spotted the problem and strongly urges the liquidation of these high-level abstractions stereotyped as "Heredity versus Environment," "since these oppositions constitute misleading constructions and not existential things and events." In expansion of his remarks, Observer explains that these terms do not put us in contact with concrete occurrences that we can relate to each other in an effort to reach understanding. Certainly, they do not point to any "forces" either. They are only words without referents. Is there, then, no help for us in teasing out the relationship between hereditary variables and behavior? This time, for assistance, we shift to a formulation by the father of American genetics, H. S. Jennings.

GENETICS A LA JENNINGS

A construct that goes back more than half a century offers quite a contrast to the theory propounded by the preceding sample of psychologists. Yet it is as fresh and novel as if it carried a contemporary date. In place of the foregoing abstractions, Jennings will put us in contact with confrontable, specific conditions and events. Here are some provocative propositions from his neglected paper "Heredity and Environment" (Jennings, 1924).

The greatest mistake about the influence of heredity is to think about it as "an entity, a force, something that itself does things—an error that has induced clouds of misconception" (Jennings, 1924, p. 225).

Heredity concerns the passing on of many discrete packets of biochemicals from parent to offspring, but, as with anything—an automobile or a tin roof—what is important is not only what it is composed of but also the conditions under which it exists. A change in any of the variables involved may change the final result.

Obviously, Jennings sees development as a long chain of connected events the final upshot of which is the completed organism ready at a certain stage of its biological evolution to begin its psychological history.

Jennings' conception of heredity does not fit the old, self-actional and mechanical "unit gene," at fertilization, producing *at a distance* a "unit character" such as "eye color," "feeblemindedness," "normal-mindedness," and so on.

Considering its early date, Jennings' statement is laudatory, but it has been improved upon in Weiss's more recent dynamic and systems viewpoint. By contrast with the traditional theory, Weiss sees any life process as an utterly complex "network of interactions among the sub- and sub-subsystems in the hierarchical organization of a living system" (Weiss, 1973, p. 11). Figure 4 represents such a system as a series of concentric shells or subsystems arranged in a hierarchy. Starting with the genes of the living organism, as indicated in the illustration, we find them embedded in the chromosomes:

the chromosomes lie in the nucleus, the nucleus is surrounded by cytoplasm (which furthermore contains organelles), the cells are incorporated in the tissue matrix, bathed by the "internal milieu" of blood and lymph, and the whole body then faces the outer environment. For each cell, the adjacent ones are evidently "environment" in which they lie entrapped. *None of the shells can ever be truly "isolated."* (P. 12, emphasis added)

Is it necessary to point out that the shells referred to serve *only* as a model for Weiss's construct?

The situation, as Weiss describes it, hardly justifies a self-actional interpretation of a unit character such as "eye color" or "feeblemindedness" encapsulated within a unit gene or a number of genes. It would be a futile job to try to trace out every one of the arrows in Weiss's illustration, demonstrating how "everything" affects "everything else," because "to be

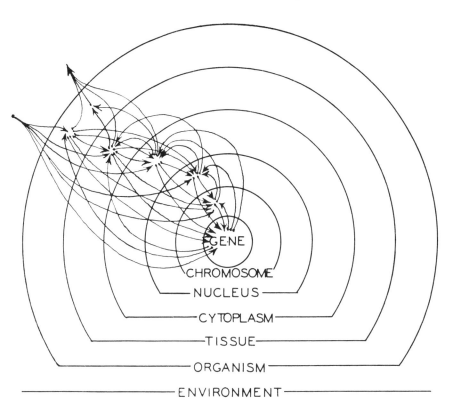

GE·NE

CHROMOSOME

NUCLEUS

CYTOPLASM

TISSUE

ORGANISM

ENVIRONMENT

Figure 4. A field view of how "genes" work. The "genes" are depicted here, not as autonomous bits of matter with specific effects, but only as aspects of an ordered system in which all component factors play a part in the total, complex transaction. (From Paul Weiss's *The Science of Life*, p. 11. Copyright 1973 by Futura Publishing Co. Reproduced by permission of author and publisher.)

is to be related." Furthermore, any assiduous study of what appears to be an integrated field event would reveal only a series of organic processes, the end result of which is the completed organism. However, no one has yet observed any psychological quality or entity in that chain of events as some would claim.

AN ALTERNATIVE VIEW

An alternative way of avoiding the problem created by the psychogenetic view is to compare biological with psychological events. While knee jerks, sneezing, coughing, and vomiting can be understood as *tissue-excitation* reactions, the same does not hold for such reactions as "a rivederci," "au revoir," auf wiedersehen," and so on. The former are ready to "fire off" at birth; the latter occur only as the result of a series of interactions between the organism and stimulus objects under specific conditions surrounding them. This involves a different historical dimension from the one that yields understanding of organismic reflexes. *In one sense*, we may say that psychology begins where heredity produces the completed organism. We must not neglect genetic and other biological factors, but, instead of treating them as causal, we regard them as *aspects* of an integrated field event or events.

For Further Reading

Jennings, H. S. (1924). Heredity and environment. *The Scientific Monthly, 19*(15), 225-238.
Observer. (1970). Innate intelligence: Another genetic avatar. *The Psychological Record, 20*, 123-130.

IDIOSYNCRATIC ACTION

Cultural or shared behavior is identified by the common stimulus functions of objects or persons and by common or shared reactions. Idiosyncratic action is, in a sense, just the opposite in that this form of behavior is developed through the individual's private contacts with "things" or events. The resulting behavior sets off the individual, in that particular respect, *apart from* the group.

In addition to conforming, people may also stray from their group's standards and expectations when they acquire reactions that no one else in their group shares with them. The so-called pet peeves and pet hates belong here. So do likes and dislikes, fears, and attitudes of a political, philosophical, or religious nature as well as those toward oneself (such as the "inferiority complex"). Let us take the last-named reaction of the "inferiority complex." While it may develop as the result of treatment by others, the point is that the behavior was not developed the same way as that person's language, manners, dress, diet, and so on. The attitude of inferiority resulted from the person's solitary contact *within the context* of treatment by others. The stress is on the manner of acquisition of a given response. For example, suppose that a child in China, one fine day, in its babble stage, had, in a hit-or-miss fashion, referred to the white, liquid product of the cow as "milk." If we were to come upon the incident at the instant of the child's vocalizing that word, we might mistakenly attribute it to some English culturalization. But we would be wrong, for we would find out that the child's vocalization of "milk" was a mere coincidence. Why? Because the response was individually, not culturally, acquired.

There are more than four hundred denominations of Christianity, which means that there were that many idiosyncrats who disagreed with the prevailing dogma and who introduced new ways of believing or of worshiping. A high degree of idiosyncrasy is to be seen in such creative products as poems, novels, painting, symphonies, and inventions. All of them are admittedly derived from cultural sources; otherwise, they would not be appreciated. But each bears an individualistic stamp. Admittedly, Antonín Dvořák had music lessons and listened to folk songs, but his *New World Symphony* is a unique creation. No one indoctrinated him to write it as he did. So for the other composers, writers, and inventors. As for composers, they have been called "dead radicals." Each introduced some new feature in his composition, perhaps an extra movement or a new musical instrument into a symphony. Rejected in their own time for their originality, they eventually were accepted as our "classical composers."

In this category, we should also include the behavior of people labeled as psychopathic. For example, Jack the Ripper develops the notion that it is his mission to rid the world of prostitutes. Another claims that he is Jesus Christ. Rokeach (1964) has made a study of *The Three Christs of Ypsilanti*, each of whom made that claim in the same state mental hospital. They were not indoctrinated to believe that; each *independently* developed that notion. When persons become desocialized, they may develop highly individualistic modes of speaking (neologisms) that no longer work to communicate with others. Thus, idiosyncratic behavior may be either socially beneficial or socially disadvantageous. However, its defining characteristic is its acquisition during the individual's singular interaction with things and not as finished ways of behaving shaped by residence in a social group. In this regard, idiosyncratic behavior may be considered the opposite of cultural or shared behavior. Its importance in social progress may be appreciated with the statement that if it hadn't been for idiosyncrats, we would still be cave dwellers.

For Further Reading

Pronko, N. H. (1980). *Psychology from the standpoint of an interbehaviorist.* Monterey, Calif.: Brooks/Cole.
Kantor, J. R., & Smith, N. W. (1975). *The science of psychology: An interbehavioral survey.* Chicago: Principia Press.

INTELLIGENCE

> [The term] "intelligent" is a word around which fantasies lurk: the belief, for instance, that intelligence is the very essence of the man, and that, somehow, somewhere inside the head, it exists in measurable amounts.
>
> Hudson (1971, p. 1)

Scientific activity starts with events or happenings, such as gravitating objects, radiation, continental drift, earthquakes, the birth, growth, and death of plants and animals, and social groups. These occurrences set the stage for observation and investigation, which procedures lead to description, explanation, or theoretical constructs. This is the normal order of things manifested in the psychologist's starting with the observation of people's loving, hating, fearing, remembering, thinking, perceiving, learning, speaking, and so on. Such a procedure conforms with general scientific method, which starts with events and terminates in constructs.

When it comes to the topic of intelligence, we experience a reversed order of things. In this case, we find constructs in search of events. Does the skeptical reader require proof of my contention? If so, look in any general psychology textbook. For example, Philip Zimbardo (1985, p. 428) tells us, "There has been little agreement on what the concept of intelligence is or how to define it." The term *define* means "to determine or identify the essential qualities or meaning of" (*Webster's Ninth New Collegiate Dictionary*). Further search for definitions yields such witticisms as "intelligence is what intelligence tests test" or "intelligence is how well you do on an intelligence test." But there are more. For example, "The ability to meet and adapt to novel situations quickly and effectively. The ability to utilize abstract concepts effectively. The ability to grasp relationships and to learn quickly" (Chaplin, 1975, p. 263).

Can the synonym *ability* be of any real help to us? If we consult *The Oxford Dictionary of English Etymology*, we learn that the term *ability* goes back to the fourteenth century, which means that it is not a scientific term but one in common, everyday usage, derived from traditional thinking. Its original meaning was synonymous with "fitness" or "power." In the sixteenth century, the term *ability* came to mean a "faculty of mind." The term *intelligence* has a similar origin dating from the Middle Ages carrying the ever-so-loose meaning "quick to understand." Both terms are hand-me-downs derived from popular psychology, adopted and imposed upon such occurrences as performances on intelligence tests. There is little, if any, difference between the lay person's remark "X is smart" or "X has a lot of smarts" and the psychologist's "X is intelligent because of his/her high IQ." The pertinent question is: What can the skeptical psychologist do, in any scientific sense, with such semantically imprecise terms?

FURTHER CRITICISM OF INTELLIGENCE

1. Both terms, *intelligence* and its synonym *ability*, are hypothetical. While hypotheses are acceptable in the sciences, they do not command respect or become useful until they are verified. Therefore, since these terms themselves require explanation, they cannot figure in the explanation of intelligence.

2. The terms *intelligence* and *ability* illustrate circular reasoning as follows. "How do you know that X has a lot of ability or a high IQ?" The answer: "Well, because of X's excellent performance on an IQ test." "Why did X perform so well on the test of intelligence?" Answer: "Because of X's abundant IQ, ability or potential." What kind of explanation is that?

3. *Intelligence, ability,* and so on represent self-actional thinking. SELF-ACTION refers to "things" that are said to act entirely on their own, as if under their own power. The IQ is thought of as a self-actional power, presumably resident within the individual *causing* that person to behave within the limits set by that individual's allotted "potential." The following comment of Dewey's (1929, p. 123) fits the standard IQ explanation: "Events are studied as if one or another factor were the whole thing."

AN INTEGRATED-FIELD VIEW OF INTELLIGENCE

The psychologist who holds an integrated-field view sees "intelligence" as referring to none other than acquired behavior. Analyze the contents of any intelligence test and you will find *no* response that the testee has not acquired or failed to acquire. Certainly, one does not come across any genetic "force" that has enabled or prevented the testee from responding to specific test items. At best, what we have in the test results is a crude kind of "summation of learning experiences" (Wesman, 1968, p. 267), experiences subject to various limiting and/or facilitating conditions. Lindsley (1964) argues for nonorganismic variables such as stimulus objects and setting factors when he claims that there are no retarded children, only retarded (or, better, *retarding*) environments. According to Sidney Bijou (1966, p. 3), "retarded behavior is a function of observable social, physical, and biological conditions."

Bijou spells out what he means by the foregoing three sets of conditions that limit behavior development. Negative biological and physical conditions include blindness, deafness, brain injuries, Down's syndrome, and phenylketonuria. These factors are not in themselves "mental retardation" but, *in time*, by severely preventing or limiting behavior development, reveal the lack of development in given individuals when they are compared with their peers. Among social conditions Bijou (1966) includes poverty with its multiple effects, child abuse, and parental or child care indifference. By taking all such factors into account, Bijou (1966, p. 238) proposes a concrete intervention program to prevent "mental retardation" particularly in the case of the less biologically defective individuals. By dealing with observable variables in the life situation of retarded persons, Bijou demonstrates the possibilities for application inherent in an integrated-field approach, by contrast with self-actional views with their main focus on internal forces allegedly residing within the person.

CONCLUSION

We have reviewed two competing formulations for understanding "intelligence." An older, established, and popular theory is stated in self-actional terms, viewing the IQ as a power-in-a-spot localized within an organism and setting limits to development. This theory is criticized as being hypothetical and as dealing in unobservables that can't be verified. As such it itself requires explanation and is, therefore, rejected for elucidating the topic before us.

A field theory, proceeding under the assumption that all behavior is acquired, deals only with observables. Under its banner, we can inventory developmental variables that hinder or facilitate progress in the acquisition of behaviors labeled as intelligent on intelligence tests. Among biological conditions, we include the following, all observable: biological injuries or defects (such as blindness, deafness, brain agenesis or injuries, and malnutrition of mother or infant), poverty with its debilitating effects, child neglect and abuse, racial and ethnic prejudice, and birth order and family size. In conclusion, our comparison of two competing formulations confronts the skeptic with another choice point. Different assumptions yield different implications for theory and practice.

For Further Reading

Bijou, S. W. (1966). A functional analysis of retarded development. In N. R. Ellis (Ed.), *International Review of Research in Mental Retardation.* (pp. 1-19). Vol. 1. New York: Academic Press.

INTERACTION

Starting with *Webster's Ninth New Collegiate Dictionary*, we find *interaction* defined as "mutual or reciprocal action or influence." This meaning is quite close to the definition of the same term proposed by John Dewey and Arthur Bentley (1949, p. 108). According to them, *interaction* can be observed "where thing is balanced against thing in causal explanation." We may understand *interaction* more clearly if we contrast it with *self-action*.

Under a self-actional approach, one variable alone (i.e., the organism or the organism's "mind" or "brain") gets all the credit for what goes on. Under interactional auspices, the organism has to share power with another variable, the stimulus object. Instead of one variable acting alone under self-actional authority, two variables now confront each other. What we can see happening on the billiard table can help us understand what Dewey and Bentley mean by this term. If you strike one billiard ball with another, action and reaction are equal and opposite as in Newton's third law of motion. Two separate things acting on each other in mutual or reciprocal action such as the hula balls in Figure 5 represent interaction.

Of special interest to us is the application of the interactional model to psychological events. When this happens, the organism is no longer in sole control of the situation, because it must now share power with another variable, the stimulus object. The psychophysical experiment of a bygone era fits the interactional framework in its attempt to define the relationship between stimulus differences and corresponding sensory experiences. S-R psychology, so prevalent on the contemporary scene, also fits the interactional paradigm. The stimulus is usually considered a *cause* and the response an *effect*.

CRITICISM OF THE INTERACTIONAL APPROACH

While, at first glance, an interactional construction appears to be superior to a self-actional one for behavioral inquiry, it nevertheless has certain defects when it is compared with a transactional view. First of all, it tends to carve out the two chief variables as "actors" with an "inter" that creates an unbridgeable chasm between them. One can almost hear Dewey and Bentley ask, "How is it that, even prior to inquiry, you decided to concentrate exclusively on the two most conspicuous factors in the situation you observed, namely, subject and object? Isn't your orientation one that you

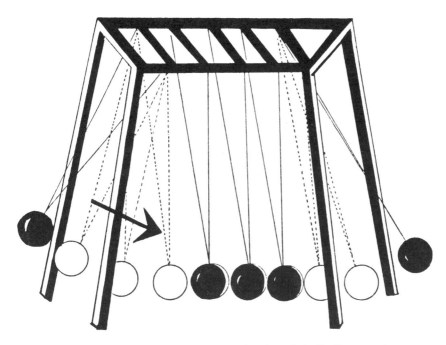

Figure 5. A simple interaction on a physical level. Hula balls illustrate that action and reaction are equal.

simply transferred from commonsense ways to a supposedly scientific investigation? And why have you adopted Newton's framework for studying mechanical things for the study of events that are not mechanical? Finally, doesn't your simplistic, theoretical structure leave variables beyond organism and stimulus object out of account?" Dewey and Bentley's hypothetical protestations will be justified if one recalls that the setting factors of behavioral events also play a definite role in those events. It should be sufficient to point out that human lovemaking, toileting, and so on are affected by immediate surroundings, such as presence of others.

Laboratory experiments, as with dogs and rats, often deal with the fragments of behavior under study as if they were independent of past behaviors. When such procedures are used, they fit the interactional paradigm of two things in causal interconnection.

PSEUDOINTERACTION

Occasionally, we find what looks like an interactional construct to be only deviantly so. Sometimes a stimulus is grudgingly acknowledged to "trigger" a response allegedly determined by "forces" within the organism. The instincts and "innate releasing mechanisms" are examples. Such imaginary Freudian entities as the superego and the id encountering each other on the battle ground of the ego also illustrate pseudointeraction. A very clear example of pseudointeraction can be seen "when small portions of organisms (visual pathways and visual cortex of the brain) are said to interact with environmental objects (light rays) as in the traditional theories of sensation" (Dewey & Bentley, 1949, p. 109). Further criticisms of *interaction* as well as advantages of a transactional approach can be found under the entry TRANSACTION.

For Further Reading

Dewey, J., & Bentley, A. F. (1949). *Knowing and the known.* Boston: Beacon Press.
Kagan, J., Havemann, J., & Segal, J. (1984). *Psychology: An introduction* (5th ed.). New York: Harcourt Brace Jovanovich.

INTERBEHAVIORAL
PSYCHOLOGY:
AN INTRODUCTION

DUALISM

Before setting down the distinguishing features of interbehavioral psychology, we need to specify what it *is not*. It is *not* a "body-mind" mode of thinking about psychology. That centuries-old way of understanding behavior conceives of an organism as consisting of a visible portion, *body*, and an invisible portion, *mind*. It is in the invisible theater of the mind that thinking, perceiving, dreaming, remembering, and so on are said to take place. In response to a dualistic or mentalistic formulation, one can hardly improve on Dewey and Bentley's (1949, p. 56) pointed question: "Who would assert he can properly and in a worthwhile manner *observe* a 'mind' *in addition to* the organism that is engaged in the transactions proper to it in an observable world?" To drive the point home in the most emphatic way possible, one wants to ask again: Who would, or who could, so assert?

BEHAVIORISM

Interbehaviorism is not to be identified with behaviorism even though the behaviorist rejects all reference to the mind. While the mentalist accepts the formula *psychology = body + mind*, the behaviorist would transform it to *psychology = body − mind*. Such a formulation limits one to bodily explanations for psychological occurrences. In so doing, the behaviorist is, nevertheless, trapped in traditional dualism, maintaining the physical aspect of that dualism while disowning the "psychical" side. Such a limited view forces the behaviorist to reduce behavior to imaginary anatomical and physiological terms. It follows that the behaviorist's approach focuses attention on the organism, particularly within its skin and contents, and especially the brain and glands as springs of action. The central question is: Do physiological explanations advance our understanding of loving, hating, dreaming, learning, and all the rest? Can physiological techniques ever attain a behavioral level? The follower of a field approach, such as the interbehaviorist, responds with an emphatic "No."

On this point, the cell geneticist François Jacob recognizes differences in the subject matters of the sciences, differences that demand separate techniques and separate ways of interpreting them. The following passage pinpoints the problem of the kind of reductionism that characterizes the contemporary approach of mainstream psychologists.

What can the notions of sexuality, or predator, or of pain represent in physics or chemistry? Or the ideas of justice, of increase in value or of democratic power in biology? At the limit, total reductionism results in absurdity. For the pretension that every level can be reduced to a simpler one would result, for example, in explaining democracy in terms of the structure and properties of elementary particles; and this is clearly nonsense. (Jacob, 1977, p. 1162)

INTERBEHAVIORISM

Such predicaments as reductionism leads to are averted with an interbehavioral viewpont by drawing a clear-cut boundary between the data of biology and that of behavioral investigation. How? Just arbitrarily? No, by observation. Right off, we learn from an examination of standard textbooks that physiologists study such processes as respiration, circulation, digestion, assimilation, excretion, and reproduction. By contrast, psychologists study such events as perceiving, learning, remembering, thinking, and feeling. How could the two be confused with each other?

We now continue with a more specific characterization of behavioral events very much like the way the chemist characterizes liquids, solids, and gases. It is to the great credit of J. R. Kantor (1924) that, six decades ago, he successfully set apart the subject matter of psychology from that of biology, more specifically, physiology. That achievement alone should have earned him an honored niche among psychologists. Anyhow, we now consider the findings of Kantor's procedure for identifying the psychologist's subject matter.

1. Psychological Events Are Historical

While we don't have to learn how to sneeze, urinate, breathe, and digest our food, we must learn how to speak, work, play, read, write, and pray. Behavioral events require a reactional history.

2. Psychological Events Are Differential

One finds a much greater specificity in behavior than in physiology. A knee jerk can be elicited indiscriminately with the proper application of a reflex hammer, ruler, stone, stick, or book; a person with a certain history would be able to give discrete verbal reactions (or names) to each of such objects in addition to other reactions to them.

3. Psychological Actions Show Integration

One may begin learning to dance "one step at a time," but eventually one can combine dancing steps with talking to one's partner, nodding to an acquaintance across the room, and so on, all of which were formerly acted separately. Now they function together in a smooth, unified pattern.

4. Psychological Activities Show Variability

Deadly monotony reigns in the realm of the reflexes. Barring changes in the supporting tissues, physiological reflexes show a constancy over long periods of time. But a cat in a puzzle box manifests changes in the pattern of its activity over a period of time, not stereotyped behavior.

5. Psychological Activities Show Modifiability

"Till death us do part," declare the bride and groom in the glow of their young romance. But when hatred manifests itself in their divorce proceedings, we have witnessed modifiability or a radical change in their stimulus functions toward each other. Schools are agencies of change or modifiability. The student who knew no French but now speaks it fluently has been psychologically modified.

6. Psychological Action Reveals Inhibition

The area of ethics and morality provides a rich source of instances of inhibition. Humans require strict privacy for their sexual activities, an inhibition not evident in the open sexual display of cats and dogs, a matter of extreme embarrassment to passing humans.

7. Psychological Acts Show Delayability

One of the items on an intelligence test involves showing a child an object placed under a cover but asking the child to fetch the object only after a certain time interval has passed. Delayability can also be observed in remembering and recall.

For Further Reading

Pronko, N. H. (1980). *Psychology from the standpoint of an interbehaviorist.* Monterey, Calif.: Brooks/Cole.

INTROSPECTION

For a start on our topic, we go back to the latter part of the nineteenth century, a time when introspection was regarded as the method par excellence. William James considered introspective observation the supreme method for studying states of consciousness, which, for him, meant "the looking into our own minds and reporting what we there discover" (James, 1918, p. 185). In his experience, James had never met any skeptic who doubted the existence of states of consciousness. Therefore, he considered beyond the shadow of a doubt, the actuality of such states "as the most fundamental of all the postulates of psychology" (James, 1918, p. 185).

Let us try to "make sense" of James's definition. If the mind is the sole agent in the body that carries out all the "psychic functions," how do *we* get into the act? It is proper to ask: *How* do we "look" into our own minds? With still another mind? Or does the mind with its own "mind's eye" "look" within itself? Followed to its logical conclusion, James's definition of introspection yields a reductio ad absurdum. As always, attempts to confine behavior to a locus within the skin of the organism break down.

It might be tempting to conjecture that such notions as William James entertained about introspection almost a century ago are dead. That isn't so. For example, according to Zimbardo (1979, p. 26), the goal of introspection is the discovery of the "contents of the mind" by questioning trained individuals about their subjective experiences.

It appears that introspection is alive and well even in contemporary psychology. When the term is uttered and heard at a superficial level, problems with it are obscured. But when one analyzes it at a deep level, *introspection* turns out to be a term without a referent. For a contrasting view of the same data as those that the term *introspection* attempts to explain, see REACTING TO ONE'S OWN REACTIONS.

For Further Reading

James, W. (1918). *The principles of psychology*. Vol. 1. New York: Henry Holt and Company. (Original work published 1890).

ISOLATION, ISOLATE

These terms are Bentleyan red-letter words aimed at pointing to the traditional verbal fragmentation of aspects of an event into its components. For Bentley, starting with a set of assumptions under which events, happenings, or occurrences are primary, to begin with preanalytic organisms or objects as if independently existing prior to inquiry is going about things backwards. If you begin with the total event, then, for certain limited purposes within that framework, Bentley would approve your teasing out the role of various factors, but you must never lose sight of the fact that the variables selected for special study are only aspects of the entire *system* under observation.

Bentley's rejection of all isolates as a starting point for inquiry is in sharp contrast to the kind of thinking in both mainstream and popular psychology based on Newtonian "particles" moved by "forces." Most definitions of psychology begin with "organisms" on the one hand and "objects" on the other. The problem with splintering events in this fashion is that one is forced to invent some kind of glue to bring the event components together again—similar to the enigma created by Humpty Dumpty after his great fall. For Bentley, events present themselves to observation as wholes and not in pieces.

The greatest obstacles to a broad Bentleyan view are our traditional beliefs and attitudes, which favor our seizing upon the enduring aspects of events to the neglect of their more transitory or changeable aspects. Certainly, "organisms" and "objects" are more attention-compelling than the less prominent and subtle factors as aspects of the system in which all are embedded.

To round out our discussion, let us consider some common isolates beyond those of "organisms" and "objects." Earlier "souls" were separated from "bodies," as were their successors, "minds," and later the more palatable "brains," the last as a controlling entity. The inventory continues with "organism" and "environment." "Consciousness" must be included, as must the "self" and "personality." The "central nervous system" versus the "peripheral nervous system" and the hormonal system are often treated as isolates. Even an "event" is sometimes handled as if it were an isolate, as in laboratory experiments, whereas every event is connected with other events and must be viewed in such context. One could go on and on, but this enumeration of blunders of scientific investigation must suffice to illustrate a need for alertness in avoiding isolating aspects of events as if they were independently existing entities.

For Further Reading

Ratner, S., Altman, J., & Wheeler, J. (Eds.) (1964). *John Dewey and Arthur Bentley: A philosophical correspondence*. New Brunswick, N.J.: Rutgers University Press.

JAPAN'S YOUNG VIOLINISTS

One hundred fifty years ago Western music was completely unknown in Japan. There were no pianos, violins, cellos, bassoons, nor any of the other instruments so familiar, down through the centuries, to symphony concert-goers in the West. The Japanese did have drums, flutes, and string instruments which resembled zithers and banjos, and which were played mostly by geishas. Visitors from Europe and America were convinced that "Oriental ears" could never appreciate Western music. They were equally certain that Oriental people would never be able to perform music by Mozart, Beethoven, Bach, or Brahms.

THE PICTURE TODAY

The musical scenario has revealed a radical change in recent times. Today Tokyo alone has three symphony orchestras. Tickets for symphony concerts are grabbed up well in advance of scheduled programs, which are similar to those offered to Western audiences. An increasing number of performers have gained international recognition, including the celebrated conductors Seiji Ozawa and Watanabe Akio. In 1981, there were four million pianos in Japanese homes (Bunge, 1983, p. 135). Television courses offer lessons in piano, guitar, and violin. The Suzuki Talent Education Institutes have produced a generation of violin virtuosos, an account of which is given in the following section.

SUZUKI'S TALENT EDUCATION PROGRAM

We focus on Shinichi Suzuki and his accomplishments because of the philosophical or theoretical implications involved. The notions that guide his work strongly contradict widespread Western ideas (and the results thereof), ideas that are found even in mainstream psychology as well as in popular thinking about musical "talent." Suzuki refuses to go along with the universal notion of an "inherited talent" for music, mathematics, art, or whatever, and his achievements support his beliefs.

Early in his teaching career, Suzuki was immensely impressed with the realization that children all over the world learned to speak their mother tongue casually and painlessly, yet very effectively. He decided to adapt this mother-tongue method to teaching music, starting with the birth of the child, by exposing it to recordings of fine music played over and over again. This is the foundation for the later achievement of pitch discrimination and the production of tonal quality. On the other hand, according to Suzuki, one can teach a child to be tone deaf simply by exposing it to unmusical sounds or to out-of-tune music. Says Suzuki (1973, p. 16), "Imagine, if you will, a Mozart or a Beethoven brought up from birth to cacophony, to every variety of unmusical sound. My own observations tell me that we would not have had a Ninth or a Jupiter Symphony."

THE NEXT STEP

In the United States, the custom has been to postpone a child's lessons on the violin, piano, or wind instrument until the age of seven, eight, or nine. No one ever questions why except Suzuki. He starts teaching children at the age of three and, in some cases, even earlier. But musical training involves the mother, who serves as a model and surrogate teacher, whom the child emulates and from whom it receives support and encouragement. Naturally, the child's first violin is pint-sized. The young student listens to recordings of violin virtuosos (e.g., Isaac Stern or Arthur Grumiaux) and tries to emulate their performance by constant practice.

Every beginner starts with "Twinkle, Twinkle, Little Star" and practices it until it reaches an accurate degree of pitch discrimination and tonal production. A stimulating musical environment and maximum participation by the child provide situations similar to those experienced by so-called musical prodigies, shining examples of which are Beethoven, Mozart, Pablo Casals, Jascha Heifetz, and many others.

After the student masters "Twinkle, Twinkle, Little Star," the teacher adds one new item at a time. After each tune heard on high-fidelity equipment is learned, the child is coached to play it. The child must keep *each additional piece* well practiced so as to be able to play any item of its repertoire on demand. Reading musical notes comes later, without stress, in this carefully graduated program.

A SUZUKI CONCERT

Because the young violin students keep alive every piece that they have studied, Suzuki is able to produce a spectacular concert in Tokyo every spring. Fifteen hundred children between the ages of four and fifteen gather in the Sports Palace. They come from the various islands of Japan to play in unison, without rehearsal, and without a fixed program, in a mass concert as shown in Figure 6. Here is a typical Suzuki program.

Figure 6. Suzuki's young violinists playing in ensemble at a concent in Matsumoto (Photo courtesy of Dr. Shinichi Suzuki.)

Weber's "Country Dance"
Bach's Double Concerto
Mozart's "Polonaise"
"Auld Lang Syne"
Vivaldi's A Minor Concerto
Vivaldi's G Minor Concerto
Schumann's "The Two Grenadiers"
The familiar "Waltz" of Brahms

One old gentleman who attended such a concert was so moved that he cried "Bravo," went to the stage, embraced the children and wept. He was Pablo Casals. Other professional musicians and teachers have been equally impressed with the children's performances, compared, by many, to the performances of college majors in Western countries.

THE SIGNIFICANCE OF SUZUKI'S ACHIEVEMENT

Two hundred thousand students have passed through the branches of the

Suzuki Talent Education Institutes scattered over the tiny country of Japan. He has created little geniuses by the gross, an achievement that can't be found anywhere else on our planet. Fortunately for the concert enterprise on earth, Suzuki does not propose to flood the concert stages with Japanese artists. He aims only to enrich the lives of all the earth's children.

The important philosophical point for us to consider is that Suzuki's achievements did not result from the application of available psychological theory. On the contrary, he rejects the notion of an inherent musical talent. Therefore, he is prepared to accept any child that can speak its mother tongue; that child can come from any continent and be of any skin color, nationality, or ancestry. Suzuki will teach such a child to play with excellence. Nor will he administer any IQ test or test of musical ability before its admission. All who can speak are welcome.

CONCLUSION

As often happens, practice will not wait for a useful theory. In fact, practice often outstrips theory, guided only by vague surmises, intuitions, and insights as to what means will achieve desired ends. Suzuki's unusual results with unselected children compelled him to reject the hoary, but still prevalent, notion that only certain individuals have been selected, or preselected, for remarkable achievement along certain lines of human endeavor. A skeptic can't help ending on an ironic note in observing the incongruity between Suzuki's remarkable achievements and the dire prophecies of Western observers of Japanese culture about "Oriental insensitive ears" to Western music, music that was nonexistent in Japan 150 years ago.

For Further Reading

Suzuki, S. (1969). *Nurtured by love*. New York: Exposition Press.

THE KALLIKAK FAMILY

The rediscovery, in 1900, of Gregor Mendel's studies on the transmission of genetic qualities from plant parent to offspring created quite a stir in the intellectual world of that time. Mendel's neat notion of dominant and recessive unit characters was especially appealing. A psychologist of that time, Henry Goddard, thought: Why couldn't Mendel's law governing the transmission of dominant and recessive characters apply to the inheritance of feeblemindedness and normal-mindedness (his terms, not mine)?

Without realizing that his surmise was only an assumption, Goddard (1935) proceeded with a study, *The Kallikak Family*, the conclusions of which continue to influence thinking about the inheritance of intelligence to this very day.

GODDARD'S RESEARCH STRATEGY

As director of the research laboratory of the Vineland Training School for Feebleminded Girls and Boys in Vineland, New Jersey, Goddard came across an interesting case of a young female resident, Deborah, classified as a moron, a term he invented. She had been born in an almshouse and had lived at the Vineland school for fifteen years following her admission there at the age of eight. She had been classified as feebleminded and, in line with Goddard's thinking, was considered a "bad seed." He decided to track down the origin of her "bad seed" in confirmation of his hereditary theory—and he "succeeded."

Goddard sent out into "the field" one of his assistants, a Miss Elizabeth Kite. Her assignment was to interview the parents, grandparents, relatives, acquaintances, neighbors, or anybody else who might throw any light whatsoever on Deborah's ancestors, their intelligence, character, reputation, child-rearing methods, and so on.

THE FINDINGS

Miss Kite's persistence paid off. By piecing together the details of her loose anecdotal survey, Goddard came up with Deborah's family tree. The fountainhead of the Kallikak generations turned out to be one Martin Kallikak, Sr., a Revolutionary soldier.

This is the story. Martin Kallikak had joined the militia in the early period of the American Revolution. At one of the New Jersey taverns visited by the militia, Martin took up with a girl whom Miss Kite labeled feebleminded 150 years later! She bore a son, presumably by Martin, named Martin Kallikak, Jr. This event made the offspring of that casual union the great-great-grandfather of Deborah and of all her defective predecessors in between. The source of the "bad seed" was "obviously," by long-distance diagnosis, the feebleminded woman who frequented that tavern and who started the successive generations of criminals, alcoholics, prostitutes, and other defective individuals culminating in feebleminded Deborah.

The Kallikak story would be interesting enough up to this point, but its denouement makes it incredible. As Goddard tells it, after the war, Martin Kallikak Jr.'s father, Martin Kallikak, Sr., reformed, married a respectable girl of good family, and started a line of descendants who were "doctors, lawyers, judges, educators, traders, landholders, in short, respectable citizens, men and women prominent in every phase of social life" (Goddard, 1935, p. 30).

To these results, Goddard had only to apply the simplistic Mendelian formula of dominant and recessive characters. The tavern habitué carried the bad, recessive seed, and Martin Kallikak's legal wife carried the good, dominant seed. This formulation made matters crystal clear for Goddard and to much of the world to which he broadcast it. Thus was launched "an intriguing and powerful social myth in western cultures during much of the twentieth century" (Smith, 1985, p. 16).

GODDARD'S CRITICS

Smith (1985) traces the influence of Goddard's study that led to the passage of the Immigration Restriction Act of 1924 limiting the quota of Italians, Russians, Hungarians, and Jews, among whom Goddard had "found" an abundance of feebleminded. Smith (1985, chap. 9) also details how Goddard's notion of the moron as a pollutor of American democracy grew to influence the eugenics movement toward sterilization of those defective individuals. The reverberations of Goddard's views are reflected in a class action suit in 1984 in Virginia on behalf of people who had been involuntarily sterilized.

There are other critics of Goddard's renowned study of the Kallikak family and the social alarmism and hysteria that it engendered. Among these are Albert Deutsch (1938) and Stephen Jay Gould. In his examination of Goddard's work, the latter (Gould, 1981, p. 171) discovered "a bit of more conscious skullduggery," namely a touch-up of photos of the bad line of Kallikaks to give them a depraved and sinister look to fit the stereotype of the feebleminded.

Goddard's study of the Kallikak family is a notorious example of how not to do research. Above all, it argues eloquently for the thorough scrutiny of one's assumptions. Goddard's failure to do so produced results that were predestined from the premises with which he started. While there is no intimation of any personal responsibility in the mischief caused by his notion of the moron, there is no doubt about the rapid growth and acceptance of his ideas, which are still alive in popular psychology as well as in the books of supposedly scientific writers.

For Further Reading

Goddard, H. H. (1935). *The Kallikak family: A study in the heredity of feeble-mindedness*. New York: Macmillan. (Original work published 1912)

Smith, J. D. (1985). *Minds made feeble: The myth and legacy of the Kallikaks*. Rockville, Md.: Aspen Systems Corporation.

LANGUAGE:
THREE APPROACHES

People living at the seashore grow so accustomed to the murmur of the waves that they never hear it. By the same token, we scarcely ever hear the words which we utter.

Ehrlich (1965, p. 119)

Surely humans are the "talkingest" of all the animal species. We spend a lot of our lives talking or listening, but both forms of behavior operate so smoothly and "automatically" that, as someone put it, we get ourselves into the middle of a sentence and trust Providence to get us out of it. But the way we take our speech for granted works against our reflecting on what goes on when we speak. For the psychologist, the question is: How shall we understand this ubiquitous form of human communicative behavior?

We explore three answers to this poser: (1) a mentalistic explanation, (2) a behavioristic one, and (3) a naturalistic, integrated-field interpretation of the same behavioral circumstance.

We start with a simple, everyday situation and note how each of the three theories handles it. Here are our data in everyday terms. Two friends, John and Jim, are chatting together at the home of Jim, as illustrated in Figure 7. Jim is looking for his pipe. From where he is sitting, John spots Jim's pipe and says, "There's your pipe."

A MENTALISTIC ACCOUNT

It is important to point out that mentalists start with the assumption that, in addition to the visible body, there is an unobservable mind somewhere in the head. Our linguistic event is said to start with an idea in John's mind directing John to tell Jim where his pipe is. The idea in John's mind is then transformed into neural impulses to the organs of speech. As a result, the speech organs utter the words, "There's your pipe." But that's only the beginning. Now, according to the mentalist, the speech uttered by John is transformed into sound waves, which are carried to Jim's ears. Next, neural impulses must transport the sound waves up into Jim's brain, where further translation results in an arousal in Jim's mind that corresponds to the idea in John's mind that started the proceedings. Note that the entire chain of events involves the following series of conversions: psychical→physiological →physical→physiological→psychical.

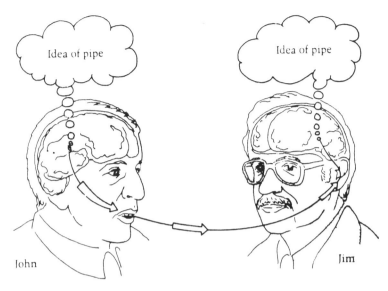

Figure 7. An account, in mentalistic terms, of a linguistic situation in which John tells Jim, "There's your pipe." The event is said to start with an idea of *pipe* in John's mind. Then neural impulses cause the organs of speech to utter the above phrase. The physical impulses reach Jim's ears, where they are said to be transformed into neural impulses, which are, in turn, alleged to be translated into an idea of the pipe in Jim's mind.

A CLASSICAL BEHAVIORISTIC ACCOUNT

A classical behavioristic account varies from the foregoing explanation by omitting the unscientific mind. For the behaviorist, the brain is made to do the work that the mind *used to do*. For example, according to Kagan, Havemann, and Segal (1984, p. 52), the cortex has certain areas that receive, analyze, and interpret speech sounds and convert them into meaningful words and sentences. These highly inferential statements (and that's all they are) are seriously offered as scientific interpretations of communicative speech.

ANALYSIS OF MENTALISTIC AND BEHAVIORISTIC THEORIES

Essentially, the preceding two theories differ less than one might think. While the mentalistic account makes blatant reference to the mind or psyche, the behavioristic story carries an implicit or subtle reference to the same. Both of them assign two functions to the flesh that we know as the brain: (1) a legitimate biological function of conduction and integration and (2) an anthropomorphic function of receiving, analyzing, and interpreting.

The homunculi that carry out the alleged activities are purely imaginary.

One wants to say "in words as hard as cannonballs" that there is no scientific evidence to prove that nervous tissue performs psychological functions. Only self-actional thinking endows the brain with all such powers, and tradition perpetuates the notion. Now, insofar as the merely hypothetical (or rather, imaginary) mentalistic and behavioristic theories do not do justice to the facts of human linguistic behavior, we are justified in exploring a third mode of trying to understand them. This is an integrated-field theory.

A DIFFERENT THEORY OF LANGUAGE

We start with the same behavioral situation as before, that is, with John's searching for his pipe. We can dispense with the illustration showing Jim and John because we will not be dealing with alleged, nonobservable entities in the mind/brain. Nor will we be *bridging* the action occurring between John and Jim, because we define psychology as *the study of the individual*. Therefore, we must dissect the behavior of each *in turn*.

Beginning with John, we observe him looking at Jim searching for his pipe. Next, John spots Jim's pipe. Up to this point in our analysis, neither of John's acts is linguistic. Why? Because both are unistimulation responses, (1) to Jim's searching activity and (2) to Jim's pipe on the coffee table.

For purposes of analysis, let us carve out the behaviors that follow as if we were to stop the action of a motion-picture recording of Jim and John. What happens now is distinctive in that when Jim says, "There's your pipe," he reacts, *within that slice of behavior*, to both Jim and the pipe. He is referring to Jim as one stimulus object and to the pipe as the other stimulus object. That's why interbehavioral psychology has dubbed such linguistic events *bistimulational* (Pronko, 1980, chap. 12).

Now, we move on to Jim's action in the episode we are analyzing. We find that Jim's response is also bistimulational because, within the slice of behavior we are inspecting, we find him reacting both to John's speaking *and* to the pipe he had been looking for. In our analysis of Jim's and John's participation in the linguistic event that we selected for analysis, we find simplicity itself, in harmony with the principle of parsimony. We find no need for mysterious translation of alleged psychic events into physiological, then physical, again physiological and psychic happenings that are supposed to travel from one mind to another in accordance with prevailing theory. All is observable and treated as such, but the full observability of linguistic action requires elaboration, to which task we turn next.

THE OBSERVABILITY OF THE SPEAKING ACT

For simplicity's sake, imagine an everyday situation of a shopper, A, involved in a transaction with B, the manager of a fruit store. There they are talking before us in full sight and sound of each other as we observe them. As A inquires about the produce and B responds, we can make complete sense of the entire episode. There is no need to look behind the scene for invisible aspects of the event, in addition to those that we can observe, as called for by traditional theory. It is astonishing how invalid theories have confounded the complete observability and understanding of human speech, transforming it into obscure happenings, allegedly within the skin of the speaking and hearing organisms.

Adherents to the mentalistic view of language verbalize, think about, and perceive humans' speaking to one another according to the mold provided by the mentalistic framework. The same is true of the behavioristic way of formulating, thinking about, and perceiving speaking events. At this point, the interbehaviorist steps in and says, "Hold on! There is still another way of formulating the event people-speaking-and-listening-to-one-another that provides a naturalistic mold in which such events are viewed as completely observable occurrences that make sense." How do you know? Just look and listen. However, the "new look" demands retraining in the way we perceive events. We must learn (or relearn) how to see only what's there.

For Further Reading

Kagan, J., Havemann, J. & Segal, J. (1984). *Psychology: An introduction* (5th ed.). New York: Harcourt Brace Jovanovich.

Pronko, N. H. (1980). *Psychology from the standpoint of an interbehaviorist.* Monterey, Calif.: Brooks/Cole.

Kantor, J. R., & Smith, N. W. (1975). *The science of psychology: An interbehavioral survey.* Chicago: Principia Press.

"LIGHTNING CALCULATORS" AND SUCH

Even those who might subscribe to the proposition that behavior makes sense, that it shows a certain law and order, would exclude some seemingly incredible human performances. There are individuals who when asked how many seconds there are in eleven years will respond accurately, "346,896,000." If you ask, "What sum multiplied by itself will produce 998,001?" they will reply (in less than four seconds), "999." Others can tell at once what day of the week it was on a specific date in the past or in the future. Many people view such performances with bewilderment, even awe; they consider them "out of this world" or believe that such people possess special gifts or powers not granted to the rest of us. Such a pessimistic attitude leads us to a dead end as far as understanding goes. Such achievements remain forever awesome and baffling, and what's the profit in that? If scientists had taken a similar stand, throughout history, on such natural phenomena as lightning, volcanic activity, and the aurora borealis, we would still be stuck with mythical explanations at best.

AN ALTERNATIVE EXPLANATION

For a different approach, let us make only one assumption, namely, that all such performances are acquired achievements built up during the individual's reactional history in the same way as that person's language, dress, customs, food tastes, feelings, religious beliefs and practices, and so on. Let us try such a naturalistic approach and see if it advances our understanding. Steven Smith (1983) comes to our help. He compares the performance of lightning calculators to the learning of language by children. The beginner proceeds slowly, deliberately, and wittingly. But with fluency, one may achieve skill as a speaker, writer, poet, or orator. So it is with touch typing. The initial stages are slow and deliberate, but, with practice, an expert can type 125 words a minute. It's the same with calculators. According to Smith (1983, p. 29), calculators show the same slow, deliberate start and gradual improvement toward their high levels of achievement. Smith (1983, p. 30) states that any child capable of speech is "a potential calculating prodigy."

Another conspicuous feature of rapid calculators' attainment is its specificity. Smith (1983, p. 30) reports twin calendar calculators, one of whom was limited to this century while the other made correct day-date identifications in centuries ranging from 4100 B.C. to 40,000 A.D. Yet neither twin was able to learn the rudiments of arithmetic; they were even unable to multiply 3 × 6. Thus, we don't see any generalized ability, but rather an over-development in a specific area and a severe underdevelopment in most other types of development.

But how can we explain such overdevelopment? According to Smith's extensive study of speed calculators, the condition in their lives that favored such unusual achievement was isolation and a lack of distractions. In his elaborate investigations of the world's geniuses, McCurdy (1957, p. 448) found the same condition present in their early lives. He noted a great deal of attention paid to the child by parents and other adults, intensive culti-vation of the child's interest, and isolation from other children, particularly those outside the family. He found that such patterns were common in the childhood of J. S. Mill, Leibniz, Goethe, Pascal, McCaulay, Voltaire, Pope, Pitt, and others whose biographies he examined. McCurdy's findings sustain Smith's analysis of outstanding accomplishments of calculating prodigies.

One more piece of evidence. It is a fact that some high-speed calculators retain their achievements into the latter decades while others lose them even in their early years. Similarly, adults reared in China or France during their childhood speak the language fluently. But let them then move to another country permanently, and the "native" language speaking achievement may disappear. One can think of other behavioral skills, such as vocal or instru-mental performances, sports such as tennis, hockey, or archery, surgery, typing, and still others, which are acquired at one point in a person's life history and which disappear at another. Again, these facts do not offer any support for the notion of an individual's innate endowment of some mysterious "power." They do fit in with the proposed naturalistic explana-tion of their origin during the individual's reactional biography. But here is a bolder statement by a contemporary calculator, Hans Eberstark, who wrote an "Introductory Comment" to Smith's comprehensive account of calculators: "If you know the multiplication tables, I could teach you how to extract cube roots in less than a week and it would take me a month or two to train you in the fundamentals to become a calculating prodigy. (You can take me up on this offer!)" (Smith, 1983, p. xv).

There is a moral to this entire enterprise. When we are confronted with some seemingly marvelous occurrence, we can either throw up our hands and declare it unnatural, which precludes further inquiry, or roll up our sleeves and search out relevant factors that will lead to its understanding, as Smith has so elegantly shown us in the area of his special interest.

For Further Reading

McCurdy, H. G. (1957). The childhood pattern of genius. *Journal of the Elisha Mitchell Scientific Society, 73,* 448-462.

Smith, S. B. (1983). *The great mental calculators: The psychology, methods, and lives of calculating prodigies, past and present.* New York: Columbia University Press.

THE LIMITS
OF HUMAN NATURE

An illegitimate male child is born to a peasant girl and a notary or clerk of a hill village near Vinci in Italy. Who would have predicted that the boy would achieve distinction as the supreme example of an all-around man of the Renaissance, "l'uomo universale" or universal man? That boy did become the world-acclaimed Leonardo da Vinci. Within the behavioral parameters of one man, Leonardo came to excel in painting, sculpting, architecture, anatomy, physiology, geology, and botany. He was also a student of hydraulics and mechanics, and as an engineer he designed engines of war, canals, and flying machines. Da Vinci's many-sided accomplishments were adequate for distribution among a dozen men.

One reaction to Leonardo's acquisition of a multiplicity of excellences would be to call it a "sport of nature, the exception that proves the rule," which is no explanation. But the rebuttal to that weak claim is that Leonardo was only one of many high achievers of the Renaissance in Italy. There is Leone Battista Alberti, who was artist, architect, and gymnast and who also strived "to appear faultless in walking, in riding, and in speaking" (Burckhardt, 1909, p. 136). But that didn't satisfy him, so he taught himself music, attaining such mastery as to win the approval of professional musicians. Then poverty nudged him into the study of civil and canonical laws over a period of many years. Physics and mathematics absorbed him next, after which he excelled in painting and modeling. To the foregoing list must be added his literary output on art and architecture; his moral, philosophical, and historical works; his Latin prose writings, poems, and speeches; and so on and on. An extended list of all-around Renaissance men should include Petrarch, Dante, Michelangelo, Raphael, and a host of others with achievements of various degrees of excellence and versatility. We begin to suspect the operation of a generalized set of factors to explain such prevalent attainments. We find such in the milieu of our high achievers, which brings us to the culture of the times.

BURCKHARDT'S ILLUMINATION

Jacob Burckhardt helps in pinpointing the new influences that the Italian Renaissance ushered in. Instead of preoccupation with the other world, there was a shift to an absorption in the present world that led to a "discovery of man" (Burckhardt, 1909, p. 308ff.) and a widespread belief in the infinite perfectibility of humans (Heller, 1978, p. 81). People were believed to be capable of doing anything on their own once they willed it. Heller (1978, p. 446) quotes Nicholas of Cusa's dictum "Nothing sets bounds to the creative activity of humanity but humanity itself."

Writing on the Renaissance, Greenblatt (1980, p. 3) argues that there is no such thing as a human nature independent of culture, that humans are "cultural artifacts," and that we are born "unfinished animals." His statement is reminiscent of Ashley Montagu's (1956, p. 14) statement that "man is custom made, tailored according to the pattern prevailing in each culture." The Renaissance men that Greenblatt writes about are Sir Thomas More, Edmund Spenser, Christopher Marlowe, William Shakespeare, William Tyndale, and Sir Thomas Wyatt, sons of middle-class families who "stumbled" into greatness because of the stimulating conditions that they found themselves in. Their accomplishments were praised, honored, and rewarded in numerous ways. Skinner would probably say that Renaissance man acted as he did because his actions were reinforced.

EXCELLENCE IN OUR CULTURE

The outstanding feature of our civilization is its thorough saturation with the notion of IQ, talent, or giftedness that lies at the bottom of high achievement or excellence. Children earning superior scores on intelligence tests or course exams are believed to be gifted and are, therefore, assigned to the "fast track." One must ask, *what* is this giftedness, talent, IQ, and so on? *How* did it get into the child, *when*, and *where*? Such questions are never asked. The implicit thinking in the acceptance of the alleged entities goes something like this. Why is X's performance superb? Because she's talented (or gifted). How do you know she's talented (or gifted)? Because of her superb performance. The reasoning-in-a-circle should be apparent. And yet such glib explanations are readily accepted not only by the lay person but also by many psychologists. Let no one doubt the entrenched nature of the notion of the gifted child. An official publication of the American Psychological Association, *Psychology Today*, included a special section, "Gifted and Talented, Nurturing a National Treasure," in its May 1984 issue. This is a far cry from the prevalent thinking of people during the Renaissance period of human history. The difference in the outcome of the two philosophies has been eloquently summed up in the following passage from Skorpen (1965, p. 12):

When . . . the Renaissance ideal of the universal man is duly recognized, in the performance of men like Alberti and Da Vinci, we may wonder if the human perfection which they instanced does not represent the peak of mankind's development in both theory and practice, such that, apart from improved techniques of scientific discovery and applied technology, little else of importance distinguishes modern man from his Renaissance ancestor. Indeed, we might wonder if modern man hasn't deteriorated in comparison.

From the standpoint of the skeptic, a fitting conclusion to this disquisition on the limits of human potential is provided by the following passage from Jean Jacques Rousseau's (1979, p. 62) *Émile*: "I know of no philosopher or psychologist who has yet been so bold as to say: this is the limit of what man can attain and beyond which he cannot go. We do not know what our nature permits us to be."

For Further Reading

Burckhardt, J. (1909). *The civilization of the Renaissance in Italy* (S. G. C. Middlemore, Trans.). New York: Macmillan.

LLOYD MORGAN'S CANON

Conway Lloyd Morgan was a celebrated comparative psychologist who taught at University College in Bristol, England, during the latter part of the eighteenth century and the first decade of the nineteenth. His name lives on to this day attached to an accepted principle or rule known as Lloyd Morgan's canon. There is an interesting story connected with the formulation of his guide to proper psychological inquiry.

We need to recall that Darwin's theory of evolution had created quite a stir by Lloyd Morgan's time. The boundary between human and infrahuman behavior was breaking down. In fact, students of animal behavior bent backwards in attributing human behavioral characteristics to the lower animals. For example, they interpreted certain animal reactions as jealousy, revenge, or reasoning. Morgan objected strongly to such anthropomorphizing and came up with a procedure for checking unbridled speculation.

Lloyd Morgan was a child of his culture, as we all are. At that time, he could be none other than a mentalist. Therefore, his canon was expressed in a mentalistic framework. Here is how it reads:

In no case may we interpret an action as the outcome of the exercise of a higher psychical faculty, if it can be interpreted as the outcome of the exercise of one which stands lower in the psychological scale. (Morgan, 1967, p. 56)

Morgan notes that false assumptions and vague generalizations are more readily entertained about mental processes than about their physical expressions or correlates. That observation holds for animal as well as human behavior. The layman often imputes the same motives to his pet as to himself or his neighbor. The psychologist should be on guard against such audacious conjectures.

Morgan illustrates the point about unconstrained theorizing with an experience involving his dog, Tony, a fox terrier pup. On their walks in the country, Morgan would carry a stick along and throw it. Each time, Tony would retrieve it and return with it in his mouth. On one occasion, Morgan took along a heavy-knobbed walking stick and threw it as he had the earlier one. Tony seized the cane by the middle as he had before, but its unbalanced position caused him to change his tactics, and after an hour or two, he seized the stick near the knob end. Presumably, that became a habitual way of handling the heavy-knobbed walking stick thereafter.

The question is: How did Tony solve, in a practical way, a problem in mechanics? Did he reason that the center of gravity lay seven inches from the knob end of the stick? No. In accordance with his own canon, Morgan offers a more conservative explanation of Tony's behavior. The dog did not perceive that the stick's "center of gravity had certain space relations" (p. 57). Tony certainly profited from past experience applied to several concrete experiences with the stick. With reference to his own canon, Morgan (1967, p. 57) states, "If I say this canon is to be adopted, then we are bound to interpret the action of the dog as performed through sense-experience alone."

As pointed out earlier, a mentalistic framework was the only route available to Morgan. But his canon is applicable in other approaches to behavioral inquiry, because the essential point concerns caution and conservatism in explaining or interpreting behavioral events. The injunction is to stick as close to the data as possible. Don't reach for the exotic, fancy, far-fetched, or imaginary explanation. Where you have a choice, take the simpler, more easily verifiable alternative.

Scientists in other fields have made statements similar to that of Morgan. Hanson (1958, p. 95), a physicist, in criticizing theories that require supplementary explanation, states, "If that to which I refer when accounting for events needs more explaining than that to which you refer, then your explanation is better than mine." A remark of Einstein's (Clark, 1971, p. 109) seems relevant as a concluding statement: "A theory is the more impressive the greater the simplicity of its premises is, the more different kinds of things it relates, and the more extended its area of applicability." Such cautionary measures as the different versions of Lloyd Morgan's canon necessitate are not alien to the skeptical psychologist. (See also OCCAM'S RAZOR.)

For Further Reading

Morgan, C. L. (1967). Introduction to comparative psychology. In A. J. Riopelle (Ed.), *Animal problem solving* (pp. 54-61). Baltimore: Penguin Books. (Original work published 1909)

MEASUREMENT: ITS FUNCTION IN SCIENCE

Our most prevalent notions both about the function of measurement and about the source of its special efficacy are derived largely from myth.

Kuhn (1961, p. 161)

Thomas Kuhn traces the derivation of the myth to the misleading image of measurement presented in science textbooks. The real function of scientific measurement is to be found not in textbooks but in scientific journals, which reflect the gradual development of scientific theories, whereas textbooks present scientific theories as finished products with presumably built-in computations and measurements. Kuhn (1961, p. 162) considers such textbook accounts misleading because they fail "to show that large amounts of qualitative work have usually been prerequisite to fruitful quantification in the physical sciences."

As a historian of science, Kuhn reports that earlier historical developments of the natural sciences proceeded without major assistance from quantitative methods. It was the rare genius of such workers as Newton, Lavoisier, or Einstein who created a theoretical upheaval (i.e., qualitative changes) in their sciences that provided "measurement [with] its overwhelmingly most common scientific function" (1961, p. 168). Kuhn stresses the point that the role of measurement as usually conceived is reversed. Theoretical genius paves the way for the experimentalists to follow with their measurement techniques. Furthermore, a lot of theoretical development is required before one can make sense of the results of measurement. In fact, if an adequate theory has been developed, the law implied by it can often be guessed without measurement.

Mario Bunge (1969, p. 61) points out the dissatisfaction among quantum physicists over the imponderable, quaint elementary particles and atomic nuclei. Despite the fact that they can calculate a number of quantities, such measurements do not advance understanding of that which is being calculated. Kuhn (1961, p. 175) echoes Bunge's assessment in stating that unless you know what you're measuring, the numbers that you obtain are just numbers.

THE CENTRALITY OF THE CRUDE DATUM

We can get another perspective on the role of quantitative statements by analyzing the physicist's equation of motion $S = \frac{1}{2}gt^2$. This formula predicts the distance traveled by an object in a given time, an object dropped (not thrown) falling freely toward the earth. Actually, the formula describes only a limited aspect of the gravitational event. But suppose that, by some magic, you had never in your life witnessed a gravitational event. What could the formula mean to you? Without prior study of physics and without the event itself, from which the formula is derived and to which it refers, the formula would be nonsensical. Above all, the formula should not be considered as if it had encapsulated or apprehended the total event, a common error that derives from identifying the formula with the event of which it is a partial description, that is, identifying the description with the thing described.

The preceding example of a gravitational event carries implications about the importance of the event per se. As long as one can readily refer to the event at one's pleasure, even an abstract formula such as $S = \frac{1}{2}gt^2$ appears to help in understanding it. Why? Because one has the gravitational event itself conveniently at hand to refer to. The description, mathematical or otherwise, and the event itself are so closely linked together that the two may be easily confused.

Let us apply the preceding analysis to a psychological situation. Suppose that X quite suddenly acts very strangely. Y explains X's unusual behavior by suggesting that "X's mind snapped." A reductionist proposes the notion of a malfunctioning brain. A psychoanalyst puts forward the notion that an id impulse, unrestrained by the ego, had found expression, manifesting itself as X's strange behavior. The proponent of any of the interpretations can believe in his or her stand by pointing to the event, the starting point of each proponent's interpretation. Here we have an example, not of an abstract formula as in the case of the physicist, but of an entirely false explanation of a psychological occurrence. Yet the charmed believer in a "mind" that can "snap," the reductionist who favors deranged brains, and one who goes for id impulses each can readily point to the event itself as a confirmation of the proposed explanation. Here is another instance of an identification of an explanation with the thing requiring explanation. This fallacy of circular reasoning occurs whether or not measurement is involved.

MEASURING THE IQ

The manner in which measurement is used (abused?) in psychology may be illustrated with the computation of the IQ from a child's performance on the Stanford-Binet Intelligence Test. Suppose that two children, Johnnie and Suzy, both took the same Stanford-Binet test. Suppose, too, for argument's sake, that every test that Johnnie passed Suzy failed, and, vice versa, every test that Suzy passed Johnnie failed. Stated otherwise, their respective behavior repertoires consist of different component reactions, yet, when their IQs are calculated, they are found to have *identical* IQs. Their very different specific items passed are somehow assigned the same numerical value, thus yielding "identical IQs."

In an article, "The Pernicious Influence of Mathematics on Science," Schwartz (1962, p. 356) states that "mathematics must deal with well defined situations." The heterogeneous test items of the Stanford-Binet that we have examined hardly meet Schwartz's criterion of "well defined situations." Nevertheless, the various test items are treated *as if* they were simple, equivalent units. And the same holds for the "identical IQs" assigned to both Johnnie and Suzy, IQs derived from such variegated tests as were passed by each testee.

STATISTICS AND PSYCHOLOGY

Statistics plays a significant role in modern psychology, a role that contradicts the definition of psychology as the study of the individual. B. F. Skinner has much to say on this subject. In his *Cumulative Record*, Skinner (1959, p. 247) is critical of the traditional manner in which graduate schools train young psychologists. Instead of scientific method, they are given courses in statistics. Because of the abstract view fostered by a statistical approach, the direct manipulation of variables for finer control is discouraged. If the numerical results are not significant, simply increase the size of your sample until you do get "significant" results. But by this time you are dealing not with behavior but with numbers, so that contact with the behavior of the individual organism has been lost. As Skinner (1959, p. 247) puts it, such preoccupation yields "a much more intimate acquaintance with a calculating machine than with a behaving organism."

To say that theory in modern physics has become highly abstract is an understatement. To take only one example, what can one make of the quarks, such as up, down, bottom, beauty, and so on? We are told that these "things" are only colorful terms for "properties of quarks that can only be described by mathematical expressions" (Gardner, 1985, p. 31).

At this point, the unskeptical psychologist who emulates the physicist in an effort to be "scientific" might ask, "If you tolerate such rarefied theory in the case of the physicist, why do you oppose my theory of hypothetical retinal images, brain traces, memory storage in the brain, mental representations, and so on?"

The skeptical psychologist's response would run somewhat as follows: "So much the worse for the physicist! What a pity his submicroscopic data are so far removed from the events of everyday life. We psychologists are fortunate that our subject matter is open to inspection. After all, we are studying organisms in interaction with either objects or other organisms in their surroundings, under specifiable conditions, all of them directly observable. Therefore, all we need to do is to detail the nature of the interrelationships of the participating variables. There is no need for any hypothetical entities to explain what is directly observable."

CONCLUSION

In winding up our consideration of the role of measurement in scientific activity, the clear implication is that measurement should not shut out the part that the qualitative aspects of natural events play in scientific inquiry. It seems that the safest simplistic rule would be to let the data dictate the relative weight of the quantitative and qualitative facets of natural events. However, the problems raised by a consideration of the role of measurement in scientific inquiry are far more complex than those touched upon here. As children of our culture, we carry so many silent assumptions about the power of measurement that assessing the proper role is about as achievable as lifting ourselves by our bootstraps.

For Further Reading

Kuhn, T. S. (1961). The function of measurement in modern science. *Isis, 52*, Part 2, No. 168, 161-193.
Skinner, B. F. (1959). *Cumulative record*. New York: Appleton-Century-Crofts.

MEMORY

Canst thou not minister to a mind diseased;
Pluck from the memory a rooted sorrow;
Raze out [erase] the written troubles of the brain?

Macbeth, Act V, Scene III

In the preceding passage, Shakespeare reveals an early intellectual ancestor of today's memory trace or engram. Compare Macbeth's lamentable appeal to the family physician in behalf of Lady Macbeth with a statement appearing in a book *Memory* by Elizabeth Loftus (1980), published almost four hundred years after *Macbeth*. We enter her discussion at the point where Loftus (1980, p. xiv) considers the "malleability of memory" and speculates about the feasibility of going to a clinic to have troublesome memories altered. As an aside, one must admit that Macbeth's (or better, Shakespeare's) understanding of memory would be right in step with that of contemporary mainstream psychology. But surely Shakespeare would be completely at sea in understanding contemporary chemistry, physics, biology, and astronomy.

The usual definition of memory refers to a "faculty" or "power" by which one recalls or remembers the store of experiences.

THE NINETEENTH-CENTURY SEARCH FOR THE MEMORY TRACE

Murray (1980) narrates a two-thousand-year-long history of speculation about the memory trace which goes back to Galen's (129 A.D.) time. According to Seamon (1980, p. 3), these speculations are still pursued today. Instead of Galen's movements of "animal spirits" running through the nerves to fixate memory, today's theory is formulated in electro-chemical terms. Kagan, Havemann, and Segal's (1984, p. 119) formulation assumes the essential features of the traditional storehouse notion as a container of our knowledge. They state that "memory is the storehouse in which we keep all this information—carefully sorted into various rooms, aisles, and bins so that we can find it." Are we to take their statement literally, and how did "we" get into the act? Reader, try to make sense out of that statement. I can't.

Criticism of the Memory-Trace Theory

1. The theory is purely imaginary.
2. It confounds understanding of memory instead of advancing it.
3. It is, consequently, useless. For example, what could one say *in terms of the alleged memory trace* to someone interested in improving one's memory?

AN ALTERNATIVE APPROACH TO "MEMORY"

A field approach to memory requires abandoning an exclusive pre-occupation with the organism. It calls for an expanded space-time framework, one that embraces the thing recalled from the past and the present recall of it into a unit event. This procedure requires a radical departure from the mechanistic, Newtonian space-time framework inherent in the traditional memory-trace theory.

Rachlin (1977, p. 373) is comfortable with working in an expanded space-time framework as revealed in the following quotation:

If a subject in an experiment is instructed on Day 1 to make response X on Day 2, the cause of response X when it is observed need not be attributed to anything inside the subject's head, but directly to events on the previous day. There is nothing logically wrong with supposing that events on Day 1 directly cause events on Day 2 without supposing a chain of intermediary events (in the mind or nervous system or elsewhere).

A radical departure from a Newtonian space-time framework is required to understand what is involved in such events as recall. A terrestrial space and clock time explained remembering by assuming a fictitious space somewhere in the head and clock time, which continuously retained an impression until some later time that required its release (or whatever).

A behavioral space-time usage goes about things differently. We start with the fact that (if you will *not misunderstand*) the term, humans, behaviorally speaking, can *transcend* space and time *as viewed from a Newtonian framework!* You can *right now*, so to speak, "jump over" to a different location and to a past time embracing them together. The verb *transcend* is not meant in any mystical sense; it derives meaning only by contrast with a Newtonian framework. The fact is that human behavior is not restricted to the *here* and *now*. If that is so, why not deal with the facts as they are instead of converting them into something which they aren't (e.g., memory traces, synaptic modifications, and so on). The only alternative is the abandonment of a Newtonian space-time framework and the adoption of a behavioral space-time derived from observable events, one that will do justice to the facts. Physics made the switch to a space-time paradigm when the old one was found wanting. Psychology still awaits a paradigm shift.

For Further Reading

Kagan, J., Havemann, J. & Segal, J. (1984). *Psychology: An introduction* (5th ed.). New York: Harcourt Brace Jovanovich.

Murray, D. J. (1980). Research on human memory in the nineteenth century. In J. D. Seamon (Ed.), *Human memory: Contemporary readings,* pp. 5-23. New York: Oxford University Press.

METAPHORS

Even a brief perusal of a book by Lakoff and Johnson (1980) will convince the reader that our daily communication with each other is shot through with "the metaphors we live by" (the title of their book). Not only are metaphors pervasive; they are used unwittingly by both the speaker and the hearer or, by extension, the writer and reader. For example, when you read the expression "shot through" in the preceding sentence, did you realize that it was a metaphor? Lakoff and Johnson make a convincing case for the widespread influence of metaphor on our everyday functioning including our ways of conceptualizing things. To underscore the inescapable and subtle power of metaphor, we note the metaphoric relationship between time and money. We *save, share, waste, run out of, spend, borrow, put aside, budget,* and *invest* our time. It is interesting how a whole cluster of related verbs applicable to talking and thinking about money has been appropriated to talking and thinking about time. Thus, metaphors are not all rare and exotic creations of poets. They constitute the warp and woof of the common language of common people. For a rich source of sexual metaphors as applied by laborers in the steel industry, engineering, electrical work, plumbing, construction, mining, and carpentering, see Merlin Thomas (1951).

TURBAYNE'S CONTRIBUTION

Turbayne's (1970) exhaustive work on metaphor teaches us how to use metaphors without being used by them. For one thing, it is not a confusion to refer to things of a certain kind in the idioms of another kind if we are aware of such use. Confusion lies in using such idioms *without awareness.* As Turbayne (1970, p. 3) puts it, "There is a difference between using a metaphor and taking it literally, between using a model and mistaking it for the thing modeled. The one is to make believe that something is the case; the other is to believe that it is."

In addition to an awareness of the use of metaphor, Turbayne indicates that there has to be an appreciation of the duality of meaning; there has to be an *as-if* or *make-believe* feature present. We realize this when Marullus in *Julius Caesar* addresses the Roman commoners as "You blocks, you stones, you worse than senseless things." But we do not realize it when we mistake a theory for a fact, as when we compare the brain with a computer or with a substance on which we can make a trace as in memory traces. The brain becomes *literally* a computer and something on which something can be written and, perhaps, even erased. When the description of an event is identified with the thing described, then, instead of using metaphor, we are being used by it. It is at this stage that we are dealing with what Turbayne calls a "dead metaphor" (p. 25). The use of metaphor calls for a great deal of discretion in its use lest we become victims of it. After all, a metaphor is only a metaphor; it is no substitute for strict, precise reference to events.

For Further Reading

Lakoff, G., & Johnson, M. (1980). *The metaphors we live by*. Chicago: University of Chicago Press.

Turbayne, C. M. (1970). *The myth of metaphor* (rev. ed.). Columbia: University of South Carolina Press.

METAPHYSICS

"Metaphysics means nothing but an unusually obstinate effort to think clearly" (James, 1918, p. 145). If it doesn't, it should.

MODELS

To speak of models in connection with a scientific theory already
smacks of the metaphorical.

Black (1962, p. 219)

Most dictionaries define the term *model* as a copy, image, or representation
of something similar in some respects but dissimilar in others, as a scale
model. As such, models are extended metaphors because they compare two
unlike things in limited ways.

We may learn something about models by studying their "birth, evolution, and death." Our first response to a new model is to deny its
metaphorical nature. When sounds were first compared to vibrations and
light to waves, everyone was aware of the fact that vibrations and waves
were *only* models, and *not* vibrations and waves. In time, however, sounds
became literally vibrations and light literally waves. Today they are dead
metaphors. In physics, forces reside in bodies and bodies attract each other,
the latter modeled after people who attract each other. The model has been
confused with the thing for which it served as a model.

MODELS IN PSYCHOLOGY

Some philosophers and scientists believe that we have entered the "Age of
the Thinking Machine" what with computers that can play chess with
humans, compose music, and spew out answers to problems with amazing
speed. With every technological advance, there is a change in the metaphor
applied to the brain. The brain is no longer a telephone central switchboard.
Today the brain is a computer and the computer is a brain, an interesting
two-way metaphor also serving as a two-way reinforcement for each other.
The brain so conceived serves as a model for the biologist as well as the
psychologist. In an article in the *A.P.A. Monitor*, "Mapping the Brain's
Circuits" (1984), the brain is compared to the internal combustion engine,
and brain researchers are said to be "at the nuts and bolts stage" (p. 39) in
their search for the specific neural elements that will help us to "understand
the intricacies of human learning" (p. 39). Because the brain is discussed
fully under the two entries THE BRAIN, we drop the matter at this point.

A provocative mechanical model derives from Freud's system of psychoanalysis. Hendrick (1958), himself a psychoanalyst, illustrates Freud's pleasure and reality principles with the aid of a seductive "blueprint" of each. The model that Hendrick relies on is a hydraulic system. The water represents the "instincts," which are under pressure by a pump. Normally the instincts are channeled and expressed through some pleasurable activity, and the internal pressure is maintained at a safe level. But, if the normal outlet is blocked, pressure increases, and you may have a break in the system. Then you have a neurosis or psychosis. Such everyday expressions as "He blew off steam," "He exploded," "She blew her top," and "Let it all out" also fit this model.

"Mental health," "mental illness," and "mental disease": these terms, in such rampant usage among lay persons, psychologists, psychiatrists, and physicians and in official government practices (e.g., the National Institute of *Mental* Health) are part of the vocabulary of the medical model. The way the medical model spells it out, "mental hygiene" is parallel to so-called physical hygiene. To continue with the medical model, just as one can have a sick or diseased body, so one can also suffer from a sick or diseased mind. What is called for is "diagnosis," "prognosis," and "treatment." In place of the medical model, Thomas Szasz embraces the notion that anxiety, despair, guilt, and fear of sickness, old age, and death are *human problems of living* to be studied *in their own right* and *on their own level*. May we conclude that the medical model applied to human problems is dead? Not at all. It is alive and well and manifests itself throughout the land. In Turbayne's sense only is it a dead model or extended metaphor. Why? Because its vocabulary is used without awareness and it is understood literally. After all, when someone *acts* in a most unusual way, don't most people exclaim, "Sick! Sick! Sick!"?

It is surely a laudable practice to view events from a number of perspectives, but, as Nalimov (1981, p. 4) informs us, "The models we are so accustomed to in science can be obtained only from premises and not immediately from observational results." The clear implication is that we must examine the premises of the models that we adopt for inquiry and note that we are *imposing* such models *on* events, not *deriving them from* events.

For Further Reading

Black, M. (1962). *Models and metaphors*. Ithaca, N.Y.: Cornell University Press.
Szasz, T. S. (1961). *The myth of mental illness*. New York: Hoeber-Harper.

NEUROLOGICAL VERSUS PSYCHOLOGICAL EXPLANATION

This is a demonstration of the difference between a neurological and a psychological explanation/description of a case borrowed from J. H. Woodger the biologist. Woodger (1956, p. 93) starts with the ancient proverb "The burnt child dreads the flame." He transforms that expression to a more scientifically useful form in the following statement: "Every child that has been burnt avoids fire." With that preliminary out of the way, assume that we are now confronted with an event described by the following two statements:

1. Tom is a child.
2. Tom has been burnt.

With the above reformulation of the proverb into a law, we can predict:

3. Tom avoids fires.

Our first question is: How valid is such a formulation: Can we check it out? As far as determining the validity of Propositions 1 and 2 is concerned, note that both are capable of verification. Because both are observable, we can check up on Tom's status as a child and whether he was actually burnt. We can do so either from Tom's testimony or from that of witnesses (parents, teachers, or others) at the scene. Please note that we have done our job without leaving the observational level simply by relating the observable factors in an event and by relating one event, Tom and fire *now*, to a similar event in the past involving Tom and fire. The result is description or explanation that yields understanding and prediction and control.

Now, suppose we try to tell the story in biological, that is, neurological, terms. According to traditional theory, we must assume that persons who have been burnt have a brain that has been changed in some way as the result of their having been burnt (brain traces, or "engrams"). When such persons are in the presence of hot objects or fire, the modified brain allegedly causes movements that produce avoidance of such things. But how do we verify our neurological theory of a controlling agent in the brain that produces movements away from hot objects? In only one way, and that takes us back to the psychological level as evidenced by the fact that we are forced to inquire if Tom has been burnt. That's all the "evidence" there is for the neurological story. There is no way of *independently* verifying the neurological account, no way of opening Tom's skull and confirming that the particular configuration of his neurons declares that he was burnt at some past time. And, to close with a punchline from Woodger derived from Bertrand Russell, "As Lord Russell has remarked, you cannot by examining a man's brain tell whether he speaks French or has visited New York" (Woodger, 1956, p. 95). The same holds true in trying to explain Tom's avoiding hot objects. There is no way of scrutinizing Tom's brain that would permit us to declare, "Yes, Tom was burnt by a flame and he avoids fire. I know that because his brain tells me so."

CRITICISM OF THE NEUROLOGICAL STORY

1. The theory is self-actional. It attributes power to a certain anatomical part of the organism, namely, the brain, with special powers to record and execute orders to muscles. This theory, far from being a field theory, might be termed a power-in-a-spot theory.

2. The neurological theory is reductionistic, interpreting a psychological observation in terms of an imaginary anatomy and physiology.

3. The neurological theory provides no basis whatsoever for either prediction or understanding. We have already noted that there is no way of opening up the organism to "read" its brain and that there is nothing helpful to read if we could do so.

4. The neurological theory is based upon a metaphor of the brain as a tape recorder or telephone switchboard. But metaphors can be given up or traded for more useful metaphors as the need arises. Knowing that, we can be freer in our use of them, detaching ourselves from them without sentiment and with a consequent lesser likelihood of our being used by them.

5. The neurological theory is a purely hypothetical account of Tom's avoidance of hot objects. As such, it should enjoy a respectable scientific status but only as a hypothesis subject to verification. Only after verification can it be used to explain our observation of Tom. But to *assume* a neurological explanation, as is commonly done, and then to act *as if it were true* in explaining the event from which the hypothetical explanation was conceptually derived is bad science. This is another instance of switching from make-believe to belief. What one appears to do in the case of explaining Tom's withdrawing from hot objects in neurological terms is to say, "Well, it *could* be, couldn't it, that 'traces' are left in Tom's brain from his first burning encounter?" In the next breath, one says, "It's so. There *are* brain traces. That's the way to explain Tom's compulsive behavior in the presence of hot objects." The neurological story is in terms of a "merely conceivable theory." Nature will not tolerate any "merely conceivable theory." The theory offered by Woodger has not just been dreamed up. It was derived from the observation of Tom *and* hot objects under definite

conditions, over a period of time. The theory also refers to those observations and not to something else imaginary.

For Further Reading

Woodger, J. H. (1956). *Physics, psychology and medicine.* Cambridge: At the University Press.

OBJECTS AND THEIR HISTORIES: DO OBJECTS HAVE HISTORIES?

A culturally pervasive thing orientation favors objects as the enduring aspects of events. In fact, in commonsense thinking, objects stand out like a sore thumb, while the situations which those objects undergo are soft-pedaled. The reason for this lopsided emphasis on objects is very likely due to the fact that objects are the highly visible and recurring aspects of events while the transient occasions that serve as their stage settings are variable and are, consequently, easily overlooked.

In conformance with an almost universal focus on objects, there exists a common belief that psychology studies people, whereas, at least under field auspices, people are only one of a number of essential factors that participate in behavioral events. But even with an expanded field view, stress is not on the factors that take part in the event but on the total event itself. However, the object-or-thing view, not the field view, prevails as a hangover of Newtonian thinking with its foundation of separate, self-actional bits of matter possessing certain forces.

A current textbook of psychology (Kagan, Havemann & Segal, 1984, p. 5) follows a Newtonian paradigm in its construct concerning the role of the brain. In the third paragraph of their initial definition of psychology, they state that of "the factors that influence behavior . . . the most important is the human brain."

These authors treat the brain as a special bit of matter with certain special powers such as thinking, planning, and remembering. The brain is also a storehouse of memory. In other words, the brain has a history of "what has happened to us—and thus helps us to learn from experience" (p. 56). What we have here is, on the one hand, an object, the brain, and on the other hand, its history, a quasi object—two separate and distinct entities. The construct of Kagan et al. reflects the common view that there are two antithetical entities: *people* and the *"things"* that happen to them, or persons *and* their biographies, the brain *and* its memories. The two are treated as separate and distinct, and to some degree contrasting, entities. The fallacy involved in such thinking has been cogently expressed by Broad (1952, p. 406) somewhat as follows. In our customary, everyday usage, we think of objects in severance from their histories, as if objects had some sort of priority over and above their histories. We also think of histories as something that happen to objects. Yet while there is no such thing as a history without an object, neither is there an object without a history. In the complex of observable events, there are only slices of history, some slow and monotonous such as continental drift or the birth and death of stars, others exciting and occurring faster such as volcanic explosions or April showers. Objects without their histories and histories without objects appear to fall into the Newtonian pattern of the universe as composed of independently existing "bodies" or particles on the one hand and force on the other. But under a broad field orientation, entities are only abstractions from complex occurrences. Thus, such things as organisms, stimulus objects, and brains are only enduring modes of characterizing the more conspicuous and continuing aspects of the flow of events in which they are embedded.

Here, in a nutshell, is the upshot of the present inquiry. Language is viewed as either facilitating or hindering inquiry. Verbally, but fortunately *only verbally*, we can carve up natural events any way we choose; but nature will not submit to our semantic infelicities. "Objects" and "histories" will not sever themselves from the total integrated situation or system; they insist on occupying a special status within the organization. As a matter of fact, events will still continue to roll on, one after another, no matter how we talk about them.

For Further Reading

Broad, C. D. (1952). *Scientific thought*. London: Routledge and Kegan Paul. (Original work published 1923)

OBSERVATION: WHAT IS OBSERVABLE?

A group of psychologists are observing a certain psychological event. Do they report their observations in the same way? Not at all! A sees an Oedipus complex going on in the invisible unconscious of the individual as the result of the superego's war against the id on the battleground of the ego. B sees "representations," "icons," or "storage" in the brain of the person involved. C sees a problem in interpersonal relationships; D sees a "frustration threshold" that was exceeded.

In his conditioning laboratory, Ivan Pavlov displayed prominently a sign that read, "Observation and again observation." Some would say that what he "really" saw was dogs salivating to whistles, bells, and meat powder. However, according to the subtitle of his book on conditioned reflexes, his work was "an investigation of the physiological activity of the cerebral cortex" (Pavlov, 1927). He never *directly* observed action in the brains of dogs. The point is that all of the preceding reported observations are not reports of crude data but of constructed data; in Hanson's (1958) terms, the observations are "theory-laden." What the various psychologists had learned prior to their observations was unwittingly imposed upon the data, or read *into* them, not read *out* of them. The moral is to be fully aware of the preconceptions or postulates that we bring to our observations.

The question of what is observable gets some clarification from a helpful discussion by Achinstein (1965, pp. 193-194). Suppose you are driving along a dusty country road in the daytime. What do you see ahead of you? You might say that you observed a car in the distance, or dust raised by a car, or simply a cloud of dust. What a person might say under the same circumstances would depend on a number of factors—that person's past experience and training, the answer expected by the questioner, and so on. Certainly an infant or an individual from a primitive tribe would not see a car. Yet you might be justified in claiming that you saw a car even if you couldn't tell what make or color it was. But a helicopter could substantiate your report that there was or was not a car ahead.

The example serves as a suitable introduction to the next scene, a laboratory of an experimental physicist who has a background in discriminating the kinds of tracks made by different subatomic particles in cloud chambers. If asked to tell us what he is observing, the physicist may answer that he sees (1) electrons passing through the chamber, (2) tracks left by electrons, (3) droplets of water condensed on gas ions, or (4) merely long, thin lines. All of the physicist's observational statements are a function of his or her knowledge, whatever the questioner may know, and whatever response appears to be called for. Achinstein rejects a single, absolutistic criterion for determining distinctions between observable and nonobservable entities. But always there must be an interaction, regardless of how attenuated, with some confrontable thing. At different times, instrumentation has made visible what had formerly been invisible. This point requires further elaboration.

INSTRUMENTALLY AIDED OBSERVATION

Before the invention of the microscope, bacteria, protozoa, and spermatozoa were invisible. And imagine Galileo's delight when, viewing the moon through the telescope, he saw the holes on the moon's surface as craters. Today, invisible astronomy depends on radio and infrared telescopes as well as apparatus sensitive to ultraviolet, gamma-rays, and X-rays to contact distant objects. Medicine has also expanded its armamentarium of instrumental aids to look into every nook and cranny of the opaque human organism.

At this point, one can hear the cognitivist and other proponents of the mentalistic approach saying, "Aha! You have fallen into our trap, for you yourself have demonstrated that that which was *invisible* at a given time was at some future time made visible. How do you know that research in the future might not uncover 'encoding, storage, and retrieving centers' in the brain as well as the real locus of the inscrutable 'mind'? And, as if with some degree of self-justification, all mentalists might add, in unison, "Look at all the conceptual entities that astronomers and biomedical workers were able to corroborate in time. And how about all the hypothetical entities that contemporary physicists deal with? And aren't there many degrees of observability ranging from seeing the sun with the naked eye to the track of an alpha particle? Why don't you treat us as tolerantly as you do the physicist?"

We would answer, "It is true that many 'things' in science, such as you have mentioned, were invisible at one time but were later visible. But they were all confrontable 'things,' the existence of which could be confirmed one way or another. To take only one example, an ultrasound determination of the sex of a fetus can be checked at birth some months later. Is there any comparable check you can propose for your 'encoding, storage, and retrieving centers'? Or are these not purely fictitious entities, which, although offered as explanations, are themselves in need of explanation?

"As to degrees of observability, one cannot argue against that assertion, but how would you refute the following proposition of Maxwell's (1962, p. 228)?

Although there certainly is a continuous transition from observability to unobservability, any talk of such a continuity from full-blown existence to nonexistence is, clearly, nonsense.

"As to your insistence on the same treatment as the physicist gets, let me point out that when physicists learned that their 'phlogiston' and 'ether' turned out to be fictitious, they abandoned them. Are you ready to follow some of your fellow cognitivists who are ready to forget about 'icons,' 'storage,' 'memory functions,' and other varieties of 'mental functions'—psychology's 'phlogiston' and 'ether'? Finally, let me point out that as highly attenuated as the physicists' theories appear to be, they have nevertheless resulted in radio, nuclear power, television, lasers, computers, and so on. Do you have any comparable applications of your theory, applications which derive from your theory and affirm its validity?"

THE SOLUTION: RETRAINING IN OBSERVATION

A retraining program will require the surrender of a nearly exclusive preoccupation with the organism in exchange for a vastly extended orientation, one in which the several participants of the event are held together in system prior to an analysis of their separate contributions to the event. If the physicists abandoned Newton's point of view, so can we. While some psychologists might insist that stimuli and responses are "rock bottom" and open to inspection by anyone, Mackenzie (1977, p. 167) claims otherwise, as manifested in the following closing quotation to this piece: "Stimuli and responses are what one has learned to see as stimuli and responses. They are not initially, but they become, *directly* observable." In summing up the history of psychology, we note that, over the centuries, psychologists have learned to "observe," each in its turn, soul, mind, brain encoding and storing, and stimuli and responses. The pertinent question is: With much practice, can we learn to see psychological events in still broader ways? Only time will tell.

For Further Reading

Achinstein, P. (1965). The problem of theoretical terms. *American Philosophical Quarterly, 11* (3), 193-203.

OBSERVATIONS
OF A SEMANTIC SORT

According to Francis Bacon, "Men suppose their reason has command over their words; still it happens that words in return exercise authority on reason." What if Bacon's assertion is true? Can our language cause us to reason as we do without our even realizing that we have been duped? At any rate, it may repay us to analyze how language operates. If we have a clearer understanding of how language works, we may know how to prevent words from exercising authority on reason.

About forty-five years ago, Alfred Korzybski (1941)* developed an analytic technique for dissecting language function and malfunction. His system, known as General Semantics, was intended to facilitate clear linguistic expression and to avoid linguistic traps of the sort Bacon recognized in his statement. We now consider some of Korzybski's chief analytic tools in relation to our field of study.

MAP TERRITORY

To anyone who has used a map in his or her auto travels, the map-territory concept is easy to grasp. As long as one's road map accurately represents the territory one is traveling over, no problem exists. But if the mapmaker shows Cleveland to be located west of Chicago, the traveler will be in trouble. The map and the territory don't correspond.

Similarly, if language is compared to a map and the territory to the world of facts, we may find a fit or misfit between our *talk* about the facts and *the facts* themselves. The "map" and the "territory" don't agree. Very often, it makes little difference in such remote situations as when we say, "The sun *rises* or *sets*." According to modern astronomy, such a map is erroneous because the sun really doesn't rise or set, but the sun will go on doing what it does anyhow. However, we may expect to find erroneous language maps of the psychological territory, and there it will matter. But before we enter upon that task, let us examine another semantic contrivance of Korzybski's, one closely related to the concept of map territory.

---

*There is much to criticize in Korzybski's basic orientation, but to do so would take us too far afield and is not necessary for our purpose.

REIFICATION

The term *reification* does not belong to General Semantics but is included at this point because it is an extension of the kind of error that derives from a word orientation. To reify is to thing-ify a "thing" that isn't a "thing." The Latin term *res* ("thing") forms the root of the word. More precisely, *reification* refers to an unwarranted extension of "reality" to something abstract, to treat the abstract as a material thing. A term (mind, gravity, life, heat, IQ, instincts, will power, good and evil, love and hate) is treated the same as something that has weight, size, shape, and so on. The conceptual is concretized and reacted to as if it were an independent entity. When schizophrenia is conceptualized as "a disease," certain behaviors have been *verbally* transformed into an entity or "thing" that a person is supposed to "have." Freud peopled the mind with many entities. The superego and the id were said to war with each other on the battlefield of the ego. The libido furnishes another example of a reification.

ELEMENTALISM

In addition to "making things" out of nonthings and creating a purely verbal world, our ancient language with its ancient assumptions also splits asunder (verbally) aspects of the world that refuse to be split. Korzybski (1941, p. 243) named this semantic error elementalism. Thus, although everything that we observe in the world involves indivisibly "matter," "space," and "time," we can split them asunder and handle them, verbally *only*, as if they were detachable and detached elements. Let us stress that whatever "splitting" occurs can occur only on the verbal level. "Nature," fortunately, will not cooperate in such intellectual crimes. (The term *nature* has been deliberately reified here as a horrible example.) What is the remedy for elementalism? The answer is: a nonelementalistic orientation which, instead of fragmenting and carving up wholes, treats them as events or integrated occurrences. Harry Stack Sullivan (Mullahy, 1952, p. 22) considers even the term *personality* too elementalistic, for there is no such thing as personality in isolation, only *interpersonal relations*.

TWO-VALUED ORIENTATION

"Either you are for me or you are against me." "You are either telling the truth or lying." "It's either night or day, black or white." Some people live in a world where there are only two, opposite values. For them, there is no twilight or dawn and no shades of gray between black and white. Such a rigid, either-or procedure has a way of apparently simplifying the complexity of the world for easier handling. The question is: Does it do violence to the facts? Korzybski has a clear answer to this question: It does, and the remedy is to apply a multivalued or infinite-valued orientation. Such an orientation acknowledges that, instead of trying to pigeonhole the world into two opposite compartments, it is preferable to recognize that phenomena range over a scale that varies by degrees. The yardstick and rainbow are convenient examples. To avoid rigidity, one should admit the possibility that there might be *some* situations requiring a two-valued orientation.

INDEXING

Indexing may be illustrated in the case of a white person who was wronged by a certain black person but who, as a result, hates *all* blacks. In other words, he or she is prejudiced. The way to help this person is to limit or allocate the hatred to the precipitating experience and to handle it on that basis from that point forward. Indexing provides a countermeasure to generalization or prejudice and facilitates its elimination. It acknowledges the specificity and uniqueness of things, people, and situations and so does justice to the richness and complexity of the world by pinpointing whatever is under scrutiny.

DATING

The workers in a factory abuse a fellow worker when they discover that thirty years ago she spent six months in a mental institution. Consequently, they cruelly refer to her as "the nut." Korzybski would come to her aid by reminding the workers that Jane Smith 1964 is not Jane Smith 1984. They are not the same individuals, psychologically speaking, and dating them in the above fashion calls attention to the fact. Yesterday is not today. We acknowledge change as well as stability.

ETC.

When Korzybski attempts to define anything, he always tacks on an *etc.*, to call attention to the "non-allness" of language. What this device does is to stress the richness of our experiences and the poverty of a language that attempts to match it. Look at your pencil or pen. Your description of it can never exhaust every minute detail that characterizes it. But if you add an *etc.* to your descriptive catalog of terms, you admit that you are aware that you have abstracted a limited number of characteristics out of the manifold of properties which it possesses. It is semantically beneficial to realize that we haven't ever said everything that can be said about anything.

QUOTES

Quotes, either the conventional ones on paper or visible finger wiggles before and after certain words during speech, are used to indicate that terms that are considered elementalistic or derived from a two-valued orientation are being used with full awareness of their contaminated origin. In this way, one signals to the communicant that one knows a "dirty" word is being used to get the message across. My use of the word "body" necessitates putting quotes around it to signal the reader that I am using an elementalistic term with full awareness that it is a partner of "mind." "Space" and "time" require quotes because of their usual elementalistic connotation. "Intellect" is another word with such a connotation.

HYPHENS

Korzybski would be pleased to see you putting a hyphen in *space-time, central nervous system–peripheral nervous system, night-day,* or *black-white,* because he would realize that you were attempting to treat as whole what an elementalistic viewpoint had (verbally) split apart. He refers to this process as "consciousness of abstracting." If we are aware of what we are doing, there is less likelihood of failure of communication and a greater likelihood of clear-cut, effective communication.

TO BE IS TO BE RELATED

"There is no such thing as an object in absolute isolation" (Korzybski, 1941, p. 61). If the preceding statements are true, then there has to be at least *another* object. If so, then there must be some *relationship* between them ready to be discovered. Conventional ways of thinking, particularly elementalism, and reification make it easy to ignore relations. The very term *relativity* hints heavily of the need for giving room to verbs and adjectives as well as nouns. But nouns prevail in traditional ways of thinking that make objects or things stand out like a sore thumb.

As Dewey and Bentley (1949, p. 138) phrase it, "The organism . . . seems in everyday life and language to stand out strongly apart from the transactions in which it is engaged. This is superficial observation. One reason for it is that the organism is engaged in so many transactions."

For Further Reading

Hayakawa, S. I. (1941). *Language in action.* New York: Harcourt, Brace and Company.

Korzybski, A. (1941). *Science and sanity.* Lancaster, Pa.: Science Press Printing Co.

Lee, I. J. (Ed.). (1949). *The language of wisdom and folly.* New York: Harper.

Rapoport, A. (1953). *Operational philosophy.* New York: Harper.

OCCAM'S RAZOR

William of Occam, an English scholastic philosopher, studied and taught at Oxford University from around 1310 to 1324. He is famous for his principle of parsimony, which dictates strict economy in explaining things. His "razor" prescribes that "what can be explained by the assumption of fewer things is vainly explained by the assumption of more things." Or, explanatory principles ("entities") should not be needlessly multiplied. Stated in still another form, the simpler of two hypotheses is to be preferred. Obviously, if one is permitted to make any number of assumptions, one can explain almost anything (see also LLOYD MORGAN'S CANON).

Traditional brain dogma illustrates violations of the principle of parsimony. We start with the conventional notion of the central importance of the brain as the seat of consciousness, awareness, introspection, memory, learning, speech, and so forth. Suppose the removal of the total hemisphere results in some paralysis but no aphasia, memory loss, or other psychological deficiencies. What then? The believer will "save" the traditional theory by "explaining" that the remaining hemisphere "took over" the functions of the missing hemisphere. That's why, the reasoning goes, the patient shows minimal deficiency with only half as much brain as before. What such a believer has done is to add another principle to the original principle, in defiance of Occam's razor. Instead of starting afresh in an attempt to develop a parsimonious theory, the diehard supporter of conventional brain dogma will patch up the old theory as needed. Goldstein (1939, p. 17) discovered evasions of Occam's razor in early attempts to localize brain functions. He has captured the situation in the following passage:

The real crisis arises when, even in the face of new findings, the investigator cannot free himself from the former theory; rather, he attempts to preserve it, and, by constant emendations, to reconcile it with these new facts, instead of replacing it by a new theory fit to deal with both the old and new facts. This error has not been avoided in the evolution of the classical doctrine.

The history of psychology is replete with needlessly multiplied explanatory "entities." Such "faculties" or powers of the mind as will, judgment, intellect, and attentiveness could lead such a parade. The procession would be joined by Freud's id, ego, and superego plus the dozen or so Freudian dynamisms. More recent explanatory entities in the extended line of march would include "innate IQ," drives (such as maternal, sex, hunger, and thirst), and the various brain "centers" exemplified by the taste center, coughing center, speech center, memory center, and all other such power-in-a-spot controlling entities. The skeptical psychologist is ever alert to the above, and any other, circumvention of Occam's razor.

For Further Reading

Goldstein, K. (1939). *The organism.* New York: American Book Co.

THE ORGANISM: SOME
PROBLEMS PERTAINING TO IT

With the immediately preceding semantic discussion as a suggested orientating framework, let us go on to a consideration of some problems pertaining to the organism. We have been accustomed to speaking of an "organism" *and* its "environment" with a resulting orientation that treats them both as isolable "things." Instead, I suggest that in nature one actually observes such ongoing events as worm-burrowing-hole, fish-swimming-through-water, plant-transpiring-air, man-riding-horse, or mother-rocking-child. These examples are meant to point out that when we observe "something," *events* are primary and that only out of context and only verbally can we label a certain aspect of the happening as an "organism." By comparison with the dynamic event that was observed, the verbal description of it is static, dead, frozen. When we say the word *organism*, then we must be constantly alert to the fact that we have abstracted only one feature out of a manifold spatiotemporal occurrence.

Note that no organism is an organism in and of itself, existing in a vacuum. Even though it is a unit thing, the surrounding air is an essential part of the series of occurrences generally referred to as an organism. Isolate it from its atmospheric envelope for a short time, and there ceases to be an "object" of physiological study. The same holds for the temperature, humidity, pressure, and other relevant conditions. Granted that these conditions are rather constant under normal circumstances, that is no excuse to overlook them. In fact, we generally take them for granted and finally completely ignore them. "Abstraction" has got in its confounding work, and the language "map" shows poor correspondence to the "territory." The result can only be an abstractionistic orientation that considers an organism as a lump or entity.

It is suggested that our language habits have much to do with the difficulties indicated. Since, in our materialistic culture, stress is on "things" or "stuff" rather than on "process" or "action," by means of language (i.e., in our talking and writing) we can pick out certain factors from the manifold of happenings about us. These are strikingly similar or recurrent in an endless variety of situations. They constitute the familiar "we," "you," "they," and "I" of everyday life happenings. In everyday terms, "the same I" over the years meets "the same you," feeds "the same dog," and cuts "the same lawn." From one standpoint, we can say that there is an ongoing stream of events with certain features repeated. We come to label them all indiscriminately as "organisms" and treat them as "things" to which "something happens." However, is it not true that *only verbally* can we do this, and that in nature the basic datum is an event or series of events or histories? It is this dynamic approach toward natural phenomena that is here proposed as an alternative to the old, static, "commonsense" view.

SEMANTIC ANALYSIS OF THE TERM *MIND*

Coming closer once again to our own subject matter, we must apply what semantic resources we can to analyze such troublesome terms as *mind, consciousness, unconscious, sensation, motive, incentive, drive,* and *instinct.* How scientifically valid are these terms? Do they provide a dependable and accurate "map" of the psychological "territory"? That is the question.

Let us seek for an answer from a different perspective. An analogy from the banking business may help. For example, a check written for an amount covered by the check writer's account is a valid check. But a check written on a checking account without any funds is worthless. So it is, according to some semanticists, with words. When our terms point to observables, they are valid because they effect proper communication. When they are purely verbal coinage, they are phony and point to nothing. As a result, we find ourselves in a verbally created world. Never in our *observations* of behaving organisms will we encounter a "mind," "consciousness," "instinct," and so on. The only way we can come into usage of such terms is to adopt the terminology of an ancient linguistic tradition and impose it upon the raw data. For the dice are loaded; our preobservation language habits will determine that we will explain them in the terminology of our cultural indoctrination. Apparently, *mind, consciousness,* and other such terms have a secure, well-established status in our culture and, in part, in the miniculture of psychology. The same holds for the organism, which is viewed as a machine with parts that perform separate and distinct functions instead of treating it as an organized unit and participant in an event.

For Further Reading

Goldstein, K. (1939). *The organism.* New York: American Book Co.

PANCHRESTON

Here is a worthwhile addition to the semantic equipment of any investigation. Garrett Hardin (1957) coined this term, derived from the Greek. He defines *panchreston* as an "explain-all," a word that explains everything and therefore explains nothing. As such, he considers it a threat to clarity, which he elucidates with an example from psychology. He states that if you try to find out what's behind such terms as *intelligence* and *the unconscious*, you are in trouble because these traditional terms "stop inquiry where it is most painful (and, it must be admitted, most likely to fail)" (Hardin, 1957, p. 393).

To be more specific, let's take the example of A telling B that C is "crazy." B agrees; both feel self-satisfied in the belief that they have explained C's unusual behavior and go on to another topic of conversation. But do we understand C's behavior any better by attaching the word *crazy* to it? Hardin would call the term a panchreston, a term which means so much that it means nothing. Instead of explaining something, it explains it away.

In an article, "Psychiatrists Use Dangerous Words," Karl Menninger (1964) emphasizes the danger in applying verbal labels to the behavior of humans. He censures the ready use of the words *schizophrenia, manic-depressive,* and *psychotic* because not only do they not explain the behavior so labeled, but they also frighten patients and relatives and induce anxiety and despair in both, as well as in their therapists. He rejects totally the notion of mental disease but accepts that of "mental illness," defining the latter as a "state of functioning, a way of behaving." One might argue with Menninger's labeling "a way of behaving" as an illness, but that is another matter. The progress shown in his rejection of the "mental disease" label must be applauded, as well as his approximation to a near-panchreston view of such labels as *schizophrenia, manic-depressive,* and *psychotic.* These panchrestons and others such as *instinct, drive,* and so on pose as "explain-alls" but in reality explain nothing; furthermore, they discourage research that might lead to their proper understanding.

In his article "The Problem of Psychiatric Nosology," Thomas Szasz (1957, p. 409) applies Hardin's newly coined term *panchreston* to the problem of schizophrenia. The trouble has been that the term *schizophrenia* has been used as an "explain-all," as when we say that a person *"has* schizophrenia." Such usage misleads us into thinking that "there is a more-or-less homogeneous group of phenomena which are designated by the word in question" (Szasz, 1957, p. 409). The ordinary use of the term *schizophrenia* can easily lead us into thinking that schizophrenia is an entity such as pneumonia or scarlet fever, whereas actually it can be properly used to label problems of living. Think of the consequences in the treatment of people bearing that label as it is defined by the counselor.

There is an important lesson to be derived from this brief exercise. One can start at the verbal level, with a panchreston, a word imported from an extraneous source and imposed on behavioral events. In that case, one ends up with a distortion of those events and an "explain-all," which explains nothing. The other approach starts inquiry without any verbal straitjackets and goes straight to the event level, with full awareness of whatever assumptions are brought to the investigation. The outcome of this procedure is believed to be derived only from the observations carried out and to be referable directly to them. As always, there are choices to be made; the matter is left to the reader.

For Further Reading

Hardin, G. (1957). The threat of clarity. *American Journal of Psychiatry, 114,* 392-396.
Szasz, T. S. (1957). The problem of psychiatric nosology. *American Journal of Psychiatry, 114,* 405-413.

PARADIGMS

Our consideration of paradigms should begin with Thomas Kuhn's (1970b) *The Structure of Scientific Revolutions,* a book that has created wide debate and one that has introduced a new view of the philosophy of science. According to Kuhn, paradigms are found wherever there is a scientific community; therefore, Kuhn starts with the latter.

A scientific community is a social psychological group that shares a more or less common education, training, apprenticeship, and introduction to a common vocabulary. Furthermore, its members read the prevailing literature, are committed to certain goals including the training and certification of those who follow, and join the approved professional organizations. For example, some affiliate with the American Psychological Association, others with the Psychonomic Society, and still others with a clinical or psychoanalytic group.

Moreover, members of a particular scientific community are initiated into the group's research techniques (e.g., factor analysis, behavior modification, or animal experimentation). Even at this point, one can sense a shared pattern of procedures, practices, attitudes, and thinking that one finds among adherents of a religious faith. Kuhn (1970a; 1970b) makes this comparison, and so does E. R. MacCormac (1976, p. 156), who, although he sees differences between science and religion, also sees similarities in the way in which both use language, particularly metaphor. In sum, the global characteristics that a scientific community shares constitute its paradigm or set of paradigms (Kuhn, 1970b, p. 182).

The term *paradigm* requires further clarification, for even Kuhn (1970b, p. 181) acknowledges that a sympathetic reviewer of his earlier work found that he (Kuhn) used the term "in at least twenty-two different ways." Therefore, Kuhn limits the term *paradigm* as it is defined in the preceding paragraph and introduces a new term, *disciplinary matrix*: "'disciplinary' because it refers to the common possession of the practitioners of a particular discipline; 'matrix' because it is composed of ordered elements of various sorts each requiring further specification" (Kuhn, 1970b, p. 182).

One of the components of the disciplinary matrix is the symbolic generalizations such as the mathematical formula of the chemist, $H_2O + 2SO_2 = H_2SO_4$. A second constituent includes the belief in models or preferred analogies that a scientific community shares. The telephone and computer models of the brain and the hydrodynamic model of Freud's system (as discussed under the entry MODELS) are examples. A third component of the disciplinary matrix takes in the values that hold the group together. Among them one must include accuracy in reporting the facts; simplicity, consistency, and economy of assumptions (Occam's razor); and values in judging theories. Kuhn holds that the fourth element of the disciplinary matrix, the exemplars, is of central importance in his analysis of a scientific community's shared attributes. Exemplars are the standard examples that the students work out in the laboratory or, with paper and pencil, solve the problems at the end of the chapters of their (very likely, standard) textbook. These constitute the glue that holds the various problems together, integrating them and providing insight into the group's overriding theory or cognitive achievement. Students have meanwhile "assimilated a time-tested and group-licensed way of seeing" (Kuhn, 1970b, p. 189). In other words, they have become firm believers, converts who will carry on the traditional practices, exemplars, and paradigms of their scientific community. As a result of their indoctrination, they eventually become the establishment, well equipped to maintain what Kuhn calls normal science, a topic that we consider next.

NORMAL SCIENCE

Once the trainees of a scientific community have mastered the paradigms that guide research, they join their mentors in solving problems as they continue to emerge. Problems that the prevailing paradigm can't handle are ignored; nevertheless, faith in it persists. Elaborate equipment, an esoteric vocabulary and skills, and a theoretical refinement that departs from everyday language follow the community members' pursuits. When these become institutionalized, members' views grow narrowly channeled and become rigid and resistant to paradigm modification. But normal science does not continue through eternity. Anomalies appear that don't fit the accepted, standard paradigm. At first, the scientific community's practitioners resort to ad hoc assumptions to patch up the threatened paradigm when it doesn't seem to work. A ready example is available from "psychoneurology." The traditional paradigm attributes great psychological significance to the cerebral hemispheres. But if one hemisphere is removed and there is little behavioral change, the paradigm is amended by stating that the remaining hemisphere "took over" (note the metaphor here) the "function" formerly performed by the missing hemisphere. However, patching up of a paradigm can proceed only so far. Eventually, it breaks down and a change is called for. When such a crisis occurs, a scientific revolution threatens.

SCIENTIFIC REVOLUTION

With the complete collapse of the old paradigm, a new paradigm emerges, initiating a new tradition of normal science. Kuhn (1970b, pp. 84-85) stresses the point that the new paradigm is not a reconstruction or extension of the old paradigm. It requires a radical shift in the way in which the scientist sees things. The Copernican and Einsteinian revolutions are fitting examples; in psychology, behaviorism and interbehaviorism demand a profound change in the way in which behavior is seen. Kuhn compares that which happens with the exchange of an old paradigm for a new one to a "gestalt switch" (1970b, p. 85).

The accompanying illustration, "My Wife and My Mother-in-law," will serve our purpose in making the point. Assume that when you look at Figure 8, you see only the old hag, nothing else. To keep the situation parallel to that of the prevailing paradigm in a science, let us assume that eventually a gestalt switch occurs and, lo and behold, you perceive the young woman in profile. A paradigm switch involves a similar psychological response. The revolutionist sees things in a different way now. However, there is a difference between the two. One can switch back and forth between "My Wife" and "My Mother-in-law." But, according to Kuhn (1970b, p. 85), "the scientist does not preserve the gestalt subject's freedom to switch back and forth between two ways of seeing." Once the established scientists and the next generation entering the field have been won over to the new paradigm, they see things only in a new way. They now share a distinctive global orientation, a different world view, and their discipline moves on once more, as normal science, until the next revolution with its call for a change of paradigms.

RELEVANCE OF PARADIGMS TO PSYCHOLOGY

A survey of psychology over two millennia reveals *not one revolution,* in sharp contrast with physics, astronomy, or biology. Predominantly, self-actional-interactional paradigms and hoary models such as the brain as a chief executive and the body-mind notion have persisted over the centuries. Should you bring up Watsonian behaviorism, I would point out that that was an aborted revolution, one that didn't "take." The old paradigms and models survived and are thriving even today. However, newer paradigms and models are available, among which are field or transactional approaches (see FIELD THEORY and TRANSACTION).

As a final commentary, this skeptical psychologist can bear witness to the possibility of "seeing" behavior as occurring in a situation extending beyond the organism and including objects or other persons under definite conditions, and setting factors, all within the context of antecedent and succeeding events. Such a "view" requires a gestalt switch from the traditional preoccupation with imaginary spots and "functions" within the organism (i.e., its mind or brain). But in view of the planet-wide saturation with the age-old paradigm, there is scanty opportunity for a revolution and a paradigm switch in psychology.

Figure 8. "My Wife and My Mother-in-law," showing that a particular geometric pattern may have two psychological possibilities, to be perceived as (1) a young woman or (2) an old hag.

For Further Reading

Kuhn, T. S. (1970b). *The structure of scientific revolutions* (2nd Ed.). Chicago: University of Chicago Press.

PERCEIVING EVENTS

The term *perception* was purposely avoided in the title because of its common psychology textbook definition as a mental state taking place in the organism's head. For example, McConnell explains perception in terms of "messages" from the visual input area to the association area of the cortex, where the "memory traces" or "images" of our past experiences are stored. From that point on, J. V. McConnell (1977, p. 194) states, "Your Board of Directors scans or compares both the past image and the present incoming sensation, and if the two are similar enough, the Board 'recognizes' what you are looking at as something it has encountered in the past." Are we to take McConnell's statement literally or metaphorically? In either case, we must ask: Has his analysis advanced our understanding of how organisms discriminate the objects, circumstances, and events in their surroundings? Now, departing from this prevalent formulation of perception, we next examine a radically different viewpoint recently propounded by an insurgent investigator of perception, J. J. Gibson, who uses a totally different paradigm.

GIBSON'S ECOLOGICAL APPROACH

Gibson's paradigm is revealed in the very title of his book, *The Ecological Approach to Visual Perception* (Gibson, 1979). His view that *animal* and environment are "an inseparable pair" (p. 8) portends a broader view of perception than the traditional, organism-centered one. He denies the prevalent notion that perception is mediated by *retinal* pictures, *neural* pictures, or *mental* pictures in favor of a view that perception of the environment is "direct" (p. 147). Gibson also rejects the stimulus-response formula as useful as it may be for physiology. Why? Because the stimulus is more than photons; therefore, he speaks of "stimulus information," coming very close to the interbehavioral theory's "stimulus function." Even this brief sketch of Gibson's position contrasts it sharply with that so prevalent in mainstream psychology. The lesson from this comparison is that if you start inquiry with different assumptions, you end up with different answers.

BEYOND GIBSON

Let us try to apprehend a still broader view than that of Gibson's ecological one, that is, a field view. We define a field as the totality of things and conditions in an integrated system. Organism and stimulus object are prominent aspects, as they are for Gibson, but there's more. The medium of contact, light for visual perception, is as essential as organism and stimulus object if these two are to confront each other. Besides light (as light and not as photons), setting factors are also important. A green patch of color surrounded by gray is not perceived the same as when it is viewed against a green background. Besides that, the prior sequence of events or the reactional biography must be considered in explaining a particular slice of that history.

As illustration of this point, note Figure 9, "An Ambiguous Figure," also known as "The Burning Tree." As you examine it, what do you make of it? One large tree and a number of smaller ones? Or is there a forest fire in the background illuminating a large number of trees in the foreground? Could the illumination be the result of a flash of lightning? Might it be the

Figure 9. An ambiguous figure. What do you observe? A large tree and several smaller ones? A forest fire in the background? A discharge of lightning? A portion of a blood circulatory system, showing arteries or veins branching into capillaries? Nerve processes innervating some tissue? Actually, the illustration is an infrared aerial photo of a river delta. (Photo courtesy of Ed Spoonts, Aero Service Co.)

representation of a blood circulatory system with a full array of veins and arteries branching into capillaries? How about a portion of a nervous system innervating some tissue? It is actually an infrared aerial photo of a river delta along the California coast. You may say, "Of course!" But what if you had observed this illustration at the age of three? Would you have been able to perceive it in the several ways specified above? Obviously not, because perception cannot be understood if we limit our analysis to the here and now. We require an expanded space-time framework comprising all your *past* reactions with forest fires, representations of circulatory systems, and so on. All are indissolubly joined together so that we can never see things fresh and pure, uncontaminated by our past behavior. In a metaphorical sense, we have lost our perceptual innocence. We cannot circumvent our reactional biographies.

SUMMARY

We have compared and contrasted three different theories of perception. The first and most popular, the mentalistic approach, localized perception within the organism. Gibson's ecological approach shifted from a fixation on speculative occurrences within the eyes and brain to a view of perception as a joint function of organism and object without any intermediaries. A proposed field theory went beyond Gibson's view with its stress on organism-object interaction and dealt with perceiving events as multi-factorial occurrences with all components held in system, unfractured prior to analysis. It is difficult to grasp because it requires retraining in "seeing" what's there. When achieved, one has experienced a gestalt switch.

For Further Reading

Gibson, J. J. (1979). *The ecological approach to visual perception.* Boston: Houghton Mifflin.

McConnell, J. V. (1977). *Understanding human behavior* (2nd Ed.). New York: Holt, Rinehart and Winston.

PERMISSIVENESS

Permissiveness is an attitude of tolerance on the part of caretakers for those subject to their authority. The English and English (1958, p. 380) *Dictionary* offers the following definition: "the attitude that grants freedom of choice and expression to another person out of respect for his personality." The term has been used with a fairly wide connotation for the opposite of *regimentation, authoritarianism, dominance,* or *punitiveness.* These same authors make a distinction between permissiveness on the one hand and indulgence and neglect on the other. However, in widespread usage, the term *indulgence* is often heard as a synonym for permissiveness. In the following passage, B. F. Skinner (1971, pp. 83-84) appears to stretch the definition of permissiveness to absence of control in an individual's development.

An all-out permissiveness has been seriously advanced as an alternative to punishment. No control at all is to be exerted. . . . Permissiveness is not, however, a policy; it is the abandonment of policy, and its apparent advantages are illusory. To refuse to control is to leave control not to the person himself, but to other parts of the social and non-social environments.

Skinner makes a valuable point here: whether under deliberate or accidental control, our behavior is nevertheless controlled. If parents are indulgent in rearing their children, their children's behavior will come under the control of their peer group, the police, the courts, the prison authorities, or, perhaps, eventually, their fellow prisoners. Skinner's point is that our behavior is a function of environmental conditions, which no one can escape, whether such conditions are contrived or haphazard.

For Further Reading

Skinner, B. F. (1971). *Beyond freedom and dignity.* New York: Alfred A. Knopf.

PERSONALITY

There are over fifty meanings of the term *personality*, but most of them would agree that personality is something within the individual that determines or influences the person's behavior across different situations and across time. In other words, personality is converted into a thing or entity with certain attributes. The parallel with the Newtonian hard bits of matter possessing certain properties should be underscored.

Once we formulate personality as an indwelling agent with powers to do things, we involve ourselves in SELF-ACTION. Self-actional notions have it that things act *on their own*, a violation of modern scientific thinking that every event involves *at least* two variables in interaction, not one variable acting solo. Also, hypothetical agents are that and nothing more, and must themselves be demonstrated before they can be used in an explanatory way.

WHAT'S THE ALTERNATIVE?

The alternative is a naturalistic account that dethrones the organism to a status no greater than the stimulus and other conditions participating in the events involving a given individual. All are viewed together in system as events or integrated fields. If we agree that psychology is the study of an individual, then our definition of personality must not violate that commitment.

Sticking as closely as possible to observable data, I suggest that personality be defined as all the occurrences or happenings involving a given individual. Because individuals are a prominent aspect of a psychological event, they become easily identified loci of relevant events collectively labeled as personality. In everyday terms, with an inevitable focus on the individual concerned, personality includes everything that the person does and can do. This would include the individual's seeings, smellings, tastings, touchings, hearings, desirings, lovings, hatings, fearings, thinkings, knowings, and so on.

The enormity of capturing a given individual's complete psychological repertoire has been grasped by Murray and Kluckhohn. They state that if we could observe and record all of an individual's psychological occurrences twenty-four hours a day from birth to death, we would acquire a massive, unmanageable document. How ponderous would it be? "If it were possible, as in music, to represent with appropriate symbols twenty-four hours of activity on 2,400 pages of paper, making five compact volumes per day, there would be 1,825 for each year, and over 125,000 for a biblical lifetime. Here, surely, filling a large library, would be the facts about one person, a truth too huge to serve" (Murray & Kluckhohn, 1948, pp. 6-7). But we must rise above the level of our crude data; otherwise we would be bogged down in them. Therefore, the following characterizations, derived from observation, are offered as generalizations toward the understanding of personality.

ORGANIZATION

Inspection of the events centering around a given individual shows that they do not follow one another helter-skelter. They are organized with respect to surrounding conditions. People speak English or Russian, practice Islam, Christianity, or Buddhism, and reject or eat pork depending on the circumstances of their rearing. Such facts support the notion that the explanation of personality is not to be found somewhere within the organism but in wider perspective, in relation to objects, people, and conditions in the individual's milieu.

STABILITY AND CHANGE

Water remains a liquid over long periods of time if the temperature is stable (above 32°), but as soon as it drops below 32°, it becomes a solid. Personality, too, can remain stable over long periods, as, for example, in a simple, isolated tribe, but let an upheaval intervene, such as a riot, revolution, invasion by an enemy, fire, flood or desertification, and we can expect personality change.

Bakker (1975) has criticized students of personality for their too-close focus on the organism instead of looking at the social contexts of personality. As a striking example, he notes the radical changes in personality that occurred under Nazi auspices. On the job, Hitler's storm troopers could commit the most abominable acts against concentration camp victims. Yet they could go home, kiss their wives, play with the dog and their children, go to church on Sunday, and act otherwise as good husbands and fathers are expected to act. After the defeat of Hitler, these same men became postmen, trolley conductors, and bureaucrats, indistinguishable from other ordinary citizens. Thus, personality manifests stability as well as change, but both are subject to a certain lawfulness and orderliness. Personality makes sense.

ORIGIN

Nothing comes out of nothing. All things have an origin—the cosmos, our galaxy, life on earth, you and I. Why should personality be denied

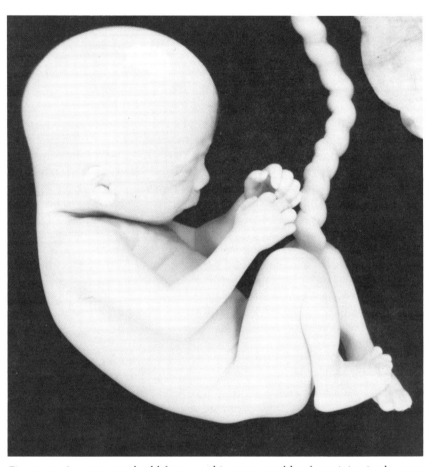

Figure 10. A seven-month-old fetus, at this stage capable of surviving in the outer world, but also capable of such learning as thumb-sucking inside the womb. (From Jan Langman, *Medical Embryology*, 3rd Edition, 1975. Baltimore, Md. Copyright by The Williams & Wilkins Co. Reproduced by permission of author and publisher.)

equal status? We know that, after the seventh month, the human infant is adapted for life outside the uterus. Is birth, then, the zero point for personality development? No, we must enter the womb to capture that moment. Liley (1972) has shown us how active the fetus is as the months progress. For example, flailings of arms and legs gradually become integrated into learned movements, as may be seen in Figure 10. Such conditions are ripe for an increasingly more directed and faster path to the mouth. At this point, we are ready to see the zero point for the thumb-sucking response and experience with gravity. But it is emergence into the outside world that provides expanded opportunities for personality development, which continues throughout life. Most theories of personality ignore questions of origin; for them personality just *is*. A counterargument asserts that personality is behavior and that it originates during the lifetime of the individual.

UNIQUENESS

When one considers the seemingly infinite series of specific events confronting each individual, it becomes easier to grasp the notion of the uniqueness of personality. In a strict psychological sense, no two siblings or even twin pairs have exactly the same life history. Therefore, their personalities are not identical.

Uniqueness is not peculiar to personality. Other sciences also contend with unique data. In astronomy, no two galaxies, solar systems, or planets are alike. The same holds for botany and for anatomy, yet useful generalizations can be derived from their investigations. For us, the uniqueness of personality can be understood in terms of the uniqueness of each individual's reactional history.

In summation, then, with a broad field approach, we learn that personality comprises all of a given individual's behavior, that it is organized or orderly, that it shows a lawful stability and lawful change, that it originates during the lifetime of the individual, and that it is unique, as are astronomical, biological, and even physical phenomena (e.g., snowflakes).

For Further Reading

Bakker, C. B. (1975). Why people don't change. *Psychotherapy: Theory, research and practice,* 12, 164-172.

Atkinson, R. L., Atkinson, R. C. & Hilgard, E. R. (1983). *Introduction to psychology* (8th Ed.). New York: Harcourt Brace Jovanovich.

POSTULATION: TO POSTULATE OR NOT TO POSTULATE

What goes without saying is what especially needs to be said. And so a thinker's first effort should be to discover and drag out into the open all his silent premises. He should lay his cards on the table face up, so that he as well as his readers may look at them.

Muller (1943, p. 21, emphasis added)

Human behavior is permeated with assumptions, hunches, conjectures, and presuppositions. For example, you expect the drivers of automobiles heading toward you to stay in their own proper lane instead of crossing over into yours. Such assumptions sometimes prove erroneous, and serious accidents may occur.

Recent developments in the sciences have produced a greater sensitivity to the influence of the assumptions or postulates that control scientific investigation. Since defining one's terms is important in any human enterprise, we must try to achieve a clear definition of the preferred term *postulate.*

A postulate resembles an axiom in one way, namely, it is a statement accepted without proof, but it need not be self-evident, as is an axiom. Postulates cannot be disproved anymore than they can be proved. A postulate serves as a guide to observation. In a manner of speaking, a set of postulates declares under what banner one will conduct one's enterprise. Postulates do not have a logical force to them. One simply acts as if they were true. For example, all the sciences act on the assumption that the world makes sense. The statements that humans are materialistic things, that the body is like a machine, and that the brain is like a computer are all postulates. It should be apparent what the outcome of observations would be under such guidelines or assumptions.

That man consists of a body and a mind is another postulate. No one can demonstrate that it is so, but the investigator operating under such a postulate would act *as if* it were true that people are made up of a visible portion, the body, and an invisible portion, the mind. Such statements go beyond the facts themselves and are accepted as being more than hypotheses. Investigators who hold to such postulates as guidelines assert them vigorously, even aggressively, and often they become hardened into dogmas. At this stage, they cease to be recognized as assumptions or presuppositions and come to be believed in as if they were demonstrated fact. Next, they are defended religiously.

Relativity physics has had a healthy effect on the sometimes witting, sometimes unwitting process by which postulates were transformed into articles of faith. The more recent advances have charged scientists to look sharply to their postulates and to make *explicit* what was, since time immemorial, *implicit* or tacit. Bringing everything into the open will make everyone more aware of what he or she is about. With the newer ways of thinking, it has been increasingly realized that postulates as guidelines are provisional and subject to change when they are not found helpful. By helpful, we mean do they advance our understanding of the facts under observation? If not, since we are not wedded to those particular guidelines, let us try other ones, because when guidelines become hardened into dogmas, we are in deep trouble. The question posed at the beginning of this section, to postulate or not to postulate, can now be answered. The answer is that postulation is unavoidable. Everyone postulates one way or another. Some do it unwittingly, their investigations guided by silent assumptions mistaken for hard facts.

Now, how about the postulational situation in psychology? The state of affairs in this respect has been recently evaluated by Lichtenstein (1980), who reports a widespread neglect of postulation by psychologists. Nevertheless, such silent assumptions as body-mind, the brain as a controlling mechanism, sensation, and consciousness control much of the field and laboratory operations.

Does it not seem desirable to be open and aboveboard in any inquiry and, where assumptions are concerned, to expose what is "hidden" and to verbalize what is "silent" *before* one enters the laboratory? Poincaré (1946, p. 134) answered this question in no uncertain terms when he stated that experimentation was not enough. What was far more important was to recognize "dangerous hypotheses" that guided experimentation. Furthermore, if we hold such unwittingly, how can we hope to give them up? All we can do is try by (1) engaging in scrupulous self-examination for hidden presuppositions, surmises, conjectures, and assumptions, and (2) testing out their validity as to whether or not they advance our understanding.

For Further Reading

Lichtenstein, P. E. (1980). Theoretical psychology: Where is it headed? *The Psychological Record, 30,* 447-458.

Poincaré, H. (1946). *The foundations of science.* New York: Garrison. (Original work published 1913)

PSYCHOSOMATIC

What does the word "psychosomatic" really mean?

Lipowski (1984, p. 153)

In his exhaustive historical and semantic inquiry into the meaning of the term *psychosomatic*, Lipowski (1984, p. 153) found not only "a lack of consensus" but even ambiguity and confusion. As a starting point, here is a definition of the term found in the *Dictionary of Psychology* (Chaplin, 1975): "1. pertaining to processes that are both somatic (bodily) and psychic (mental) in nature. 2. pertaining to the relation of mind and body." A bit of reflection reveals that the term refers to theoretical matters implying, or taking for granted, that there are actually such things as bodies and minds. And yet this formulation, in universal usage for almost two-thousand years, is today the basic framework for interpreting human behavior. There is little or no appreciation of the fact that psyche and soma are only paradigmatic, based on a model expropriated from the matter-spirit duality.

ENTER VISITORS FROM ANOTHER PLANET

We are now ready to entertain visitors from another planet, which is to say, living beings equivalent to earthly humans, but not contaminated by our planet-wide ways of understanding ourselves. We take them on a tour of our industries, businesses, and transportation systems and show them people operating machines, cranes, bulldozers, trucks, automobiles, subways, and so on. They see others buying and selling, cooking and serving food, playing musical instruments, and lecturing to classes of students.

At this point, we introduce our Milky Way visitors to a fundamental bit of earthly psychology. We inform them that the humans whom they observed are really psychosomatic or dual organisms, that is, that they consist of a psyche, or mind, and a body. With true unworldliness, our visitors remonstrate, "We didn't see any minds or bodies. We saw only living, breathing organisms in action. Why didn't *we* see minds and bodies?" And with proper justification, they ask, "Say, how do you *know* that humans consist of a mind and a body?" At this point, we leave the scene pondering the most basic question of all: How *do* you know?

A PROPOSED RESOLUTION OF THE PSYCHOSOMATIC PROBLEM WITHOUT PSYCHE AND SOMA

Suppose we are workers in Ivan Pavlov's conditioning laboratory confirming Pavlov's (1927) finding on the salivary response to direct introduction of meat powder in the dog's mouth. This is the well-known unconditioned response to an unconditioned stimulus, in reality a physiological response to a stimulus eliciting a tissue reaction, in the salivary glands, by direct contact. We measure the amount of secretion in cubic centimeters in this physiological situation.

Now, we engage in some conditioning by introducing a metronome into our experiment. We set the metronome going and note the amount of salivary secretion, which is nil. We proceed by presenting the metronome followed by meat-in-mouth for fifty trials. Now, we present the metronome alone. Lo and behold! We get a sizable secretion to the metronome alone. We have established a conditioned or psychological response. And we can actually measure the specific amount of secretion produced as a physiological response as well as the amount yielded as a psychological response. We must not lose sight of the significance of our finding. We have successfully measured the secretion yielded on the basis of a tissue-excitation reaction. And we have achieved equal success by determining the amount of secretion produced as the result of a historical connection between our animal and the conditioned and unconditioned stimuli. A bit of history made sense of the experimental findings and *without recourse to the dog's psyche and soma.*

This simple paradigm can serve as a model for the data subsumed under the traditional term *psychosomatic*. Reduced to simplest terms, this means that in addition to reacting on a physiological basis, human hearts, stomachs, lungs, bowels, and so on get involved or incorporated into people's angers, resentments, fears, and anxieties on a historical or reactional biography basis. The student's heart rate under relaxed conditions or while jogging can be understood on a physiological basis. But that same student's heart rate after a summons to appear at the dean's office can no longer be understood with physiological probe bodies alone. Only a historical dimension between that student and authority figures in the present or past can make sense of the heart rate, which may be the same as in jogging, only now that student is standing still. If we can make sense of such (and other) situations without *psyche* and *soma*, why do we need *psyche* and *soma* or *psychosomatic*?

For Further Reading

Lipowski, Z. J. (1984). What does the word "psychosomatic" really mean? *Psychosomatic Medicine, 46*(2), 153-171.

Pavlov, I. (1927). *Conditioned reflexes: An investigation of the physiological activity of the cerebral cortex.* (G. V. Anrep, Trans. and Ed.). London: Oxford University Press.

PUBLIC VERSUS
PRIVATE RESPONSES

"The subject matter of psychology is behavior and experience." It would be interesting to know how frequently such a definition of psychology has been uttered in classrooms across the land during the first session of an introductory psychology course. The clear implication of the statement is that two different matters will be considered during the semester: (1) behavior and (2) experience.

Should eager students in such an instructor's course run to certain dictionaries of psychology or perhaps even to their own textbook, they would learn that *behavior* refers to the actions of an organism, the whole organism, or to its neuromuscular or glandular response. They would also discover that *experience,* by contrast, refers to an *inferred* mental, psychic, or conscious occurrence transpiring within the organism's mind and/or brain. They would also ascertain that behavior was visible or public and experience invisible or private.

In *Science and Human Behavior,* B. F. Skinner (1953, p. 257) has a section entitled "The World within One's Own Skin," with the clear implication that there is an outer world, whereas science knows only one world. Skinner localizes my toothache in that private world because *you* can't experience it. Of course not. Why? Because two entirely different behavioral fields are involved, one including me and my own tissue conditions plus the other field factors and the other involving you and your own tissue and other variables. Why should we expect two very different events to be identical? Isn't this inability to get inside me and experience my toothache the same condition that pervades any investigator of natural events? The anatomist cannot enter into the froghood of the frog he is dissecting, and the physicist cannot *be* a gravitating object or an astronomer a supernova, and yet each of them can advance understanding of the thing he or she chooses to study. It is only the witting or unwitting hangover from ancient psychic doctrine that has raised this pseudoquestion. Localizing behavior within the skin of the organism always causes theoretical embarrassment.

Another point that needs to be raised here concerns the proper use of inference. It is possible to argue that psychologists may even have an advantage over other scientists in studying things that are more like themselves. Is it not true that people in intimate relationships can know "what's going on" behaviorally with the other person, even to the point of discerning what the other is thinking? I would argue that an inference about the occurrence of a behavioral event is not to be equated with an inference about a hypothetical explanation such as remembering in terms of brain traces. The latter cannot be validated; the former can be because it is observ*able*.

Let us proceed to a possible happening. The teacher announces to her class that yesterday her purse was stolen. She observes that a certain boy acts in a very embarrassed manner. She suspects him and infers that he must have been the culprit, but she can't prove it because she didn't actually observe him steal it. She has made an inference about an observable event that occurred prior to her announcement to the class. Now, to make a long hypothetical story short, let us assume that the janitor did observe that very boy steal the purse and has so stated. An inference from one datum to another is checkable, but an inference about brain traces or id-ego conflicts is not. Therefore, whether by inference or by other ingenious procedure, the naturalistic psychologist rejects the notion of public and private response and deals with subtle and gross actions alike as observable in the only world known to us. Such a view offers no greater handicap than that which confronts the nuclear physicist or the astronomer dealing with black holes, cosmic rays, or gravity.

For Further Reading

Kantor, J. R., & Smith, N. W. (1975). *The science of psychology: An interbehavioral survey.* Chicago: Principia Press.
Skinner, B. F. (1953). *Science and human behavior.* New York: Macmillan.

THE QUEST FOR CERTAINTY

In casting about for a suitable entry under the letter Q, I happened to recall Dewey's book *The Quest for Certainty* and found its theme compatible with my general purpose. Frustrated by a ceaselessly changing world of apparent chaos, philosophers have long been engaged in a quest for certainty. What they sought was something persisting and unchanging behind all the transient changes. With Newton, it looked as though that search had come to a satisfactory conclusion.

No longer would the world have to fear that nature would fall apart and revert to chaos. Newton saved the day with his invention of solid, hard, massy, impenetrable, movable particles with their inherent, eternal properties. It was these indestructible entities that provided a sense of security and certainty, because whatever changes were observed were superficial and incidental manifestations of those intrinsically unchangeable particles, the foundation of all that exists in nature. Thus, classical philosophy's quest for certainty ended in a fiction, a spurious reality, something behind all knowing but also incapable of being known. Why? Because Newton's alleged building blocks of the universe were fictions based only on inference and hunch. The "blind alley" in which Newton and his followers found themselves as a result of their quest for an absolutely unshakable certainty proved that "pure thought" alone in an ivory tower may get you nowhere, but the Newtonians didn't know that; they were convinced that they had achieved the ultimate theory of natural phenomena and, with it, certitude at last.

ENTER MODERN PHYSICS

The first three decades of our century saw developments that sent shock waves throughout physics and the rest of the scientific and philosophic world. All the fundamental concepts of Newtonian physics were gradually shattered—the notion of absolute space and time, the elementary solid particles, cause-effect, and so on. The hard, indestructible atoms of Newton were found to consist of vast spaces in which small particles moved. The newly discovered, highly abstract subatomic units themselves would not stay put, sometimes appearing as waves and sometimes as particles. Another disturbing finding came from the discovery of one after another of the so-called elementary particles, which today number over two-hundred, forcing the adjective *elementary* into obsolescence. But that isn't all; in addition to their dual nature, particles appear to transform themselves into other particles. Nor can a particle be treated as having a separate existence, because it makes sense only in its interaction within a context. Today physics has entered even a stranger world, that of invisible quarks with their outlandish names such as *charm* and *strangeness*. These have proliferated just as the other elementary particles proliferated, frustrating the continued search for the simple, basic building blocks of the universe. But each advance brings us no nearer to our goal in the continuing quest for certainty.

For Further Reading

Dewey, J. (1929). *The quest for certainty*. New York: Minton, Balch & Co.

RACE

Man's natures are alike: it is their habits that carry them far apart.
Confucius (551-478 B.C.)

Despite its ubiquitous usage, or probably because of it, the term *race* has acquired a confounded and confounding meaning. For that reason, we start with the more inclusive term *species*, which, according to Howells (1971, pp. 5-6), is "the real and ultimate unit." *Species* is generally defined as a population of individuals all members of which are potentially fertile, but which are unable to mate with members of other species. According to Dobzhansky (1971, p. 14) humans "have existed as a single species since at least the Pleistocene epoch, some half a million years ago." The human species, then, is a single evolutionary unit that makes all humans scattered over planet Earth evolutionary brothers and sisters of the human family.

RACE DEFINED

Before we attempt a definition of race, let us perform an imaginary "experiment." Let us agree to adopt a single criterion, namely, skin color, in an effort to determine how it is distributed among our planet's human populations. Let us ask the blackest person to head the line by standing at the left. Next, to the left of that person we place the next blackest one, continuing our procedure through the so-called brown skins and the reds and yellows, ending at the extreme right side of the thousands-of-miles-long line with the "whitest" human on earth, realizing that, as George Bernard Shaw said, "a truly white person would be a horrible sight to see." So-called white people are really more pinkish than white, as can be demonstrated by holding a sheet of white bond paper alongside the face of a Caucasian.

Now, if we inspect closely our seemingly endless line of individuals, ranging from one extreme to the other, we find a color gradient or gradual transition from one shade or tint to another. We end up with a continuous sequence or color spectrum with no break or gap that would permit us to say, "At this cut-off point, one subdivision or race stops and another begins." However, if we should ask two individuals from that lineup, one from the darker end and one from the distant, lighter end, to step forward out of line and stand close together, the contrast in skin color would be quite apparent.

Scientifically speaking, continuous variation is the rock-bottom fact in a consideration of anatomical/physiological attributes of the human species. But, particularly in the United States, "race" has become distorted to emphasize negro-white differences, particularly the notion that blacks are on the average "inferior to whites in mental capacity" (Howells, 1971, p. 7).

WHAT THE ANTHROPOLOGISTS SAY

Some anthropologists such as Carleton Coon (1962) support the notion of race. Others discard the term and proceed to work without it. Over many decades, Ashley Montagu (1965) has argued that the belief in "race" is a widespread contemporary myth in the Western world, comparing it to a former belief in witchcraft. He denounces the popular belief that different human groups inherit different abilities according to their skin color, thus yielding a natural hierarchy of "races." Naturally, according to the popular myth, whites have achieved more, and that fact proves that whites are biologically superior. In opposing such a racist notion, Montagu (1956, p. 48) argues that not only are all biologically normal members of the human species psychologically equipotential today, but the same characterization holds for "different populations or races . . . in the history of mankind." As Montagu (1956, p. 108) sees it, "Man is the most plastic, the most educable, the most malleable of all the creatures on the face of the earth; the creature beyond all others, which makes ridiculous the reductionist fallacy which has it that man is 'nothing but' a functioning of his genes."

The fundamental question that skeptics are likely to ask is this:

How does "race" enter into our understanding of a person's psychological nature? What does the individual's skin color, hair texture, limb-to-body-height ratio or any other hereditary, anatomical characteristic have to do with his or her attainment of excellence as a Metropolitan Opera star, an atomic scientist, a chemist, violinist, conductor, composer, military strategist, or poet? Today the evidence for high attainment is occurring on a global basis, irrespective of continent, nationality, religion, or "race" (Pronko, 1969, p. 83).

One can never *disprove* a negative proposition such as "Human races are unequal in 'natural endowment.'" Rather, it is the obligation of the proponents of that claim to *prove* their case. Until they do, we can say with certainty that, as of now, *"the races cannot be shown to be* unequal" (Howells, 1971, p. 9).

For Further Reading

Howells, W. W. (1971). The meaning of race. In R. H. Osborne (Ed.), *The biological and social meaning of race* (pp. 3-10). San Francisco: Freeman.
Montagu, A. (1956). *The biosocial nature of man.* New York: Grove Press.

REACTING TO ONE'S OWN
REACTIONS: AN ALTERNATIVE
TO INTROSPECTION

Psychological theorizing reveals a peculiar difficulty. There is no problem as long as the "thing" to which one responds is *another* person or object. Theoretical difficulties arise when people respond to their *own* organism or to their *own* action. *Introspection* was invented to explain or interpret the latter situations. There is another way of understanding such data, but, before we get into that, we need to establish what the facts are.

One can kill another person (homicide), and one can kill oneself (suicide). I can notice a skin blemish on your face, and I can notice one on my face. I can hear your stomach "growling," and I can hear my own. I can disapprove an act you performed yesterday, but I can be equally critical and repentent of a past disgraceful act of my own. Kantor and Smith (1975, p. 43) offer the constructs of endogenous and exogenous stimulus function. The former refers to stimulus functions that originate in the psychological and biological acts and conditions of the individual. The latter applies to all other conditions. The main point here is that no new principle is needed to explain behavior involving oneself as compared with behavior involving other variables.

In expansion of that point, a study by Secord and Jourard (1953) asked their subjects to indicate on a scale of 1 to 5 what parts of their anatomy they were satisfied with, what parts they were dissatisfied with, and which they worried about and would like to change. They learned that their subjects reacted with varying degrees of satisfaction or dissatisfaction with their various anatomical aspects, which included body build, height, legs, weight, teeth, facial complexion, and so on. The construct of endogenous stimulus function can handle such findings whereas others prefer the notion of self-consciousness.

GALLUP'S EXPERIMENT

Starting from a mentalistic framework, G. G. Gallup (1977) argued that consciousness was bidirectional, manifesting itself either as *consciousness* or *self-consciousness*. He wanted to know if he could demonstrate self-recognition (self-consciousness) in the chimp. In briefest terms, he introduced chimps to mirrors; the chimps acted very much to their mirror image as if they were observing another member of their own species. This he called other-directed behavior. But after prolonged confrontation with mirrors, Gallup observed self-directed behavior. But was this self-recognition?

To test this point, with the chimps under deep anesthesia, Gallup painted a portion of the eyebrow ridge and the top half of the opposite ear. Following recovery, as a control, Gallup counted the number of times the chimp "spontaneously," that is, without benefit of mirror, touched the painted portions. Reintroduction of the mirror increased touching by a factor of twenty-five times when compared to the test period (without benefit of mirror). Gallup concluded that self-recognition is not an exclusively human attribute—that the chimp is capable of experiencing self-consciousness as well as consciousness. However, if one eschews making the assumption of an indwelling consciousness in the chimp, one can handle the facts more conservatively with Kantor and Smith's endogenous stimulus function. Reader, take your choice.

For Further Reading

Gallup, G. G. (1977). Self-recognition in primates. *American Psychologist, 32*(5), 329-338.

Secord, P. F., & Jourard, S. M. (1953). The appraisal of body-cathexis: Body-cathexis and the self. *Journal of Consulting Psychology, 17*, 343-347.

REALITY: WHAT IS IT?

The butcher, the baker, and the candlestick maker have no problem with reality. In fact, they may go to their graves without once pondering the question: What is reality? For them, it is enough to work with the flesh, the flour, dough, and ovens, and the wax and wicks each works with, plus their tools, customers, and other observable aspects of their respective trades. When you, gentle reader, are crossing the street and see a car bearing down on you, you don't leisurely reflect, "Is this for real, or is it only an appearance of reality?" You dart out of the car's way. This is not the language of the traditional philosopher.

CONVENTIONAL PHILOSOPHY

As a basis for our discussion of reality, we start with a statement by the English philosopher F. H. Bradley: (1959, p. 429) "We have found that no one aspect of experience, as such, is real. None is primary, or can serve to explain the others or the whole. They are all alike *appearances*, all one-sided, and passing away beyond themselves" (emphasis added). That which the butcher, baker, and candlestick maker perceive is, for Bradley and other followers of the classic philosophical tradition, only "surface aspects" of a "true," transcendent reality beyond the merely perceivable. The merely perceivable is transient and in a state of flux.

The fundament, or what we might characterize as "real," reality, is said to lie behind the appearances. The change so prominent in the perceivable is contingent on so many things because it is subject to chance that cannot be eliminated. Therefore, it is said, reality must be sought in the universal and the absolute, the fixed and eternal—in short, the "ultimate reality" which is said to somehow mirror and shape the surface appearances of that reality. The search requires knowledge of a higher, a priori order than that exercised by natural scientists in the practical world of change.

COMMENTARY ON ULTIMATE REALITY

The notion subscribed to by Bradley and his supporters that "things are never what they seem" is an assumption. It assumes that that which is knowable or known is somehow subordinate to that which is not knowable or not known by means of human confrontation. It is a blatant contradiction to assert or believe that things outside of human contacts are observed or observable. What a far cry from the approach of the seeker after ultimate reality to that of Dewey and Bentley (1949, p. 86), who rule out interest in anything inherently nonobservable (whatever that might be) or inquiry based on an intuitive or purely speculative methodology.

There seems to be no more fitting close to the question posed at the beginning of this article than the following eloquent statement by Dewey and Bentley (1949, p. 87): "Nothing 'more real' than the observable is secured by using the word 'real' or by peering for something behind or beyond the observable to which to apply the name."

For Further Reading

Bradley, F. H. (1959). *Appearance and reality*. Oxford: Clarendon Press.
Dewey, J., & Bentley, A. F. (1949). *Knowing and the known*. Boston: Free Press.

REDUCTIONISM AND HOLISM

First of all, we should define our terms. The term *reductionism* refers to a philosophical position held by some scientists and laymen, according to which, in the hierarchy of sciences, arranged as in the accompanying chart (Figure 11), phenomena at one level are to be explained and understood by "reducing" them to the data or explanatory principles of a science at a lower level. Thus, according to reductionists, social events are to be explained in psychological terms. In turn, psychological happenings are to be understood in terms of the underlying anatomical and physiological factors, and so on down the ladder in the chart.

Philosophers and scientists who are opposed to reductionistic explanations find holism a more congenial approach in understanding events. According to the holistic position, an organism is more than, or different from, the sum of its parts. Instead of trying to understand an organism or any other thing by dissecting it into its component parts, the holistic investigator sees things whole or in system. The ecologist who studies an animal integrated into its niche in nature illustrates a holistic procedure.

REDUCTIONISM IN BIOLOGY

According to molecular biologists, cells are a bunch of molecules and so are organisms. But according to P. A. Weiss (1969, p. 365), the cell has certain characteristics above and beyond its constituent molecules. In fact, Weiss states that "all living phenomena consist of *group behaviors,* which offer aspects not evident in the members of the group when observed singly." Living systems are complex, not as a haphazard collection, but as an orderly entity that is not determined by its component elements. In fact, tracing out the constituent molecules of a cell would offer no help in understanding the cell because *the cell is a system in its own right.* "Coordination" and "control" seem to be necessary in describing cellular functioning. Furthermore, more predictions can be made about the action of the cell than about the action of the constituent molecules. Also, variability is greater for the latter than for the former. The cell is a system, and according to Weiss (1969, p. 370), "in the system, the structure of the whole determines the operation of the parts; in the machine, the operation of the parts determines the outcome."

REDUCTIONISM

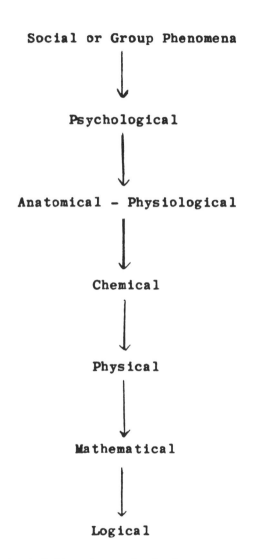

Figure 11. Hierarchical "ladder" showing levels of organization required by the theoretical reductionism that purports to explain phenomena at one level in terms of the next lower level.

PRINCIPLE OF HIERARCHICAL ORGANIZATION

The next step that Weiss leads us to is hierarchy, a notion that he considers a necessity for biological inquiry. Starting with the living cell, he reminds us that a slide of a cell under the microscope is a dead cell "frozen" at a single instant of its once-living phase, during all of which period it showed ceaseless, dynamic change from one moment to the next.

However, as a unitary entity, the living cell is a system comparable in its organized functioning to a big industry that manufactures different sorts of things in different departments, combining each into finished or semifinished products and sending them into storage or for export. Within the cell, there are subsystems organized within themselves for their own specific functions. One can go downward in analysis until one arrives at the molecular level, at which the organization seen above that level disappears. Thus, there is a hierarchy of subsystems beginning at the supramolecular level. Despite the diversity of the individual components of each subsystem, each subsystem shows an overriding but limited "authority" over the functioning of those components. Furthermore, each higher subsystem operates under rules of order that apply to the dynamics of the whole system, that is, the cell. The organization of cells into tissues, of tissues into organs, and of organs up to the organism itself follows the same "principle of hierarchical organization" as governs the functioning of an explanted cell. The term *hierarchy* refers to a collectivity such as the army organized into orders or ranks, each subordinate to the one above.

One more point about the various levels of the biological hierarchy. According to Weiss, as one crosses over from one level to another (say, from cell to tissue, or from tissue to organ) one finds *discontinuity* or, as some have referred to it less satisfactorily, an "emergence" of new qualities not found in the lower levels. For example, a tissue is more than, or different from, a bunch of cells, and an organ is more than, or different from, a bunch of tissues. By contrast, an atomistic or reductionistic explanation would presume an unbroken continuity starting at the molecular level continuing without break up to the organismic level (or beyond). Weiss's lifework has forced him to reject the reductionistic assumption simply because he finds no evidence for what he terms "micromechanical cause-effect chain reactions" (1969, p. 390). Instead, he advocates the notion of levels of integration.

Because of the discontinuity at each of the levels of the hierarchical array of life phenomena, Weiss seeks understanding by studying the role of the variables that make up the system at any particular level. Understanding will not be found by jumping up or down the various levels or strata, because, according to Weiss, determinism is *stratified*. It is to be discovered at each stratum in terms of factors interrelated at the given stratum.

SUMMARY OF THE HOLISTIC VIEW IN BIOLOGY

In summarizing Weiss's major interest, that is, to understand the functioning of the living cell, he found no way of "reducing" it to a physicochemical level, for example, in terms of molecules. Why? Simply because the cell has properties at the cellular level that cannot be observed at the "lower" molecular level. In fact, even within the cell there are subsystems (which we need not go into) that function in ways not explainable in terms of molecules. However, all the activities that go on in the cell show a certain unity, pattern, order, or integration characteristic of the cell as a whole, not found in the molecular components of that cell.

Weiss also finds distinctive features at levels above the level of the cell. Tissues are not to be explained in terms of the attributes peculiar to cells that compose them (such as muscle, cartilage, bone, or nerve); they have their own characteristic unity, pattern, order, or integration. At the organ level (lungs, heart, gland) even though they are each aggregates of tissues, each organ nevertheless has its own unity, pattern, order, or integration. And, of course, the same is true of an organism. It has properties not found in its component organs or organ systems. In fact, the very word *organism* connects one to *organization*, which is the hallmark of the organism, plant or animal.

Two final points: (1) The levels from the cellular subsystems, the cell, the tissues up through the organs and organ systems (like the glandular, circulatory, and respiratory systems) up to the organism are discontinuous, manifesting characteristics not seen below. (2) Any attempt to explain those varieties of properties by reducing them all to the same physicochemical entities such as molecules in different combinations as building blocks simply won't work.

For Further Reading

Weiss, P. A. (1969). The living system: Determination stratified. *Studium Generale,* 22, 361-400.

REDUCTIONISM IN THE
INVESTIGATION OF
SOCIAL GROUPS

Can the investigation of social groups be "boiled down to" (i.e., reduced to) the action of the individuals composing a given group? This is the question before us now. To all such queries, Émile Durkheim (1893, p. 349) had a clear answer, as manifested in the following quotation: "Every time that a social phenomenon is explained by a psychological phenomenon, we may be sure that the explanation is false." Obviously, Durkheim was not a reductionist.

Despite Durkheim's caveat of many decades ago, sociological or group phenomena are often reduced to psychological levels of explanation. When young people gather by the thousands at beaches in the spring or at musical festivals at any time of the year, they are said to have a need to socialize (in older terms, because of a gregarious instinct, which should be immediately recognized as a form of circular reasoning). All of the above explanations are also self-actional.

Clearly opposed to such reductionism stands Leslie A. White (1949), whose work will serve as a reference base for observing how the problem of reductionism versus holism works in the sciences that study group phenomena. In his analysis, White first considers the role of biological factors in explaining the vast differences in the behavior of human groups. I feel that White would agree that, as a species, *Homo sapiens* has changed biologically little if any over perhaps the last fifty thousand years. Superficially, skin color, hair texture, and other such differences do appear but in more fundamental ways such as nervous, muscular, and glandular systems, they are notably uniform. And when one considers the tremendous variation of human behavior in various groups on earth, "all evidence points to an utter insignificance of biological factors as compared with culture in any consideration of behavior variations" (1949, p. 124).

Therefore, in his study of culture, White considers "man as a constant, culture as a variable" (p. 124). He holds that the diversity of languages, customs, religions, diets, dress, fashions, and fads is not determined by inherent biological or psychological variables localizable in the constituent individuals of a given group. In fact, the differences that one observes in the behavior of various groups is determined by the culture that shapes them.

Here White completely turns the tables on the familiar, traditional formulation that we have been used to. White would surely agree that when a certain Papuan tribe engages in a cannibalistic ritual after a victorious battle, cannibalism isn't to be explained by alleging some factor in the psychological or biological makeup of the individual tribe members. It's the other way around. It was the tradition of cannibalism persisting in this tribe that made the individuals behave in a cannibalistic way.

Perhaps it is time again to refer to the reductionistic diagram (Figure 11) showing the hierarchy of sciences. If we heed the example of Weiss, we recognize the various levels of integration. This means that the different levels are discontinuous in the sense that a new quality appears at a given level, a quality not apparent at other levels. There is a strong implication that the phenomena at each level are to be explained in terms of factors observed *at that particular level* without resorting to explanatory principles from lower levels of integration. This proposition also suggests that the data at each level are independent of the data (and the principles derived from their study) at lower levels. White might say, "Yes, cultural data are psychological (in part) but they are not *merely* psychological." For White (1949, p. xviii), culture consists of a distinct set of events that continue from generation to generation. The determinants of culture are to be found in the prior and present cultural factors and processes. The explanation of customs, beliefs, ceremonies, and such are to be explained in cultural terms because culture is self-contained and self-determined.

White's unambiguous stand places him among the holists; his propositions clearly constitute a declaration of independence for his pursuit of culturology. He finds his explanatory principles at the level of culture because, in his opinion, culture should be studied "*as if* it had a life of its own, quite apart from human organisms" (p. 144). Grammar, language, the mother-in-law taboo, the effect of the automobile on the family, the divorce rate—all can be studied *as if* individual human beings didn't exist. Nevertheless, explanatory statements can be derived from an analysis of group data. The important final point is that any principles or laws pertaining to culture will be stated in terms of culture and not merely in terms of psychology or biology. Thus, as in any other science, so in the social sciences, we have the choice of inquiry from a holistic or reductionistic approach.

For Further Reading

White, L. A. (1949). *The science of culture.* New York: Grove Press.

REDUCTIONISTIC PROCEDURE IN PSYCHOLOGICAL INQUIRY

A glance at the diagram of the science hierarchy (Figure 11) reveals that a reductionistic procedure in psychology requires the explanation of behavioral phenomena at the anatomic-physiological level.

"No psychosis without a neurosis." Decades ago, this was the slogan for handling any psychological disturbance. Hallucinations, delusions, and amnesias were all considered to be the result of a malfunctioning of the patient's nervous system, which was said to be in a state of tension, damage, or irritability. And if such nerve damage or dysfunction could not be demonstrated, the belief was that at some future time, more powerful microscopes would reveal the *real* causes for the psychological troubles in the patient's "biological substrate." The "cause-effect" type of thinking here should be transparent. A neural condition (cause) was said to produce a psychological condition, that is, a delusion, hallucination, and so on (effect).

The reductionistic formula has been, and is still, applied not only to "abnormal" behaviors but to all behaviors without exception. The phrase "no psychosis without a neurosis" can be expanded beyond its limited meaning above to indicate that there can be no psychological response without a neural correlate. Thus, the memories, learnings, attitudes, beliefs, skills, and aptitudes of an individual are considered to be "effects" of an organ such as a brain or gland conceived of as "cause." This is how reductionism has been made to work in psychology.

The full significance of the brain as stated in standard textbooks of psychology refers to it as a kind of computer that "stores" all of our experiences over a lifetime and codes them for future use. In fact, everything that we think or do simply reflects the physical activity of the brain. Therefore, the secret of understanding ourselves lies in our ferreting *out* the secrets of brain action. In other words, the authors of such psychology textbooks recommend that, if we want to understand people, we should apply ourselves to the assimilation of the knowledge explosion of recent years in neurobiology. It is hardly necessary to point out the comparison between biologists who descend to the molecular level in their biological study and psychologists who drop down one step in the hierarchy of sciences and couch their explanatory terms in the language of anatomy and physiology. And, of course, sociologists who do their work by stepping down to the psychological level in interpreting group behavior are still another variety of reductionists.

THE REFLEX ARC AS A MODEL
FOR PSYCHOLOGY

In 1896, John Dewey published his paper "The Reflex Arc Concept in Psychology." Fifty years later, the editor of the *Psychological Review* Jubilee issue announced that Dewey's article had been voted, by leading psychologists, first among twenty-five of the best papers published in that journal in the preceding half-century. It is still judged to be one of the classics in the history of the functionalist school of psychology.

In that paper, Dewey objected to the adoption of the reflex arc as a model for psychology by the psychologists of his day. Although Dewey didn't criticize William James by name, he did make a fleeting reference to James's *Principles of Psychology*. In fact, as if with tongue in cheek, he cites the very page, and only that, on which James presents the reflex arc as a basic paradigm for his *Principles*. In the opening chapter of that classic work, James (1918, p. 4) stated that the universal acceptance of the brain as the immediate bodily condition of all things mental permitted him to say so and go on. This naive assumption made it easy for James to conceive of an explanatory system for psychology. James's reflex-arc theory is important (1) because it provided psychology with an enduring paradigm and (2) because Dewey attacked it as an unsuitable model for psychology. James argued that a two-segmented reflex arc involving only the lower centers would never enable a child to refrain from reaching for a candle flame. He speculated that fortunately, neural impulses from the lower centers must also run up to the cortex, where they must leave traces, so that association occurs between the burning and withdrawal movements. That is why "the burnt child dreads the flame" and is no longer at the mercy of the machinelike reaching reflex effected by the two-segmented reflex arc of the lower centers.

DEWEY'S OBJECTIONS TO THE REFLEX-ARC PARADIGM

Dewey (1896, p. 359) failed to see the child's seeing and reaching for a candle flame as constituting a series of mechanical, neural acts. Instead of dealing with a fractured happening, Dewey saw a comprehensive unity in which stimulus and response were phases of a common event, one in which seeing and grasping were so intimately connected that they reinforced each other. He also viewed stimulus and response as correlative, thus veering away from an organism-centered approach that looked within the skin of the organism for explanatory principles.

Another example that Dewey used in explaining his position as differing from James's concerned a person's hearing a sudden, loud sound. It depends on whether that person is on guard, reading a book, or at work in a noisy factory. A reflex-arc analysis isn't of much help here, because that sound will have a different "meaning" in different settings. Besides, all events are a function of antecedent events.

Another split that disturbed Dewey was the common cleavage of the organism into body and mind. In his paper, he tried to free himself from the ancient dualism by insisting that, instead of treating body and mind as separate entities, we learn to view behavior as being so integrated that it will be impossible to split it up into two things. His was an attempt to treat behavior naturalistically.

Dewey's criticism of the reflex-arc concept was a strong protest against the artificial fragmentation of his day. He considered such a paradigm no more satisfactory than the former atomism of "ideas" as bits of consciousness that had to be unified by a soul, mind, or ego. Did his noble attempt have any lasting effect on psychology? Not if one examines a contemporary textbook in psychology such as Kagan, Havemann, and Segal's (1984), Zimbardo's (1979), or Atkinson, Atkinson, and Hilgard's (1983). We should give Dewey extra credit for having written in 1896.

For Further Reading

Dewey, J. (1896). The reflex arc concept in psychology. *The Psychological Review, 3,*
357-370. Also in *University of Chicago Contributions to Philosophy* (1896),
1 (1), 39-52, and in John Dewey, *The early works, 1882-1898: Early essays*
(pp. 96-109). Carbondale: Southern Illinois University Press.

THE RETINAL IMAGE:
FACT OR FICTION?

Contemporary accounts of vision accept the "eye-as-a-camera" theory of vision, drawing point-by-point comparison between parts of the eye and parts of the camera. The stimulus for vision is said to be not objects but light waves, which are at bottom electromagnetic radiation (Kagan, Havemann & Segal, 1984, pp. 258-271). For a thorough consideration of the "picture-on-the-retina" theory, we lean heavily on Arthur Bentley's (1954) comprehensive research in this area.

ANALYSIS OF THE RETINAL IMAGE

First of all, we should note that for over three hundred years physical optics, physiology, and psychology have held the belief that, during vision, seen objects form an image or picture on the retina.

1. A tradition that old dies hard. This is our first barrier to a more valid interpretation.

2. Another problem was created for us when in 1625 Father Christophorus Scheiner took the enucleated eye of an ox, looked through it, and "saw an image" on its retina. All that he demonstrated with his experiment was that the eye contains an optical system that doesn't have much to do with seeing in a living organism. Why? And here Bentley quotes recognized experts in vision who testify that, while the retina is almost perfectly transparent during life, it loses its transparency and becomes opaque shortly after death. A transparent medium simply doesn't reflect an image any more than looking through your window or your spectacles. An opaque medium does. Thus, Scheiner's image on the dead eye of an ox is as highly artificial as the blind spot obtained only under the very special conditions of perimetric examination. In other words, both are artifacts, neither of which prevails in real-life situations. Therefore, inference from either incident to the living eye is unwarranted.

3. Conditions that work against a clear image on the retina include a rich network of nontransparent blood vessels (except at the fovea) that the retinal image must penetrate. Logically, one would expect the receptor cells of the retina to be in its very first layer. They are not. But the retinal image has still other handicaps to overcome. It must get past a layer of ganglion cells, a layer of bipolar cells, and still another of rod and cone cells, the very last layer. In addition, there is the blind spot, which should leave a hole in

our seeing but which doesn't. Then, there are tearing and blinking, "astigmatisms, aberrations, accommodation difficulties and phorias. How *good* a picture could be imaged on it? What would you do with your Kodak, if you found it working like this?" (Bentley, 1954, p. 274).

4. According to geometrical optics, the image on the retina has to be upside down. But how do we see things right side up?

5. The retina is made up of ten layers. We are not told which one contains the image.

6. There are still other problems. We see objects in three dimensions, but the presumed retinal image can be projected in only two dimensions. How does the third dimension get in there?

7. How can the spatial coherence of the retinal image be preserved as it is presumably transmitted along the nerve fibers, and what happens when "visual messages" split up at the optic chiasm? And how does the image get fused in the visual area when it is finally transmitted to the two cerebral hemispheres as separated structures? If you should answer that these two portions of the brain are connected through the corpus callosum, Ranson (1942, p. 288) would refute your argument. According to him, there are "few, if any" neurons interconnecting the specific visual areas of the two hemispheres. Therefore, we should see a crack or break right down the middle of whatever we are looking at, but we don't!

8. Finally, let us assume that, by some magic, the picture on the retina has been transmitted to the visual area of the cortex. What mind's eye is there to see the "picture"? Here's another dead end.

Any one of the above points should justify the skeptical psychologist in raising a serious question about the existence of the retinal image. Whoever requires further persuasion is invited to examine Bentley's (1954, pp. 274-284) total of thirty-eight pieces of telling evidence against the existence of the retinal image, which, in closing, he acknowledges "as a region of phenomena to be inquired into and not a reality to be guarded to the death" (p. 282).

Well over a century ago, Auguste Comte (1855, p. 25) stated that "no conception can be understood otherwise than through its history," a statement that applies with special force to the notion of the retinal image. The eye-as-a-camera model on which it is based can be traced back to 350 years ago. Not only that, but a comparison of the ancient and modern accounts reveals an incredible similarity, a dreary sameness that has survived over several centuries, leaving us with a doctrine that has come down to us, essentially, in its original form!

For Further Reading

Bentley, A. F. (1954). The fiction of "retinal image." In *Inquiry into inquiries* (pp. 268-285).(Ed. S. Ratner.) Boston: Beacon Press.

THE SELF

Because the self is a metaphysical creation, we start with the following definition offered by H. H. Titus and M. S. Smith (1974, p. 547): "the person, subject, ego, knower or the 'I,' the unity that persists through changes." While the term has some practical referential value in everyday life situations, it is not a scientific expression derived from observation of confrontable things. Indeed, Titus and Smith as much as admit that when they state that "the self has, up to the present time, defied adequate description" (p. 34). It is a term in search of a referent. But these authors feel the need for such a term to explain the unity and continuity of behavior. Therefore, they postulate an "I" or a "me," an entity that is in charge and keeps records.

In their interpretation, Titus and Smith have endowed the organism with the total explanatory burden of perceiving, feeling, remembering, and other psychological occurrences. Their only recourse is to *verbally* create an "entity" (their own term) dwelling within the organism to carry out those functions. We should note that the usual definition of entity is something that has an independent, separate, or self-sustained existence.

Among others, Mahoney (1975, p. 865) has decried the use of behavioral prime movers. He doesn't look for any first cause, either inside or outside the organism, because the organism and its environment are in a constant and close reciprocal relationship. Skinner (1953, p. 283) also considers the self as a hypothetical cause of behavior, used only by ignoring the stimulus conditions in the organism's milieu. The alternative is to attribute their functions to a verbally created self-actional entity within the individual.

For Further Reading

Mahoney, M. J. (1975). The sensitive scientist in empirical humanism. *American Psychologist, 30*(8), 864-867.
Skinner, B. F. (1953). *Science and human behavior.* New York: Macmillan.

SELF-ACTION

Webster's Ninth New Collegiate Dictionary defines *self-acting* as follows: "acting or capable of acting of or by itself: automatic." Here are some examples of self-action from prescientific times. When the ancients found maggots in their meat, they believed that those maggots developed by a kind of "spontaneous generation" out of rotting flesh. Today, we recognize the maggot as the larval stage of the housefly, developing from eggs deposited by the female fly. Another example is provided by the ancient Egyptians. They held the belief that lice arose of themselves from human sweat and mice from the mud of the river Nile. It was also an old belief that fireflies originated from fire and that waterbugs came from water puddles left behind by the rain. Self-actional ways of explaining things are an archaic heritage of the human species.

DEWEY AND BENTLEY ON SELF-ACTION

A specialized usage of the term *self-action* is provided by Bentley (1935) and by Dewey and Bentley (1949). In their joint work, they (Dewey & Bentley, 1949, p. 108) define *self-action* thus: "where things are viewed as acting under their own powers." According to an antiquated psychological tradition, the mind (or brain) initiates and generates desires, thoughts, dreams, and so on. According to faculty psychology, there are resident within us three "faculties," intellect, feeling, and will, which are conceived to be "actual forces or powers which were supposed to give rise to the separate ideas, feelings, etc." (Pratt, 1929, p. 143). All of the above explanations illustrate self-actional theories.

SELF-ACTION IN CONTEMPORARY PSYCHOLOGY

Self-actional explanations are by no means a thing of the past. They flourish in contemporary psychology as well. Suppose we inspect ten jumbo-sized textbooks of general psychology such as are commonly sent to instructors of introductory courses and that turn up in such reviews as those of Gerow (1978) and Popplestone (1978). Without mentioning specific authors, we commonly find a number of entities viewed as acting under their own powers, thus meeting the definition of self-action.

SELF-ACTIONAL ENTITIES

"Mind," "consciousness," "drive," and "motive" head the list. According to one author, a motive is "the *urge* behind behavior." Another writer states that motives "*direct* the organism to a goal or goals." All the texts assign a heavy self-actional role to the brain. We are told that a cellular analysis of the nervous system "will permit us to go beyond a general understanding of what the brain does to *how* it enables us to start, stop, talk, listen, make love or war, in short to be human or to act inhumanely." Unanimously, the brain is said to contain the "physiological mechanisms of memory." It processes information, coding, storing, filing, and retrieving it. There are supposed to be different mechanisms for "short-term memory" and "long-term memory." The brain also "coordinates" and "filters" sense data and contains a "sleep" and "appetite center," and "the very high level of human IQ comes from the cerebral cortex." There are many more examples of self-actional entities, all of which posit powers or forces that are alleged to do the work solo. If our samples are representative, and I believe they are, then large areas of contemporary psychology fall into the self-actional category.

CRITICISM OF SELF-ACTIONAL EXPLANATIONS

Modern science subscribes to the view that the events that it studies always involve *at least* two variables. When things are said to "act on their own," self-actionally, they violate this dictum. Another way to see the problem is to ask, "How can a thing be the cause of itself?" When we stuff the entire explanation of psychological action within the organism, we only obscure our understanding of it. How does it help to say that a child performs with excellence because it is "gifted"? And when we ask, "How do you know the child is gifted?" to be told circularly, "Because it does so well." Self-actional explanations are always in terms of some imaginary "agent" or "agency," for example, "She has a 'good brain' or a 'talent.'" As Dewey (1929, p. 229) put it, "The more evident and observable is thus 'explained' in terms of the obscure, the obscurity being hidden from view because of habits that have the weight of tradition behind them." Psychology began to make greater progress when it broadened its observational base to include other variables beyond the organism, as it did when it tried interactional and transactional views of behavior.

For Further Reading

Dewey, J., & Bentley, A. F. (1949). *Knowing and the known.* Boston: Beacon Press.

SETTING FACTORS:
AN EXPANDED ACCOUNT

Question: "How much do you weigh?" Answer: "One hundred fifty pounds." The unthinking person is likely to state that if you weigh 150 pounds on Earth, why shouldn't you weigh the same on any other planet of the solar system? Isn't your weight an abiding feature of you? Not so. Assuming that you took along common spring scales on your trip to the moon and our sister planets, because such scales work against gravity, you would not weigh the same. On the moon, you would weigh only 16½ pounds, on Venus, 84, on Jupiter, 250, Uranus, 84, and on Neptune, 114. Even walking, so taken for granted, does not work the same everywhere in the cosmos. The astronauts who visited the moon seemed to be bouncing along instead of walking. It took some time for them to adapt their locomotion to the unaccustomed gravity of the moon.

The moral of this little lesson is that we often either ignore or take for granted the conditions under which events occur. Even such an apparently simple thing as a person's stepping on a scale isn't at all simple, for, as we have seen, the *same person's* standing on the *same scale* shows radically different weights depending on where the two are located.

The foregoing example, properly assignable to the science of physics, demonstrates that even gravitational events must be studied by taking into account the specific conditions under which they occur. Chemical interactions also vary depending on the temperature, the atmospheric pressure, the fineness of the interacting components, and so on. Therefore, it should not be a surprise to learn that the way in which organism and stimulus object act toward each other is a function of the context in which they are embedded.

SETTING FACTORS IN BEHAVIORAL INQUIRY

Setting factors constitute the surroundings, background, or ambience in which organism and stimulus object confront each other. For example, Liddell (1956, p. 37) reported that, in order to achieve any conditioning in his work with sheep, he had to tether another sheep in the laboratory within sight of the experimental animal.

Setting factors may be found on the side of (1) the stimulus object, (2) the organism, or (3) the surroundings in which the event is set. On the side of the stimulus object, if you should take two pieces of the same patch of gray paper and place one on a white background and the other on black, you would find that the one on black looks much brighter than the other. Thus, the immediate surroundings of the stimulus object play a role in the event. So does the organism. Whether drugged, fatigued, starved, sickly, or injured, such organismic conditions also contribute to the outcome of the psychological event. But so do the other aspects of behavioral events, that is, the more peripheral variables. If you were to "crack a safe," would you prefer to do your work in privacy, during the dark hours of the night, or with others peering over your shoulder, in broad daylight? Behavior appropriate at wedding celebrations or at a cocktail party would be considered offensive during a funeral service. A forceful illustration of the determining role of setting factors in human situations is provided by Hudson's (1975, p. 69) description of a gynecological examination in a medical setting.

Every day throughout the Western world staid women of all ages allow men they do not know, often accompanied by groups of young students of both sexes, to examine and discuss parts of their body that they normally shelter even from their husbands or lovers—parts of their bodies around which center the elaborate gradations of self-disclosure and self-expression that go to make up their sense of themselves as women. Yet, *If the situation is defined as "medical,"* they bare themselves on the instant to the probing hands and by no means entirely impersonal gaze of complete strangers (emphasis added).

As integral aspects of behavioral events, the preceding examples point to a need for extreme sensitivity in identifying the variables in the immediate locus of the stimulus object and responding organism.

For Further Reading

Kantor, J. R., & Smith, N. W. (1975). *The science of psychology: An interbehavioral survey*. Chicago: Principia Press.

SITUATION

The term *situation* gets special consideration because its elaboration may give an additional and supportive insight into the notion of an integrated field.

We start with Arthur Bentley's (1954, chap. 8) "Situational vs. Psychological Theories of Behavior," in which he dissociates himself from psychological theories that interpret behavior as transpiring inside the organism in the form of "experiences" or "consciousness."

Bentley unfolds his argument by quoting Woodbridge's redefinition of consciousness as seeing and hearing and all the rest. He then expands seeing, hearing, and all the rest as "double-barreled" words, better stated as "sights-seen and sounds-heard" (p. 142). By taking "sights" and "seen" and hyphenating them so as to produce a single term, Bentley denies any preferential treatment to the organism's "seeing" or to the object "seen." The two are viewed together in indissoluble union.

Bentley now faced the inevitable problem as to the locus of the behaviors seeing, hearing, and all the rest. If the behavior is not localizable in the organism or the confrontable object, where is it "to be looked for and found"? First of all, behavior is not a thing but an occurrence or happening localizable in a situation. The situation includes an organism and stimulus object—not as things having a separate existence in a static way but as phases of something going on, a process or event.

Bentley's process approach differs radically from traditional views, which assume an entity such as "consciousness" or "mind" residing within the organism and emanating from it after the Newtonian paradigm of "matter" and its propellant, "force." The participants in events such as sights-seen, sounds-heard, and so on do not possess independent powers of their own. It's just that *something takes place* when the two are brought together under certain definite circumstances. The traditional analysis of a situation that, in everyday terms, can be stated in the form "I see it" is faulty when that event is (verbally) broken up into an "I" that "sees" and an "it" that is "seen." Our elementalistic habit of seeing things as acting under their own powers traps us into fragmenting an occurrence into an "actor" ("I"), an act, "seeing" and an "it," the object seen. Now how do you glue the three disparate factors together again? Such a problem does not arise with a situational approach, because the unity of the situation is kept intact as it undergoes analysis.

For Further Reading

Bentley, A. F. (1954). *Inquiry into inquiries.* Boston: Beacon Press.

SOCIOBIOLOGY

Edward O. Wilson's evolutionary perspective embraces the whole range of animal species and eons of time in explaining contemporary human nature or mind. According to Wilson (1978, p. 17), "the will—the soul, if you wish," is too slippery to study, so we are forced to study the will's or soul's material basis, the brain. Right off, we apprehend Wilson's silent, dualistic assumption of matter and spirit that guide his investigation. Therefore, he seizes on the brain as the key to understanding the mind, which can only work within the limits set during the brain's evolution by means of natural selection. Wilson believes that those mental functions which turned out to be adaptive ensured such brains continued survival.

Starting, as he does, with the assumptions that Wilson adopts, one might guess what the outcome would be. Sure enough, his at-a-distance, blurred view of "man as though seen through the front end of a telescope" (1978, p. 17) reveals, to him, behavioral similarities across entire societies, human and infrahuman. Therefore, these resemblances prove to Wilson that they are genetically determined, an assumption that he started with and one that itself needs to be demonstrated.

CRITICISM OF SOCIOBIOLOGY

1. Sociobiology is reductionistic and self-actional. It reduces complex behaviors such as altruism not only to brain functions but still further to a spot in a gene millions of years ago.

2. Wilson offers no genetic evidence for his genetic claims.

3. As Midgley (1980, p. 25) points out, "the remoteness of causes by no means increases their explanatory force. If it did, the original big bang would be the only true explanation of everything, and we all ought to be doing astrophysics, not evolutionary biology."

4. Rose (1980, p. 166) adds another point concerning the models that we adopt for our investigations. "We are in constant danger of being seduced by our models, of being so enchanted by the fact that they 'fit' the data that we ignore the fact that an infinity of *other* models could equally well fit one's observations."

5. "A theory is only a license for research" (Washburn, 1980, p. 258) and must be testable, not merely show reasoning in a circle.

CONCLUSION

What can one say for *On Human Nature?* In all conscience, not much. Wilson is a distinguished scientist, but neither the distinction nor the science is much in evidence here. Where he offers us scientific hypotheses, he rarely provides the evidence to support them, and he frequently does not stop to consider how one might set about collecting relevant evidence. Where he offers us his political and social views, he does so as though the respect due to science would lend them added authority. It does not (Mackintosh, 1980, p. 341).

For Further Reading

Washburn, S. L. (1978). Animal behavior and social anthropology. In M. S. Gregory, A. Silvers & D. Sutch (Eds.), *Sociobiology and human nature* (pp. 53-74). San Francisco: Jossey-Bass.

Wilson, E. O. (1978). *On human nature*. Cambridge, Mass.: Harvard University Press.

"SOUL": THE TRANSFORMATION OF "SOUL" TO "MIND" AND "MIND" TO "BRAIN"

Our habits of talking about things serve as a straitjacket in the manner we think about and understand them. This is as true of soul as of mind. As the historical predecessor of mind, the intangible, invisible soul was for a long time believed to be an inhabitant of the human (but not the infrahuman) body. According to Bentley (1935, p. 6), for almost two thousand years, soul was so taken for granted that there was no question about its reality, only its attributes. Each soul stood apart from nature to be later judged by its maker.

For René Descartes, all things psychological transpired in the soul. According to him, although the soul was joined to the whole body, it performed its functions, not in the whole brain (a modern view) but in its innermost, centrally located pineal gland. Descartes believed that it was from the pineal gland that the soul radiated throughout the body via animal spirits, nerves, and blood, producing movement in the limbs.

J. R. Kantor (1969, pp. 94-97) has traced the changes that took place in the way *soul* was conceived over the centuries. During the Enlightenment, in the eighteenth century, *soul* began to lose its theological and sacred attributes and was "transformed into prosaic mind, the seat of man's desires and of the power to move toward satisfying them" (Kantor, 1969, p. 96). In time, *experience* and *consciousness* (standard, contemporary terms), were assigned to the mind. Although these alleged functions were still intangible and invisible, they encouraged investigators to look at human behavior in a more naturalistic manner, a step toward seeing the data in a different light.

How the brain became a successor to mind has been punctiliously chronicled by Kantor (1969, pp. 247ff.). He reports extensively on the burgeoning of the biological sciences during the nineteenth century. Prominent stars of the era were Pasteur, Darwin, and Mendel, but countless others contributed to histology, physiology, embryology, bacteriology, and still other branches of the science of living things.

Of special interest to us is the influence of the series of new biological findings on the emerging science of psychology. First, we need to note the spread of French and German materialism during the eighteenth and nineteenth centuries. The recognized elusiveness of mind (spirit) required a solid basis in matter (the body). "Those who accepted the existence of both mind and matter regarded the latter as the external base or cause of sensory awareness or experience" (Kantor, 1969, p. 186). The brilliant work of

Broca, Fritsch, Hitzig, Flourens, Gall, and Spurzheim revealed much about the functioning of the brain. But with what consequences to psychology? The upshot of all this research was to saddle the materialistic brain with the functions of the immaterial mind. Thus was the brain made successor to the less scientifically palatable mind. And that's the way it has been ever since: soul → mind → brain.

For Further Reading

Kantor, J. R. (1969). *The scientific evolution of psychology.* Vol 2. Chicago: Principia Press.

SPACE-TIME: AN ACROSS-THE-BOARD VIEW

What then is time? If no one asks me, I know; if I wish to explain to one that asketh, I know not.

Saint Augustine

Time looked at from a distance seems so familiar and obvious; viewed more closely, it becomes a complete stranger. Our purpose is not to solve such profound problems as are attacked by Fraser (1975), Smart (1964), and Whitrow (1961). Our modest objective is to achieve such a view of time as will advance our understanding of behavior. As a starter, we adopt an overall view from different perspectives.

A homely illustration of time as an integral aspect of events can be seen in the instant replay (in slow motion) on the television screen. In such cases, note that only one variable, the temporal factor, has been changed, with radical consequences to the pattern of movements displayed. As another example, note that astronauts don't walk with the same tempo on the moon as on the earth. In that case, a gravitational difference produces a difference in the temporal aspect of the pattern of locomotion giving it a distinctive form. Indulging in a bit of science-fiction speculation, continued space exploration may reveal that gravitational differences on different planets might yield still greater variation in the walking, running, dancing, and work movements of future cosmonauts. If and when such a time comes, gravitation will have to be included "in" events. It has been easy to overlook it because of its relative constancy on our planet.

Coming back to earth, more radical behavioral consequences can be demonstrated by simply speeding up the motion-picture projector. By changing only the time variable, we can manufacture farce of the Mack Sennett comedy variety. Imagine how a motion-picture projection of a tragic funeral can be profaned by a simple manipulation of the temporal variable alone.

Further examples can be found in the auditory sphere. For example, time is the very nature of music. Remove time from music and you have killed it, but less radical time alterations can also produce startling changes. For a convincing demonstration, let the reader take a Beethoven sonata record (recorded at 33⅓ rpm.) and play it at 78 rpm. The effect is ludicrous. Now, take a whistle of a constant pitch and sound it for a period of one minute.

With both whistle and responding organism in fixed position in relation to each other, the organism reports an *unchanged* pitch of the whistle. Now, let the organism stay put but sound the whistle at a constant pitch on a vehicle traveling at a fairly fast speed past the organism. This time the observer reports a higher pitch at the approach of the vehicle and a lower pitch as it moves away. By simply manipulating the spatial and the temporal variables in the situation, we get different results than we did before. Thus, space and time are "in," or are phases of, events labeled as pitch discrimination. Such events have traditionally been known as the Doppler effect. A similar shift (from red to blue) occurs when a light source moves toward an observer. Therefore, we may say that space and time are also involved "in" the discrimination of a source of light. But because in everyday situations things and people mostly "stay put" in relation to each other, space and time as aspects of events are easily overlooked.

For Further Reading

Smart, J. J. C. (Ed.). (1964). *Problems of space and time.* New York: Macmillan.
Whitrow, G. (1961). *The natural philosophy of time.* New York: Harper & Row.

SPACE-TIME IN BIOLOGY

While much of biological inquiry ignores the spatial-temporal aspects of the data that it deals with, not all biologists' work should be so characterized. J. H. Woodger is such an exception. As an example of his uncommon theoretical stand, let us note how he thinks of the heart. But first, by contrast, most people think of the heart, after it is dissected out of the cadaver, as the epitome of concreteness. The medical student, particularly, feels that here, at last, is something solid that one can grasp, measure, weigh, and so on.

For J. H. Woodger (1929, pp. 328-329), the pickled heart in the museum jar is a totally *abstract object*. If an anatomist should apply the term *structure* to such a specimen, Woodger would argue that *structure* can properly apply only to certain limited aspects of the heart abstracted out of its temporal dimension. However, as observed during its biological career in the living organism, the heart has an exciting and complex history. But the dead heart has "only a tame history as a uniform physical object" (p. 328).

When the heart is alive and functioning, pumping action reveals highly dynamic and variable changes in structure. That's because we have included the necessary spatial-temporal aspects of the events before us. Now, we note the variability in the dynamic ongoing sequence of events as a function of increased or decreased physical exertion on the part of the organism, threatening or frightening psychological conditions, and so on.

Here's the important implication of our analysis of (1) the pickled heart and (2) the throbbing, pulsating, ever-changing heart in the living individual. We won't go wrong if we realize that abstraction is necessary in all the sciences. However, if we make the mistake of treating the pickled organ as somehow more basic or "real" than the living one, then we have fallen into the "fallacy of misplaced concreteness" (Woodger, 1929, p. 329). We have exalted the purely spatial aspect of the dead organ, abstracted from its temporal dimension, to a higher status than the heart considered as "something going on" in a four-dimensional framework.

There is a side effect of the "fallacy of misplaced concreteness." This fallacy may beget yet another fallacy, namely that of "structure *versus* function." If we mistake what anatomy teaches for the concrete four-dimensional event of the living, pulsating heart, then we get into the insoluble problems of structure *versus* function. Woodger (1929, p. 329) suggests that "there is no such antithesis in nature. The antithesis springs solely from our modes of apprehension and from the separation of space and time."

What Woodger (1929, p. 330) urges us to do is to give up our Newtonian notion of structure as a merely spatial entity, as something over against function, another entity. This way of thinking is elementalistic. No longer need we be trapped into conceiving of nature as lumps of matter set into action by forces. It is possible to think of nature in terms of process, something going on, with structure as an aspect of an ongoing event. Verbally, but only verbally, we can isolate structure, but the living organism is a spatiotemporal structure, and this spatiotemporal structure is the activity itself. Furthermore, temporal characteristics are as important a feature of the living organism as its spatial aspects.

Woodger's heart illustration provides us with an impressive paradigm of biological inquiry conducted under the auspices of a fully recognized space-time framework. At the same time, it reveals the pitfalls of alternative procedures that fail to recognize the spatiotemporal aspects of biological events. It should be apparent that the model provided by the heart as we have analyzed it herein is also applicable to other types of biological investigation.

Paul Weiss, a cytologist with a distinguished research career in developmental biology and neurobiology, has taken a clear stand on the role of space-time in biological investigation. In an article with the eloquent title "A Cell Is Not an Island Entire of Itself," Weiss (1965, p. 182) criticizes the conventional, self-actional view of the cell as manifested in such quotations as "'the cell does,' 'the cell acts,' 'the cell controls,' envisaging Lilliputian homunculi endowed with powers of will, decision and authority."

Continuing his disapproval of the prevailing notion of the cell as if an independent entity, Weiss explains that cytology was, for a long time, dominated by the microscopic study of fixed and stained (i.e., dead) cells. But the visual appearance of such dead cells no more advanced understanding of the living cell than the ruins of an ancient city illuminate the life style of its inhabitants. *"Life is a process in time. No static image can reflect that time dimension"* (Weiss, 1965, p. 183, [emphasis added]).

Another biologist, a cytologist, who appreciated the need for incorporating the spatiotemporal aspects of biological events was Alexis Carrel. Over a half-century ago, Carrel (1931, p. 297) criticized his colleagues' handling of cells and tissues "abstracted from both space and time. In fact, they [cells and tissues] have been stripped of their reality." He might have said that cells and tissues studied as in fixed slides in a Newtonian framework "at an instant," are as meaningless as a single chord ripped out of the context of a Mozart piano concerto. He considered a tissue as a durational affair that changes from moment to moment. He saw time as a fourth dimension of living things. *"Cell colonies, or organs, are events which progressively unfold themselves. They must be studied like history"* (Carrel, 1931, p. 298, emphasis added).

For Further Reading

Carrel, A. (1931). The new cytology. *Science, 73*, 297-302.
Weiss, P. A. (1969). The living system: Determination stratified. *Studium Generale, 22*, 361-400.

SPACE-TIME IN PHILOSOPHY

Down through the ages, philosophers have pondered over space and time. Passing over traditional notions, we restrict our consideration of space and time to their formulation by the philosopher Alfred North Whitehead, who is closer to our own time.

With his down-to-earth orientation, Whitehead always starts with that which he encounters in nature, namely events. Events have durational and extensional aspects to them, that is, they occur *somewhere* and they *take time*; they are not instantaneous. As regards time, Whitehead (1957, pp. 65-66) suggests that we must decide whether, à la Newton, we are going to consider time as having an independent existence prior to nature or whether time (along with space) is to be found in nature as an aspect of ongoing events. To assume that time is absolute and prior to nature is to raise metaphysical questions beyond the scope of our enterprise.

It is not a risky venture to guess that Whitehead's characterization of time applies to space as well. His succinct statement on this point augments our remarks on space and time from a philosophical standpoint. "There can be no time apart from space; and no space apart from time; and no space and no time apart from the passage of the events of nature. The isolation of an entity in thought, when we think of it as a bare 'it,' has no counterpart in any corresponding isolation in nature" (Whitehead, 1957, p. 142). As Lawrence (1974, p. 33) puts it, "It is nearer the truth to say that space and time are 'in' events rather than that events are 'in' space and time." In our practical, everyday life, we may extract from the continuity of events an abstract space and time which we are at liberty, *in thought*, and by yardsticks and clocks, to carve up without limit, but the flow of natural events will not stand still so as to be dissected.

But no one has stated the matter more succinctly than Whitehead (1957, p. 66) in the following single sentence: *"There is time because there are happenings, and apart from happenings there is nothing"* (emphasis added). The same statement holds for space.

For Further Reading

Lawrence, N. (1974). *Alfred North Whitehead: A primer of his philosophy.* New York: Twayne Publishers.

Whitehead, A. N. (1957). *The concept of nature.* Ann Arbor: University of Michigan Press. (Original work published 1920)

SPACE-TIME IN PHYSICS

NEWTON'S VIEW

According to Newton (cited in Smart, 1964, p. 81), "Absolute space, in its own nature, without relation to anything external, remains always similar and immovable," and "Absolute, true, and mathematical time, of itself, and from its own nature, flows equably and without relation to anything external." Thus was born the commonsense notion of space as a container or receptacle for the world's furniture. And all changes in the physical world were described in terms of the separate dimension time. Material particles, small, solid, and indestructible, made up those elements of Newton's world. His dedicated mission was to determine precise laws that described the "force" acting between the material particles. Because Newton considered space and time as prior to, and independent of, the natural world, he concentrated all his attention on matter. It has been about three-hundred years since Newton did his work, but even today, most people consider space and time to be as real as matter. Since psychologists are children of their culture, they too absorb the prevailing Newtonian space-time framework; thus was the stage set for an interactional procedure for behavioral inquiry still extant today.

RELATIVITY VIEW

We have seen that the space of classical physics was an absolute three-dimensional space, independent of the matter contained therein, but dependent on the laws of Euclidean geometry. Time was a separate entity flowing at an even rate independent of the material world. Scientists and philosophers held this paradigm to be an inviolable and inherent property of the universe, until Einstein came along and changed all that.

Einstein was able to convince scientists and philosophers that rather than being inherent in nature, Euclidean geometry was a human invention imposed on nature. Only then were physicists free to develop a theory about space and time based on observations of nature and in conformity with those observations. The new view was based on the discovery that spatial and temporal specifications of events were no longer absolute but were relative and dependent on the observer. The union of space and time was announced in Minkowski's (1964, p. 297) electrifying statement to German natural scientists and physicians at Cologne in 1908.

The views of space and time which I wish to lay before you have sprung from the soil of experimental physics, and therein lies their strength. They are radical. Henceforth, space by itself, and time by itself, are doomed to fade away into mere shadows, and only a kind of union of the two will preserve an independent reality.

If we could look around with a fresh glance, we would perceive that "every object is related to every other object . . . not only spatially, but temporally. . . . As a fact of pure experience, there is no space without time, no time without space; they are interpenetrating" (Suzuki, 1959, p. 33). Such a statement contrasts the relativity view of a cohesiveness or unity in nature with the Newtonian fragmented view, which saw only (1) discrete material particles and (2) forces acting between them, all set in absolute space and absolute time, also as separate entities. This scanty account of Einsteinian space-time is intended to make only one significant point, namely, that when physicists found one way of handling space-time inadequate, they didn't persist in sticking with it because of sacred tradition. They showed flexibility in their approach and tried another way, and they found that it worked better. Mainstream psychology has taken Newton's space and time for granted without questioning its suitability for behavioral investigation.

For Further Reading

Smart, J. J. C. (Ed.). (1964). *Problems of space and time*. New York: Macmillan.

SPACE-TIME IN PSYCHOLOGY

> Behavior is serial, not mere succession. It can be resolved—it must be—into discrete acts, but no act can be understood apart from the series to which it belongs.
>
> Dewey (1930, p. 412)

The preceding statement of John Dewey's shows that, over a half-century ago, he was groping toward a spatiotemporal framework for behavioral inquiry. In his statement, he reveals an appreciation of the sequential nature of behavior by his attack on the traditional notion of the stimulus. Ordinarily, stimuli and their correlated responses have been treated as independent units. But, according to Dewey, these take their meaning only within the context of ongoing behavior.

Had Z. Y. Kuo been a contemporary of Dewey's he could have buttressed Dewey's argument with such statements of his as the following (Kuo, 1967, p. 27):

The importance of developmental history on behavior cannot be over-stressed. Indeed, I often wonder whether we gain much knowledge about an animal's behavior if we merely subject the animal to a laboratory experiment or observe its movements in the field without being familiar with how and under what conditions it has been reared.

The danger of dealing with behavior as fragmented, independent S-R units, is clearly expressed in Kuo's comment. Kuo elaborates on this point in his further observations on what psychologists once called an "aggressive instinct." For example, he painstakingly studied one dog, Bobby, over a span of time and found that Bobby's aggressive behavior was a complex affair, contingent upon numerous variables. For example, whether or not Bobby would attack another dog in his daily peregrinations was a function of the following factors:

a. Whether or not Bobby was well fed.
b. Whether the temperature was hot or cold.
c. Whether or not Bobby had already been in a fight.
d. Whether or not the other dog was aggressive.

e. Whether or not the other dog fell on his back.

f. Whether or not other friendly dogs attacked the other dog.

g. Whether or not the other dog had defeated Bobby as a pup.

h. Whether or not the other dog was a female in heat.

As an aside, the specificity of behavior—or, stated otherwise, the importance of setting factors—looms conspicuously in Kuo's inventory. Even more so, perhaps his list shows the need for taking the historical dimension into account in understanding behavior, for it reveals that what happens at a certain point in the behavioral stream is a function of what happened, or did not happen, at an earlier point. Both Dewey and Kuo argue for the preservation of the essential integrity of the durational aspects of behavior. Assuming that the skeptical reader accepts the proposition that behavior "takes time," we move on to a consideration of instantaneity. What is the relationship between duration and the instantaneous?

Webster's Ninth New Collegiate Dictionary defines *instantaneous* as "done, occurring, or acting without any perceptible duration of time." The question is: Can anything happen "in no time flat," as the saying goes? For example, can John, in a rage over an insult, rise to his feet *instantly*, ready to attack? Or does his act of rising to his feet (as fast as it might be) take time? What is *instantaneity*? Let us have a look at photography. Electronic flash lasting 1/1,000 second can adequately freeze most action being photographed. But a high-speed flash of 1/50,000 second will arrest the action of a drop of milk falling onto a glass plate, water running out of a faucet, or the flight of a pigeon. However, stroboscopic photography deals with flashes of 1/1,000,000 seconds at a rate of 100 flashes per second producing, for example, a multiple-exposure motion study of a golf swing (Carraher and Chartier, 1980, pp. 155-157). Human vision is incapable of "stopping" such action. As fast as the speeds encountered in high-speed flash photography, they can't compare to the time intervals with which computer technology measures its events. Here, we encounter such useful units as *nanoseconds* or one billionth of a second, and *picoseconds*, one trillionth of a second. Recently, IBM researchers invented a machine that delivers the "World's Shortest Light Pulse" (1985). The unit of measure for the light pulse is 12 *femtoseconds* or 12×10^{-15} seconds. As brief a time as such events take, they do not happen "in no time flat" or instantaneously. More than six decades ago, Bentley (1926, p. 38) realized that, in physics, a science that deals with high speeds more than any other science, nothing happens instantaneously. Even the electrons, in their mad whirl about their atomic orbits, "take their time," brief as it may be. It appears, then, that duration is built into the very warp and woof of occurrences, and that nothing happens instantaneously.

With this synopsis of the preceding argument, we are ready to consider the manner in which time and space are treated in mainstream psychology. Let us deal with the spatial aspect first; this procedure is permissible on account of traditional psychology's splitting of space and time.

TRADITIONAL PSYCHOLOGY'S TREATMENT OF SPACE

If you think about it, you will observe that, ordinarily, we have no trouble localizing (i.e., assigning a definite place to) objects or happenings in our environment. We say, "It's on the top shelf," or "in the middle drawer," or "the accident occurred at Twenty-first and Broadway." What can we say about the locus of the mind? Only that which we have been trained to say, which is, "It's in my head." To which the proper retort is, "Yes, but *exactly* where? Show us the very spot."

Both recent and more remote studies have shown little hope for locating the mind in the brain. Recently, some cognitivists (Haber, 1983, pp. 2-3) have searched for an "information-processing center" in the brain, the retina, the neural units subserving the photoreceptors, or the photoreceptors themselves. Others are ready to give up the search. In their survey *Brain Damage and Recovery*, Finger and Stein (1982, p. 6) pose the following question:

After almost 200 years of making lesions to specify the "organs of the mind," one might ask why there is so much confusion, so little agreement, and why such limited progress has been made.

They suggest (in a paraphrase) that we may have been "barking up the wrong tree" and that maybe a new paradigm is called for. Such contradictions are not new. Almost a half-century ago, a celebrated American neurosurgeon, Harvey Cushing, who operated on hundreds of brains, declared:

Being obliged because of his hazardous tasks to keep his feet on the ground, the neurosurgeon is very much puzzled about the mind, which in all of his exploring he has never been able to locate, much less feel or see even in the left hemisphere where it is reported to abide (Cushing, 1940, p. 181).

In a review of attempts to find a locus or place of residence for the mind, I call attention to Wilder Penfield's work *The Mystery of the Mind*. After a lifetime devoted to neurosurgery, Penfield (1975, p. x) declares that some philosophers would charge that "since the mind cannot, by its very nature, have a position in space, there is only one phenomenon to be considered, namely, the brain." After conceding that the mind is transspatial, Penfield (1975, p. xiii) confesses, "I, like other scientists, have struggled to prove that the brain accounts for the mind. . . . [But] the nature of the mind remains, still, a mystery that science has not solved." After two-hundred years! Instead of trying another paradigm to guide research, Penfield expresses the belief that "it is . . . a mystery that science will solve some day" (p. xiii). Hope springs eternal in the human breast.

Bentley (1954, p. 50) makes a significant contribution to behavioral space-time with his notion of *pseudolocalization,* which applies particularly in attempts to find a site for the mind. It is an astounding actuality, if you give it any thought, that the nonspatial mind's alleged residence in a space-occupying brain has been accepted for centuries as if it were an established fact. And, yet it is only a far-fetched assumption, which, it is hoped, will be somehow cleared up when "the spatial fog clears up." Well, the spatial fog has not cleared up even after two-hundred years! Perhaps the assumption guiding such a prodigious search might be exchanged for another assumption, one that will be explored after we conclude our examination of mainstream psychology's handling of time, our next undertaking.

TRADITIONAL PSYCHOLOGY'S TREATMENT OF TIME

In announcing the next piece of music, Mendelssohn's Octet, the radio commentator divulges that Mendelssohn composed this piece of music at the age of seventeen. Most listeners react with traditional astonishment and disbelief at such an outstanding accomplishment at so young an age. Here is an application of a calendar measuring rod to a psychological development, a measuring rod that is more suited for such matters as determining the age of the earth's rock strata. It is not the mere passage of time that explains any behavioral achievement, but what happens during that passage of time. Misapplying a Newtonian scale to such achievements as those of Mendelssohn leads only to mystification, not understanding.

A behavioral time scale would take into account the specific historical details of Mendelssohn's musical development. One of his biographers furnishes a hint or two of the factors that need to be searched out in monumental detail in order to understand Mendelssohn's achievement. Here they are: "Since Mozart's childhood, no young man's head had been so crammed with music" (Jacob, 1963, p. 54) and "Composing was a responsible kind of work. It was far more difficult than writing" (Jacob, 1963, p. 56). Since biographies are not written from a truly psychological standpoint, we have only such scraps of helpful information as have been noted. Only a radical change of paradigms will sensitize biographers to gather details that fit into a behavioral continuum. (For the results of such an approach see GENIUS, GIFT, TALENT, etc.).

A NEW NOTE IS SOUNDED

Donald Baer of the University of Kansas comes to my support at this point with his felicitous phrase "An Age-Irrelevant Concept of Development" (Baer, 1970). Baer indicates that his work in child development has not included age as an independent variable, and yet he feels that his work belongs in the area of child development. He refers to a study in which four-year-olds could learn to make right-left discriminations, which seven-year-olds "normally" make under a traditional calendar schedule. Quoting another study, Baer (1970, p. 243) states, "a behavior change over time was unsatisfyingly mysterious to me. I wanted to know the *process* which produced the change, not just its outcome or its typical calendar schedule." The important point that he makes is that the results of a learning procedure are determined by its introduction at the proper point in the entire behavioral sequence. "The 'right time' was not an age, but a point in a sequence of experiences" (Baer, 1970, p. 243). In his statement, Baer approximates a behavioral space-time framework in his abandonment of the traditional Newtonian clock and calendar times useful for other purposes. Traditionally, it is the calendar that determines children's entrance into the first grade at the age of six, regardless of their reactional biography. This is contrary to the implication of Baer's view.

Baer's significant insight leads us to a consideration of our next weighty question: If the use of a Newtonian space-time framework is unsatisfactory, what kind of substitute construct will advance psychological inquiry? But before we get into the matter of erecting a new structure, it would be well to clear away the deadwood, and so we proceed to that task.

In his book *Relativity in Man and Society*, Bentley (1926, pp. v-vi) properly warns us against the many misconceptions from everyday life that follow us into our scientific work without realizing that they affect its outcome. To illustrate this point, here is Dewey's pertinent confession; this is the noted philosopher John Dewey at the age of eighty-four, after a previous lifetime of discussing and thinking about such matters as have concerned us here. In a letter to Bentley, he writes, "You have finally got through my skull the necessity of sufficiently extensive durational-spatial events to describe anything scientifically" (Ratner, Altman & Wheeler, 1964, p. 153).

As for the rest of us, it is well-nigh impossible for us to recognize how many false notions today influence our ways of thinking about things. One hint comes from the misconceptions that handicapped our predecessors. For example, the earth "used to be flat." A cartoonist makes the point, in a facetious manner, in a sketch of Queen Isabella and Columbus at the wharf discussing matters before his departure for the Indies. The queen suggests sailing only one ship over the Westward Sea. Why risk three vessels going "over the edge"? It must have been difficult for our progenitors to get accustomed to thinking about the earth as round, that we are not at the center of the universe, that air has weight, and so on, and on. But all this raises the question: What false "knowledge" hinders us from seeing things more clearly? I nominate the following as candidates for possible rejection in building a more adequate space-time construct as a guide for psychological investigation. Is it not always prudent to clear away the deadwood before erecting a new structure?

THE DEADWOOD

The elaboration of a behavioral space-time framework requires confrontation with the following propositions and a response to them.

1. Exclusion of all such entities as "organisms," "bodies," "minds," "actors," "acts," "objects," "environments," and so on where each is isolated and apart from each other, each "doing its thing" alone, but which must be somehow glued together again.
2. Rejection of the mechanistic characterization of "bodies" or "minds" and their correlative "objects" viewed in a cause-effect relationship after the Newtonian paradigm of bits of "matter" and "force."
3. Rejection of the practice of fragmenting the continuity of the "behavioral stream" into as-if, independent, separate elements, such as S-R units.
4. Abandonment of the notion of instantaneity or an alleged series of such, and acceptance of duration as an integral aspect of events.
5. Recognition and repudiation of the quasi localization or pseudolocalization of presumed "mental states," "functions," or "encoding" and "storage processes."
6. Repudiation of clock time and the calendar as the standard for behavioral research.
7. Disavowing of such Newtonian space scissoring of psychological happenings as would refer their spaces to the brain or parts thereof, or to the organism's skin as boundary, or to the "whole organism," when stress is on the whole organism's gross body movements.

WHY NOT ADOPT RELATIVITY PHYSICS SPACE-TIME?

In considering a space-time framework for psychology, one might be tempted to ask: If modern physics has evolved a space-time construct superior to Newton's space and time, why not adopt it as a guide for psychological investigation? This is why not. Newton's construct of absolute space and absolute time worked for him in his handling of matter and motion. But it did not work with Newton's successors in their investigation of electromagnetic phenomena, light and radiation, and subatomic research. Here is where the contributions of Einstein and company came to the rescue; they developed a theory, including a way of handling space-time, that worked. But why should we expect a construct evolved from the investigation of gravity, cosmic rays, light, and nuclear phenomena to be lifted and transferred, totally or in part, toward the investigation of such events as speaking, learning, remembering, seeing, hearing, and all the rest? The clear implication is that psychologists must derive their theories, not by borrowing from the physicist, or, for that matter, from the physiologist or anatomist, but by observing speaking, learning, remembering, seeing, hearing, and all the rest of their own distinctive data.

TOWARD A BEHAVIORAL SPACE-TIME FRAMEWORK

As a springboard for our consideration of a space-time construct for psychology, let us start by examining Figure 12. I am going to assume that you are one of the people for whom the illustration is, at first glance, an amorphous blob. Keep looking at it until, at some point, you exclaim, in surprise, that you see "a cow." You may even volunteer a description of the cow, explaining that the cow is staring straight at you, the right side of her head in deep shadow, with four black spots on an otherwise white flank. There is a fence on the left side of the picture and trees in the background above the cow. Let us assume that, for you, the former meaningless blob is now "very much a cow," no doubt about it.

Six months later, we meet again. I show you the onetime meaningless blob, and at once you recognize the cow in all its cow-ity, just as you finally did six months earlier. We establish that you have not seen it in the interim. The episode provides us with an appropriate behavioral specimen that will permit us to apply both a Newtonian and a non-Newtonian space-time framework.

A TRADITIONAL NEWTONIAN CONSTRUCT

Reduced to its essentials, the cognitivist's approach would explain your *second* encounter with the cow as the result of imaginary events in your brain/mind that had occurred upon your *first* encounter with it six months previously. And what are these events? According to Wessells (1982, p. 36), "both computers and people may be thought of as processing systems that encode, store, retrieve, and manipulate information." In other words, what permitted you to recognize the cow after six months was the result of what had been "encoded, stored, and retrieved" six months previously. The brain/mind, by means of "images" or "icons," kept the original impression of "cow" alive *continuously, moment by moment,* until six months later. The use of the clock and calendar time should be apparent.

A NON-NEWTONIAN APPROACH

An alternative to the Newtonian approach is simplicity itself. The fact is that you did perceive a cow in the figure six months ago and that's why you

Figure 12. What do you see? If at first glance you see only a meaningless blob, keep looking until another discriminative response emerges: a cow. To help developments, on the left side of the illustration, look for the head of a cow looking straight at you with large black ears, black eyes, and her muzzle partly in deep shadow. Her left flank is white with scattered black spots on it.

discriminate it at once later. In accordance with the principle that present events are a function of antecedent events, had you not had previous contact with it, you would have had to undergo, essentially, the earlier experience. In simple terms, you saw the cow on a later occasion "because" you had seen it earlier.

At this point, the reader accustomed to a Newtonian framework may remonstrate, "But don't you require a brain 'trace' or 'engram' to carry the cow response forward from the earlier to the later experience?" The response to that question is, "Not if you adopt a field paradigm to work with. If you arrange the complex of factors that worked on the first occasion, you get the same event on the second occasion. Just as when it rains, it rains because the same factors (moisture in the clouds, temperature, pressure, and so on) come together as they did on a previous occasion when it rained. No need to ask, where is the rain when it isn't raining; likewise, no need to ask, where is my cow response in between my separate responses to the figure at intervals of clock time?" (Here is a serviceable use of clock time.)

In dealing with gravitation and light, for example, Newtonian physicists hypothesized an intermediary ether that explained "action at a distance." Modern physics has learned to do without that fictitious entity. Mainstream psychology's "ether" is the "engram" and "storage" of "images" and "icons," purely imaginary entities.

H. A. Rachlin (1977, pp. 373-374) has grasped the notion of connecting events with one another without any intermediaries. The following quotation expresses his clear stand on this point.

If a subject in an experiment is instructed on Day 1 to make response X on Day 2, the cause of response X when it is observed need not be attributed to anything inside the subject's head, but directly to events on the previous day. There is nothing logically wrong with supposing that events on Day 1 directly cause events on Day 2 without supposing a chain of intermediary events (in the mind or the nervous system or elsewhere).

It takes some reorientation for those accustomed to imaginary brain or mind events to handle the continuity between Day 1 and Day 2. Rachlin (1977, pp. 373-374) draws a parallel between such theorists and physicists of the nineteenth century. Here is his statement:

When Faraday first suggested that physical forces could act at a distance, the response of other physicists was to infer a series of imaginary hooks bridging the gap between a magnet and an iron filing. But, as time has gone on, the notion of action at a spatial distance has come to be generally accepted without the intermediary hooks. Similarly, action at a temporal distance ought to be accepted without the intermediary . . . neural circuits or cognitions that are usually invoked to bridge the gap.

In his discussion of models and metaphors of memory, Marr (1983, p. 13) draws a parallel between classical physics's handling of action with its invention of an all-pervading ether and cognitive psychology's "search for an understanding of the structure and mechanics of the mental aether. . . . Psychology has been replete with mental aethers that mediate between stimuli and responses." Apparently, at least some psychologists are ready for a paradigm change.

ARE ALL INFERENCES EQUALLY PROPER?

In connection with the highly inferential entities proposed by cognitive and other types of psychologists, the question of the propriety of inference is likely to arise at this point. Isn't an inference an inference? Aren't all inferences on the same level? Not at all. An inference about an *imaginary, unobservable* entity is not on a par with the inference that, because you saw a cow readily in the figure referred to above, you must have been in contact with it on a prior occasion. The latter inference concerns an observ*able* event, even though at the moment it is not here and now observable. It *can be* verified; "icons" and "images" have not been supported, because they are unobservable.

We must draw a lengthy discourse to a close with a few brief observations.

1. Regarding the cow figure, here's a point that shows the irrelevance of clock time for behavioral inquiry. It really doesn't make any difference, does it, whether the interval between the two episodes with the cow is one month, five months, or five minutes? The important point is that the two episodes be viewed jointly together in order to be understood.

2. Romeo and Juliet can carry on a conversation, even without being visible to each other, separated only by the thickness of the wall between them. But they can have just as intimate a conversation in continuance of their love affair with Romeo in Hong Kong on a business trip and Juliet left behind in Verona. Their interaction can surmount the span of thousands of miles that separates them as effectively as the wall between their family estates, this time facilitated by international telephone. In this instance, space measured in units of meters, feet, or miles makes no psychological sense.

3. Can you recall some childhood event? Everybody does. Here we have a behavioral event that may span vast stretches of space and time, as viewed in everyday matters. The span of time involved may range over twenty, thirty, forty, or more years, that is, clock or calendar time, and thousands of miles or, for that matter, within the same family home, as in reminiscence. A behavioral space-time, derived from observing behavioral events themselves and not by superimposition of Newtonian space-time, is not at all embarrassed by such events. It views the event reminisced and the act of reminiscing as linked together by means of a substitute stimulus (an old letter, old photo, and so on), simply in accordance with the principle that present events are a function of antecedent events. The job can be done without any "hooks."

Much more can be said, but this much must serve as an introduction to this fascinating topic.

For Further Reading

Bentley, A. F. (1954). *Inquiry into inquiries.* Boston: Beacon Press.

Kuo, Z. Y. (1967). *The dynamics of behavior development.* New York: Random House.

SPECIFICITY, PRINCIPLE OF

"What makes people murder, rape, or embezzle corporate funds?" Such questions are likely to be tossed at psychologists by students or lay persons who expect a clear and definite answer. The unskeptical psychologists who happen to walk into such a trap extemporize an answer to the best of their ability. Skeptical psychologists would answer somewhat as follows: "You will not find anywhere in psychology any general statement that would explain all murders, rapes, or embezzlements taken collectively or separately. In simplistic terms, we would find that people engage in such activities 'for various reasons.' It seems appropriate to say that each case is a law unto itself. If you want to know the planets of the sun in any thorough fashion, you will have to focus on them individually, for each is unique. And this brings us to the principle of specificity."

According to the principle of specificity (Kantor, 1978), scientific investigation requires the observation of specific, concrete events in their full richness of detail. For example, instead of grappling with murder in general, we are content to try to understand Jane Smith's murder of her husband John, that is, a particular case of murder, by direct observation of it in relation to surrounding circumstances. The term *events* signifies that we are not concerned with the class of murderers, but specifically with each *individual's* concrete activities subsumed under the term *murder*. In an expanded sense, we should be reminded occasionally that psychology does not study *people* but the *activities* in which we find them engaged under specific conditions.

There are certain advantages accruing to research under the guidance of the specificity principle. It encourages us to search out the interrelationships among the components of events, analysis of which yields understanding. For example, our understanding of the role of the various factors involved in a conditioning experiment permits us to bring those variables together so as to "repeat" an event. We can make it happen again.

If inquiry conducted under the specificity principle permits us to "make sense" of psychological events in terms of the interrelationship of observable participating factors, then we have eliminated any need for hypothetical explanatory entities. For example, a number of current psychological textbooks start with such high-level abstractions as "emotion," "personality," "love," and "memory." If we consider memory as a topic, we are told right off that "memory involves the question of how knowledge is encoded, stored, retained and retrieved" (Zimbardo, 1980, p.

159). By failing to consider the specifics of humans actually involved in remembering events, such investigators are free to engage in unrestrained speculation as to imaginary, explanatory entities. In accordance with prevailing models or other analogies, the favorite current one is the computer. Is it necessary to point out that such explanatory entities were not derived from observation but from cultural sources? It should be obvious that such conjectural, and unverifiable, entities are superfluous in investigation pursued under the specificity principle.

There is still another benefit to be derived from a strict observance of the principle of specificity. Its emphasis on observable data sensitizes us to the variability that data may show. It is easy to think of personality as a more or less abiding or enduring entity, whereas personality is a highly dynamic "thing," meaning that the same individual may be involved in a series of behavioral events that seem incompatible or contradictory until we pay attention to changing conditions.

Pronko (1980, p. 211ff.) has pointed out the striking behavioral changes of people under different conditions. It is easy to think of Hitler's henchmen as being "thoroughly evil" and monstrous individuals as verified by the victims of their atrocities in the concentration camps. But could they not be devoted, affectionate husbands and fathers during their off-duty hours at home? Why not? Different specific conditions yield different personality reactions.

THE CASE OF ELDRIDGE CLEAVER

In his book *Soul on Ice,* Eldridge Cleaver (1968) describes his career as a criminal involved in drug dealing and rape and facing charges of attempted murder in a police shootout, after which he fled the country. But in a later book, *Soul on Fire,* Cleaver (1978) tells about his conversion to Christianity and his return to the United States to face imprisonment for his crimes. He has been out on bail, studying and preaching the gospel. The account of Cleaver's personality changes might just as easily have described the behavior of two different biological organisms, but, in this case, they involved the same, legally identifiable individual. If we adhere to the specificity principle, such discoveries do not surprise us. To the contrary, we are aided and abetted in seeking them out, because of our sensitivity to the specific details of the flow of events.

SUMMARY

1. The specificity principle commits us to confine ourselves exclusively to that which we can observe, that is, field events with their complex of relevant factors in system. Such a view offers the advantage of yielding understanding solely in terms of observables.

2. If our procedure results in understanding, then the pursuit of

nonobservable hypothetical entities, as traditionally practiced, is uncalled for. Our theory was derived from observables and is directly referable to observables in a tight fit.

3. Our sensitivity to specifics alerts us to keep an eye on every possible variable that may account for the differences between events, such as the preceding observations on personality demonstrate.

For Further Reading

Pronko, N. H. (1980). *Psychology from the standpoint of an interbehaviorist.* Monterey, Calif.: Brooks/Cole.

THINKING OR
IMPLICIT ACTION

"It's all in your mind." "I can do that problem in my head." "I can see it in my mind's eye." "That situation is mind-boggling." "Won't you change your mind and say yes?" "I'm not a mind reader, you know." "You are going to end up being a mindless person if you don't quit using mind-altering drugs." "That incident blew my mind." "She can't be in her right mind." "A sound mind in a sound body." "In the inner recesses of his mind, he knew better." "I have a mind to go." "Her mind snapped." "You are out of your mind." "The novel was his first brainchild." "It's all in your head." "He lost his head." "Keep that in mind." "I talked off the top of my head."

At the same time that I apologize for the unduly prolonged list of common, everyday expressions in the preceding paragraph, I must explain why I do so. I want to emphasize, with that dreary list, that it is only a small sample of the hundreds of expressions in common usage to refer to thinking or other varieties of implicit action, our present concern.

In addition, my intention is to let the preceding inventory of popular idioms illustrate how such linguistic forms straitjacket our thinking about psychological matters which we come to accept without question. In my opinion, in the absence of research on this point, research which is badly needed, I venture to assert that close to 100 percent of the earth's population (and that includes psychologists) believe that thinking takes place in the brain or in the mind, which is located in the brain. Listen to your radio or television set, or read the newspapers, magazines, or any other literature, and you will find human behavior explained in such terms as are listed in the opening paragraph of this article. My own melancholic opinion is that our entire civilization is so thoroughly saturated with silent assumptions to the effect that thinking occurs within the person's brain or mind that other views have no chance whatsoever of acceptance. The only slim possibility would be a revolution as broad in scope as the Copernican, Darwinian, and Einsteinian revolutions. Who would be so reckless as to wager on such a high-risk enterprise? Just the same, we must not let this handicap inhibit our exploration of alternative views of thinking or implicit action. That task lies before us.

PERCEIVING AS A HALFWAY HOUSE TO IMPLICIT ACTION

In the article PERCEIVING EVENTS, we noted that in any perceptual event, our reaction is not to the thing before us as if we had never seen it or anything like it in our past life. No perceptual event starts from scratch. We are never perceptually innocent simply because present events are a function of antecedent events. The historical connectedness of events is ever present, or, stated otherwise, we need an expanded space-time framework that will connect a present perceptual event with similar prior events as depicted in the illustration of "The Burning Tree" (Figure 12).

As you examine it, what do you make of it? One large tree and a number of smaller ones? Or is there a forest fire in the background illuminating a large number of trees in the foreground? Could the illumination be the result of a flash of lightning? Might it be the representation of a blood circulatory system with a full array of veins and arteries branching into capillaries? How about a portion of a nervous system innervating some tissue? It is actually an infrared aerial photo of a river delta along the California coast. You may say, "Of course!" But what if you had observed this illustration at the age of three, would you have been able to perceive it in the several ways specified above? Obviously not, because perception, according to Kantor (1933, p. 153) is "semi-implicit," a term requiring special attention.

"The Burning Tree" is a suitable illustration for defining the term *semi-implicit*, which may help us here. This term calls attention to the fact that we react to the pattern in that illustration, not only as it is before us, but also in terms of meaningful things in the past which resemble that pattern—lightning, forest fires, and so on.

FROM SEMI-IMPLICIT TO FULLY IMPLICIT

Suppose I should say to you now, "Without looking once more at the illustration of "The Burning Tree,' describe the pattern depicted there as best you can." And you do so; you give a creditable description of it in complete absence of the picture. This is a case of a fully implicit response. In everyday discourse, you carried out your reaction "by thinking about it." Is this an exception to psychology's generally accepted principle "No response without a stimulus?" No, because, in this case, I provided you with a *substitute* stimulus when I requested, "Without looking once more at 'the Burning Tree,' describe the pattern depicted there as best you can" and you did it quite successfully. We must be prepared for a certain detachment observed in behavioral events not to be seen in physiological events such as knee jerks or in physical events such as billiard ball interactions. You can react to events in your past or anticipate that the balloon being blown up is about to burst.

A comparison of perceptual and implicit responses reveals another distinction between them. When you interact with the illustration in front of you, the stimulus object offers a *direct stimulus function* to your perceptual response. But when you respond to the absent stimulus object via my request to "simply think about it," my request has served a *substitute stimulus function*. In other words, my verbal request has substituted for the absent visual stimulus object. It should be apparent that the space-time framework that the acts of recognition, recall, remembering, forgetting, reasoning, and so on demand is different from that found in physiological and physical events.

As elsewhere, we have choices to make in the way we think about thinking or implicit reactions to absent stimulus objects. (1) We may think of such interactions as a kind of "replay" of a kind of "tape recording" laid down on a prior occasion in the person's brain or mind. The space-time framework of this construct is akin to a Newtonian view of space-time. (2) An alternative approach is comparable to action-at-a-distance via an enlarged field embracing a prior perceptual event and the given interaction involving the absent stimulus object but without "hooks" or any other factor to carry the prior response forward in time. The alternative view incorporates a space-time construct compatible with the relativity view of physics but distinctively its own.

For Further Reading

Kantor, J. R., & Smith, N. W. (1975). *The science of psychology: An interbehavioral survey*. Chicago: Principia Press.

TISSUE EXCITATION

The term *tissue excitation* can be an additional serviceable criterion for distinguishing between the subject matter of biology and that of psychology. The most unambiguous illustration of tissue excitation is the muscle-nerve preparation. The student of physiology can learn much about muscle fatigue by excising a frog's leg and attached nerve (the rest of the frog may be discarded). Now, by hanging a weight on the muscle and sending an electrical impulse over the connected nerve repeatedly, such a student can discover how muscles function and how they fatigue. This is sound physiology. Thus, this biological branch of biology can profitably study parts of organisms, systems, or even organs such as a beating heart removed from a turtle.

There is nothing comparable to tissue excitation in psychology. We can't get much out of pieces of an organism but must always start with a complete, preferably intact, organism. There are other features of such reflex responses as the muscle-nerve preparation alluded to. They are highly organized, that is, they are very definite, highly circumscribed acts. They also manifest a certain automaticity in that a certain tap on the patellar tendon causes a heavy leg to rise in the familiar knee jerk. Reflexes are also more or less permanent. Given the same conditions, the leg muscle will always respond in the same way even over decades. It is true that biologists also deal with total organisms when they study such activities as respiration, circulation, digestion, excretion, and reproduction, but surely these functions can't be confused or identified with such psychological action as perceiving, remembering, forgetting, learning, thinking, and so on. For further distinguishing features of psychological events, see the entry under INTERBEHAVIORAL PSYCHOLOGY. At any rate, *tissue excitation* can serve as a handy standard by which to distinguish between physiological and psychological subject matters.

For Further Reading

Pronko, N. H. (1980). *Psychology from the standpoint of an interbehaviorist.* Monterey, Calif.: Brooks/Cole.

TRANSACTION

It is not hard to imagine Dewey and Bentley arguing that, had we not been reared to see things through self-actional or interactional spectacles, we would all view the happenings around us transactionally. If so, then this is what we would not do. We would not, from habit, and prior to observation, isolate organisms and the things or organisms that participated in those happenings. For, once we split them asunder, as separate entities, we would have as leftover ingredients that which happened between them. Our job would be to glue them all together again. Instead of such fragmentation, a transactional view would enable us to see things as whole.

For insight into the meaning of transaction, let us take a business transaction. But before we get into details, we must stress that Dewey and Bentley (1949, p. 104) insist on "unfractured observation," which means seeing the unified totality in the scene before us *first* before analyzing its various aspects. With that admonition before us, we are ready to proceed with our "business deal." On this point, Dewey and Bentley (1949, p. 133) use the analogy of a loan negotiation to illustrate *transaction.* They emphasize that a borrower cannot borrow without a lender to lend and vice versa. They see no other way to handle such a *situation* than one involving a reciprocal relationship between borrower and lender. Behaviorally speaking, each is jointly and mutually involved with the other. Since observation shows this to be so, then we must deal with the whole situation in its integrated totality. That is the meaning of *trans*action, and so we proceed.

Having focused on the lender and borrower, we must be careful not to let them crystallize out as entities or elements, because then we have the "relations" between them as leftovers. If we do that, we create the problem, as with Humpty Dumpty, of getting things together again. To avoid such troubles, we need to stress that we observe not "things" but *action*, a highly dynamic occurrence that is taking place before us. The terms *situation, system,* and *field* may also help us to achieve a transactional view of the event before us. The old ways of imagining something going on within the lender's and borrower's brains or minds must be given up in order to see transactions, which demand abandoning customary ways of seeing for a fresh, new look at happenings.

We need still more help from Dewey and Bentley. For one thing, they insist that, with their broad observational base, everything is open to direct observation. There are no unobservables; the alleged "unobservables" are only the result of too narrow an observational framework, as under self-actional auspices, when the organism is forced to carry too heavy an explanatory burden.

A last example from a somewhat unfamiliar field may facilitate the kind of observational orientation that Dewey and Bentley are recommending. Suppose we look at a photo of a galaxy much like our own Milky Way with a diameter of 100,000 light-years, making one revolution every 210,000,000 years. Figure 13 is such a photo. It would be futile to look for a "controlling center" that sends "messages" to the billions of bodies telling them what to do. It is senseless to try to isolate any "actors" or other components out of the totality to fit a self-actional or interactional framework. We are left with a transactional approach that compels us to deal with the total immensity-in-unity, dealing with whatever phases of the transaction call for treatment, but always with "unfractured observation," just as we find the event.

Our understanding of Dewey and Bentley's distinctive point of view may be further aided by explaining their naturalistic postulate. Let us go about the matter by noting that, at one time, earthquakes, blizzards, hurricanes, and floods were considered "acts of God." Some people still view them as suspensions of natural law as God's warning or punishment. The scientific view is that all the above phenomena as well as others can be understood without appeal to supernatural intervention. When it comes to human behavior, some people also place it *apart from nature*. But Dewey and Bentley operate under the assumption that human achievements, joys, sorrows, knowings, speakings, hearings, desirings, and so on are as natural as gravitation, electricity, storms, volcanoes, and earthquakes. In other words, they consider human behavior *a part of nature*, not outside it. As such, the assumption is that, if studied properly, human behavior will make sense.

Durations and extension are the last notions that we need to explore. For Dewey and Bentley, events have a history, some long and some short, but nothing ever occurs in an instant. This enduring quality of events cannot be "represented adequately and exclusively by such specialized devices as clock-ticks and foot rules" (Dewey and Bentley, 1949, p. 100). Just as physics, since Einstein, worked out its space-time framework, so behavioral inquiry has to elaborate whatever space-time specification is called for for the behaviors under investigation. People have recollections and re-cognitions, which events connect with past events. People also "project" plans and arrange dates which are related to future time. Traditional explanations, relying on a Newtonian space-time framework, interpreted such events by imaginary brain traces. For example, with a Newtonian space-time framework, if you learned a poem as a child and can now recite it, the temporal span between the original learning and the recitation would

Figure 13. The spiral galaxy Messier 81 (NGC 3031). This galaxy with its billions of suns and their planets demands a holistic approach because the entire galaxy operates as a system. There is no possibility of stating that an action *starts* in one spot and affects other spots, as self-actional events allow. We are forced to deal with the total immensity-in-unity with "unfractured observation." (Photo Lick Observatory.)

be carried by the hypothetical brain traces. For further discussion of these points, see the entry SPACE-TIME IN PSYCHOLOGY.

For Further Reading

Dewey, J., & Bentley, A. F. (1949). *Knowing and the known.* Boston: Beacon Press.

TRUTH

Truth is not selected because it is true; it is true because it has been selected.

Attributed to Simmel in a
quotation by Bentley (Ratner,
Altman & Wheeler, 1964, p. 247)

Traditional thinking, opposed by Dewey, has it that the universe possesses a rational or true structure that is waiting to be discovered simply upon human contact with it. The things that make up the universe and their inherent properties are thought to be independent of the fact that humans stumble on to them and come to know them. In other words, they would be eternal verities even if there were no humans. It's as if it had been preordained that everything in the universe should be absolutely true for ever and ever.

According to Dewey, of course, things existed before humans discovered them, but they are only raw materials for knowledge. Only by means of inquiry or indoctrination under recognized or tacit assumptions are they transformed into objects of knowledge.

At this point, one wants to ask, "You seem to be talking about scientific method. What does that have to do with determining what is true?" Dewey would reply, "It has everything to do with truth."

Dewey firmly believed that the very same scientific procedures of careful observation, scrupulous formulation of hypotheses, and thorough experimental testing can advance inquiry into moral and other human problems, just as they advanced the study of physical nature. Dewey's method was a thoroughgoing pragmatic or instrumental and experimental procedure for verifying what was true. Scientists had no difficulties in identifying the true with the verified in scientific settings, but because of traditional beliefs, they could not bring themselves to transfer the same attitudes and procedures to the wider, human situation. Dewey (1949, pp. 128-129) argues persuasively in behalf of such a transfer in the following passage:

If ideas, meanings, conceptions, notions, theories, systems . . . succeed in their office, they are reliable, sound valid, good, true. Confirmation, corroboration, verification lie in works, consequences. . . . That which guides us truly, is true-demonstrated capacity for such guidance is precisely what is meant by truth. . . . The hypothesis that works is the true one; and truth is an abstract noun applied to the collection of cases, actual, foreseen and desired, that receive confirmation in their works and consequences.

As logical as Dewey's argument sounds, one shouldn't expect his definition of truth to make the headlines. The world will probably continue, for a long time to come, to cherish the traditional notion of truth. *Webster's Ninth New Collegiate Dictionary* defines truth in ways more congenial to popular thinking. In it, *truth* is defined as "(1) the state of being the case, (2) the body of *real* things, events and facts, (3) the property (as of a statement) of being in accord with fact or *reality*" (p. 1268, emphasis added).

P.S. Not all philosophers of science aim at finding Truth. Hanson is satisfied at achieving *understanding* of an event. In a clarifying statement, Hanson (1958, p. 94) writes that explanation is reached when events can be related to each other in an intelligible pattern. Hanson's pronouncement is akin to Toulmin's (1963, pp. 85-86) goal of inquiry leading to "rock bottom" and "understanding." Einstein (1954, p. 292) also holds to a modest aim of attaining comprehension via "the production of some sort of order among sense impressions, this order being produced by the creation of general concepts, relations between these concepts, and by definite relations of some kind between the concepts and sense experience."

Apparently, contemporary scientists are willing to settle for much less in their inquiry than everlasting Truths. Even Dewey seems to have lost interest in the use of the antithetical terms "truth-falsity." Several years before he died he wrote Bentley that, while formerly he had fretted about truth and falsity, more recently, he came to the conclusion that those terms were synonymous with "valid-invalid," a less ambitious criterion (Ratner, Altman & Wheeler, 1964, p. 598).

For Further Reading

Dewey, J. (1949). *Reconstruction in philosophy.* New York: New American Library. (Original work published 1920)

THE UNCONSCIOUS

Sigmund Freud is usually considered the "inventor" of the unconscious, and it is he who is usually identified with it. But, as with many other notions, Freud did not start from scratch in developing this aspect of his theory. Gottfried Wilhelm von Leibniz (1646-1716), first, and then Christian von Wolff (1679-1754) developed the notion additively. However, it was Johann Friedrich Herbart (1776-1841) who elaborated the unconscious practically in the form in which Freud (1856-1939) referred to it, including the idea of a "threshold" between the conscious and the unconscious.

More specifically, by the unconscious, Freud (1933, pp. 99-110) means a "mental province" (p. 102) where dwell the instincts, wishes, and strivings that were never conscious, and thoughts and feelings that were conscious at one time, as in infancy, but that had been completely repressed into the unconscious. As an aside, we need to note the pseudolocation of the "province" of the unconscious before we continue.

Of all the compartments of the mental apparatus, for Freud, the most important is the unconscious because our lives are largely ruled by it. In a sense, we do not really live our lives; our lives are lived by the unconscious. The conscious compartment plays a minor role in human behavior, as does reason. According to Freud, it's the instincts and repressed impulses in the unconscious that initiate human behavior. In other words, unconscious motivation explains our slips of the tongue, the pen, the typewriter, our forgetting important anniversaries, and so on. But, according to Freud, we don't recognize the sources of these motives; they are hidden from us.

Now, we come upon a most interesting reference to Freud's (1933, p. 104) reference to space and time in the following passage:

We are astonished to find . . . an exception to the philosopher's assertion that space and time are necessary forms of our mental acts. In the id [unconscious] there is nothing corresponding to the idea of time, no recognition of the passage of time . . . even impressions which have been pushed down into the id [unconscious] by repression, are virtually immortal and are preserved for whole decades as though they had recently occurred.

At this point, we want to ask Freud, "How did you know about the impressions that you claim had been 'preserved for whole decades'?" Surely his answer would be, "By probing into my patient's dreams, past life, and having him or her recall and report a traumatic emotional experience." Let us be charitable and assume that Freud validated such reports by his patients and let us deal with, our main consideration, his space-time framework.

What space-time framework? Freud doesn't have any space-time framework. He simply acknowledges, on a crude datum level, that a certain behavioral event can be connected with another behavioral event that occurred "whole decades" before, and he leaves it at that.

Validated recollections of past events can be handled within a behavioral space-time framework as I have elaborated it in the article on MEMORY. Here, briefly, suffice it to say that the recall of an event, B, in adulthood, of an incident, A, that occurred in childhood, thirty or forty years earlier, can be handled with the fewest assumptions in line with the principle, event B is simply a function of event A. If we put the matter in the form of everyday speech, we may ask: Why did Freud's patient report an incident, B, during analysis? Because an incident, A, occurred in the past. Had such an (authenticated) incident, A, not occurred in the past, incident B would not have occurred either. For who, except in fantasy, recalls incidents that never happened?

NON-FREUDIAN USAGE OF UNCONSCIOUS

There are "no less than 39 distinct meanings of *unconscious*" (English & English, 1958, p. 569). Perhaps that is why it's such a slippery term. But we use it now, in one other way than the Freudian, to tag off, in everyday terms, the following type of behavior: any activity of which the person is unaware. We are unaware of which leg muscles we should contract and which to flex every time we take a step forward in walking. Nor do we attend to all the activities going on within us, our breathing, the circulation of our blood, the normal churning of digestion, or the secretion of the endocrine glands. Even our speech, gestures, and facial expressions go off, as we say, "automatically."

AN OLDER VIEW

How shall we understand such behavior? As usual, there are alternatives. An older theory explained such acts as manifestations of an unconscious mind. But such an explanation offers neither understanding nor any application. Have you gained any insight by being told, "Your unconscious or subconscious mind made you do it?" Also, how can you work with such a purely hypothetical entity as an unconscious or subconscious mind?

A SECOND VIEW

With this approach, we start with the simple and proceed to the complex.

Let us start with my noting that you have a beautiful "Grecian nose." But I can look, via a mirror, at my own nose and declare that it is too large. Next, I hear your stomach gurgle, and I can also hear my own stomach gurgle. Both episodes illustrate the *principle of the self-reaction,* which means that, just as you can serve as a source of stimulation, so can all the aspects of my biological makeup, my size, shape of various portions, defects in complexion, and so on. We need no new principle when we shift from you to me as a source of stimuli.

If we now move on to a consideration of your behavior and mine, again we don't require a new principle. Assume that yesterday you committed an outrageous act. I react to it with shock and amazement. Now, let *me* commit an outrageous act. When I "am myself" once more, I react with shock and amazement at what *I* have done. Psychologically nothing new is necessary to understand my shock to my behavior as compared to my shock to your behavior. The notion of self-reaction suffices.

HOW ABOUT APPLICATIONS?

Suppose we consider such habitual responses as swinging one's leg with crossed legs. There you are swinging your leg rhythmically without knowing that you are doing it. Let us label such action unwitting. Now, at some point, I call your attention to the rhythmical swaying of your appendage. You laugh and stop the action. I caught you "in the act," at which moment your action changed from unwitting to witting. Why? Because, at that instant, you changed from (1) not reacting to your swinging leg to (2) reacting to what was going on, involving your own leg right under your own nose.

Since we're doing a lot of supposing, let's do some more of it. Suppose you get a part in a Broadway play, one that requires you to swing your leg in one scene. There you are in rehearsal. The director asks you to start swinging your leg, now slower, now faster, and you respond appropriately. Your action in this case is not unwitting, because you must constantly monitor your action in accordance with the director's instructions. This is witting behavior. No longer do we need to appeal to imaginary entities such as unconscious or conscious minds ordering action. In simplest terms, our explanation rests on an observable relationship between a given individual's reaction to his/her own action. (A much fuller account is available in the article REACTING TO ONE'S OWN REACTIONS: AN ALTERNATIVE TO INTRO-SPECTION.

Now, we have only one more supposition to make. Imagine this time that you want to stop your chronic habit of leg swinging. How can we do it? Not by appealing to the imaginary unconscious mind. But we can do it by making the unwitting witting. We have you do your leg swinging by prescription. Over and over, we ask you to swing your leg while you monitor your action, eventually bringing it under control, integrating it with the rest of your behavior. At this point, we have made behavior that was unwitting witting. The learning of the correct response by stressing and practicing the wrong response has been called negative practice.

For Further Reading

Kantor, J. R., and Smith, N. W. (1975). *The science of psychology: An inter-behavioral survey.* Chicago: Principia Press.

VALUES AND SCIENCE

According to traditional views, the so-called world of facts belongs to science, but values belong to philosophy. Why? Because, so the reasoning goes, science deals with "reality," with the observable and measurable, with such things as chemical interactions, planetary motions, energy transformations, and living organisms. But according to the prevailing view, values seem to belong to a different realm. They are considered higher, fuzzier, ethereal, transcendental, ultimate, and eternal; therefore, they are assigned to the philosophers to be judged as to whether or not they are properly considered valuable. One looks in vain for "Value(s)" in the index of popular psychology textbooks. "It seems commonplace to encounter behavioral scientists today who maintain either that they *cannot* scientifically investigate the value issue or that they *should not* or simply that they *will not*" (Canning, 1970, p. 61). "Cannot," "should not," "will not": what a baffling statement! And what a tacit implication it carries that value events do, in actuality, exist. Could it be that such events have been improperly identified with their traditional descriptions as insubstantial psychic happenings and, for that reason, should be ignored or abandoned? At any rate, that question urges us to look at humans-in-action to determine if any of their activities warrant the value label.

What does our panoramic view of human behavior reveal? Conspicuous in our survey are the conflicts, even to the point of violence, among various human groups. It's Arab against Christian, but also Muslim against Muslim as in Sunni contra Shiite, Protestant Christian against Catholic Christian as in Ireland, Jew versus Arab, but also Jew against Jew as illustrated by Ethiopian Jew and Israeli Jew, white Afrikaner versus black African, but also black African versus black African. Why this incredible and seemingly nonsensical discord among human groups if it is not due to antithetical nationalistic, religious, humanistic, and other value systems that lead their adherents to self-sacrifice, to war, murder, impoverishment, and suffering? If additional samplings of human valuings are needed, consider the following folk sayings and aphorisms of various individuals.

"Give me liberty or give me death."
"Time is money."
"Taxation without representation is tyranny."
"My country right or wrong."

"I'm the greatest!"
"We are a government of laws and not of men."
"Don't trust anyone over thirty."
"I am a student. Please do not spindle, fold, or mutilate me."
"If you can't stand the heat, stay out of the kitchen."
"Winning isn't everything. It's the only thing."
"The ballot is stronger than the bullet."

It would be an easy task to add hundreds of other statements to the above list, statements that succinctly express a preference of one value over another. What's the point of all this? To show that everyday human life is shot through with reactions of evaluating things, conditions, the behavior of others as well as oneself, and so on. Assuming that that point is established, how is it with science?

Despite a reputation for being obstinately objective, we find that scientists also engage in making evaluations of various sorts. Some would evaluate science and the methods and procedures of science as above other human activities. And the "hard" or "exact" sciences are rated above the "soft" ones. Traditionally, measurement or quantitative procedures are adjudged superior to qualitative ones. Narrowing our view to psychology, we find that, where experimental subjects are concerned, one investigator prefers gerbils or rats above college freshmen, another favors chimpanzees or gorillas under natural conditions, while still another prefers pigeons in a Skinner box. Then there are some who endorse statistics or the nervous system or sensory organs or factor analysis as the ultimate research area. Don't all these *preferences* illustrate evaluative responses? But there's more to come. Canning (1970, p. 64) helps out in calling attention to terms found in the behavioral sciences, whether wittingly or unwittingly used, that parallel value judgments, for example, "mental health," "progress," "well-adjusted personality," "natural state," "self-actualization," "advanced culture," "emotional maturity," "meaningful frame of reference," "creativity," and "highly developed civilization." Assuming the skeptical reader is convinced that neither scientist nor nonscientist can escape making evaluative reactions, let us move on to an attempt at making sense of evaluative behavior.

PSYCHOLOGY OF VALUES

The trouble with the term *value* is that, as commonly used, it is a highly abstract word pointing to no specific referent. The proverbial man or woman from another planet, asking to be shown "earthly values," would be bemused to be told that there are no such entities to be seen on earth. They would have to be instructed that there are only individuals who weigh, appraise, or evaluate things, persons, activities, and so on in certain ways.

Diamonds, gold, platinum, and silver are precious metals, but on an earth without a single human being, obviously, all would be valueless. This brings us to the main point, that while diamonds and the rest are essential for valuing occurrences to happen, equally essential are humans who prize such things. Never one without the other; it is their response that identifies valuing events. The following incident provides a further insight into the psychology of value.

Off the southeast coast of Africa lies the island of Madagascar. The natives, Malagasies, breed a Brahma type of cow with huge, spreading horns and a fat lump on its neck.

If you were to make a count of the number of such cattle, you would find more cows than people, with the cows numbering about 8 million. Immediately, one thinks, "Ah, these cattle are being raised for economic profit." But that is not so. Those cows are not exported, and they are not eaten or milked. Nor do they have any religious significance, as do the sacred cows of India. Well, of what earthly good are they? They are a status symbol, because the more cows a Malagasy owns, the greater the prestige. Should you comment on the foolishness and artificiality of such a custom to a Malagasy citizen, you are likely to be asked (glancing at your huge diamond rings), "Of what earthly use are your diamonds?" (Pronko, 1980, pp. 186-187)

Both cows and diamonds help to make the further point that objects, activities, conditions, or situations, because humans endow them with desirable or esteemed qualities or characteristics, acquire such stimulus functions and operate in that manner thereafter. Leonardo's *The Last Supper*, Michelangelo's Sistine Chapel paintings, education, friendship, wisdom, patriotism, wealth, fame, status, power, and the Purple Heart are some of the myriad "things" that elicit valuing responses from people. One can observe, as Kraft (1981) has, how objects acquire their stimulus functions. Speaking in a statistical sense, Kraft (1981, p. 34) tells us that the first value descriptions of objects such as "nice," "good," "nasty," and "disgusting" appear toward the end of the second year. Terms denoting "good" and "bad" *behavior* appear in the third year, and so on. Thus, we can observe how evaluating interactions and their correlative stimulus functions evolve during the individual's behavioral history.

We advance one step further to show that, just as one can evaluate other things, or other people's behavior, so can one also evaluate one's own behavior (either positively or negatively) via the formulation of the self-reaction. Banks (1970, p. 90) recounts the following charming story of a little boy whose self-evaluation was modified as the result of a single incident involving a sensitive waitress. Banks writes:

I think of a seven-year-old boy who attempted to order lunch in a restaurant. His mother and sister, without consulting him, informed the waitress that he wanted a hamburger. Ignoring the others, the waitress turned to him and said, "Sir, what did you say you wanted?" He replied, "I'll have a hot dog." The sister intervened, "Yes, a hot dog with mustard for Billy." Again, the waitress turned to the boy, "What did you want on the hot dog, son?" "I'll have catsup, please." As the waitress walked away, the boy turned wide-eyed to his family and offered this verdict, "You know, she thinks I'm real!"

We have come a long way from the consideration of values as transcendental, a priori, eternal properties inherent in things to a naturalistic view in which things come to acquire valuable stimulus functions through the person's valuing interactions with them. Incidentally, we have laid bare a valuable source of human evaluating data, data heretofore totally ignored because of faulty assumptions about them.

For Further Reading

Canning, J. W. (Ed.). (1970). *Values in an age of confrontation.* Columbus, Ohio: Charles E. Merrill.
Kraft, V. (1981). *Foundations for a scientific analysis of value.* Dordrecht, Holland: R. Reidel Publishing Co.

WHY? IS WHY A PROPER SCIENTIFIC QUESTION?

Why does water freeze at 32° Fahrenheit and why does it boil at 210° Fahrenheit? Why is chlorine gas a greenish yellow color with a pungent odor? And why, when you combine plumbous chloride with potassium chromate, do you get a yellow precipitate, lead chromate? Why should it be yellow and not red, green or blue? Any why a precipitate? And, while we're at it, why is there light? And why gravity?

In evaluating the authenticity of the series of questions listed above, we turn to Stephen Toulmin's (1963) work *Foresight and Understanding.* In this book, Toulmin offers us an unambiguous answer to such questions. They are all of them inappropriate. Why? Because they are directed at what Toulmin (1963, p. 42) calls "rock bottom." By "rock bottom" Toulmin refers to the condition in which every investigator reaches a point beyond which he cannot go. For example, why is there a universe? One starts with the bare fact that there *is* a universe; that's rock bottom. Why on this planet are there psychological organisms? That, too, is rock bottom or the starting point for any investigation. One can go no further than that. Science is built up on a principle of regularity or natural order in which the fundamental nature of things (such as matter) is accepted as requiring no further explanation. Therefore, there is no need to ask further questions about them. In fact, they are the bedrock or starting point for explaining other things.

We emphasize Toulmin's concept of rock bottom with a striking illustration that he provides for us in discussing Newton's work. Newton established his inverse square law of gravitational attraction with strong observational support, but beyond this point he could not go. "He could demonstrate no mechanism to account for the gravitational interaction [which had to be] accepted as a brute fact" (Toulmin, 1963, p. 85). In other words, he could not answer such a question as was posed at the beginning of this article: Why is there gravity? All he could say is: That's the way it is. "It's the nature of the beast."

In his comprehensive biography of Einstein, Feuer (1974, p. 352) writes as follows:

The history of science has been marked by a series of . . . heroic renunciations—most severe of all was the ascetic abandonment for teleological explanations, the "why" of things, in favor of a modest satisfaction with descriptive uniformities, the "how" of things.

Dewey and Bentley (Ratner, Altman & Wheeler, 1964, p. 644) support Feuer's statement when they point out that the natural sciences made no steady progress until they rejected such questions as why.

Our brief consideration of *Why* as a suitable scientific question suggests that we should not ask, "Why do planets orbit?" or "Why is there light?" because these are "brute facts." Here is where we hit "rock bottom" and are stopped in our inquiry. Instead of asking the question *Why?* we might make greater scientific progress if we asked: *How* does gravity work? *How* does light work? with additional help from *What? When?* and *Where?* they work.

The following quotation from Newton's (1946, p. 202) work constitutes a fitting conclusion to the question *Why?*: "I have not been able to discover the causes of those properties of gravity. . . . it is enough that gravity does really exist, and act according to the laws which we have explained." Newton realized that he had reached "rock bottom."

For Further Reading

Toulmin, S. (1963). *Foresight and understanding: An enquiry into the aims of science.* New York: Harper & Row.

WOMEN

A woman should be seen, not heard.

> Sophocles (496?-406 B.C.), *Antigone*

A woman should be good for everything at home, but abroad good for nothing.

> Euripides (484-406 B.C.), *Meleager*

Woman may be said to be an inferior man.

> Aristotle [384-322 B.C.], *Poetics* XV

A fickle and changeable thing is woman ever.

> Virgil [70-19 B.C.], *Aeneid,* Book I

Nature doth paint them [women] further to be weak, frail, impatient, feeble and foolish.

> John Knox (ca. 1514-1572), *The Monstrous Regiment of Women*

Frailty, thy name is woman.

> Shakespeare (1564-1616), *Hamlet*

Women are to be talked to as below men, and above children.

> Lord Chesterfield, (1694-1773), *Letters to His Son*

Woman: A rag and a bone and a hank of hair.

> Kipling (1865-1936), *The Vampire*

Regan advised the *Washington Post* . . . that many of the paper's female readers would not understand "throw weights or what is happening in Afghanistan or what is happening in human rights. Most women . . . would rather read the human-interest stuff of what happened."

> *Time*, December 2, 1985

The preceding list of characterizations of women shows that, down through the ages, women have had a bad press. However, the discerning reader will note that the series of putdowns was not devised by women. But regardless of their authorship, such derogatory utterances have convinced not only men but many women about the inferiority of women. At least, that has been the state of affairs until comparatively recent times with the burgeoning of the women's movement. Are women psychologically inferior to men? That is the focal question of immediate concern to us.

"ANATOMY IS DESTINY"

The pervasive notion that woman is "the weaker vessel" (1 Peter 3:7) is a derivative of the Judeo-Christian religion. The implication is that woman is biologically inferior to man. Because psychoanalysis has had considerable influence on the way we think, we need to note what Freud had to say on this subject. According to Freud (1933, p. 170), the anatomical distinction between the sexes lies at the bottom of woman's sense of inferiority. The drama begins with the little girl's Oedipus complex at the time the sight of the genital organs of the other sex initiates her castration complex. Shocked at her lack of a penis,

she feels herself at a great disadvantage, and often declares that she would "like to have something like that too," and falls a victim to *penis-envy*, which leaves ineradicable traces on her development and character-formation.

The castration complex forces a turning point in the life of the girl. One road leads to sexual inhibition or to neurosis, the second to behavior changes that culminate in a masculinity complex, and the third to a passive surrender to normal femininity with its full acceptance of her castration. The masculinity complex or Adler's version of the "masculinity protest" is of special interest to us. It is this "constitutional factor" (Freud, 1933, p. 177) that permits her to avoid the passivity of femininity in favor of "a greater degree of activity, such as is usually characteristic of the male." While Freud doesn't spell matters out definitively, presumably the masculinity complex provides the drive for woman's competition with the male. To sum up Freud's contribution, strictly speaking, it is not true that "anatomy is destiny"; it is the manner in which the woman reacts to the perceived anatomical difference between the male and female. Or, if we forget psychoanalysis, is Freud saying anything more than this: some women become homemakers, some become career women, and some are successful at both jobs, as our subsequent consideration of the available data will show. But, if anatomy is not destiny, how about hormones? Don't they account for macho men and gentle, nurturing women? As help in finding an answer to this question, we move on to a remarkable paper by an endocrinologist.

HOW ABOUT HORMONES?

In a paper, "Sex Hormones and Executive Ability," E. R. Ramey (1973, p. 237) starts out by rejecting Freud's notion that anatomy is destiny. She scorns Freud's claim that the female reproductive system has "kept women emotionally unstable, submissive, passive, masochistic, and devoid of creative intellectual potential" (p. 237).

Ramey considers the important question raised by "a bastardized endocrinology," which claims that the behavioral differences between men and women are to be explained in terms of hormonal differences. According to the stereotype, estrogen makes women "biologically fragile, unstable, intuitive and irrational" and testosterone creates men who are "biologically strong, stable, hard-headed and rational" (p. 228). But according to Ramey, neither empirical nor experimental studies support such claims.

The facts are much more complex than a one-to-one relationship between a hormone, on the one hand, and masculinity or femininity on the other. For how is one to explain the extreme diversity manifested in such facts as bisexuality, homosexuality, pedophilia, zoophilia, fetishism, complete sex role reversal, or the total repression or rejection of the sexual response? For example, is the bisexual response to a male or female sexual partner regulated by a switch from testosterone to estrogen or vice versa? Ramey (p. 239) prefers to think that people are sexually neutral at birth but are shaped by life experiences that permit "the development and perpetuation of diverse patterns of psychosexual orientation and functioning."

Ramey presents other lines of evidence against a strict hormonal interpretation of human sexual behavior. Departing for the moment from Ramey's text, how shall we explain, in endocrinological terms, the sexual behavior of the citizens of classical Greece? K. J. Dover (1978, p. 1) tells us that Greek culture of that period not only recognized but showed wide acceptance and sympathetic understanding of "the alternation of homosexual and heterosexual preferences *in the same individual*, its implicit denial that such alternation or coexistence created peculiar problems for the individual or for society." Furthermore, the Greeks appeared to relish the unrestrained treatment of homosexuality in their literature and visual arts. If you were to press Dover (1978) for an explanation for that state of affairs, his response would be that "they accepted it because it was acceptable to their fathers and uncles and their grandfathers" (p. 2). For Dover, this was a more conservative explanation than one based on presumed hormonal factors.

HOW ABOUT AGGRESSION AND LEADERSHIP?

The role of testosterone as the "take-charge" hormone has appealed to many investigators in explaining aggression and leadership. Experimental work with subhuman animals has yielded contradictory results. Certainly, we find no one-to-one correlation between testosterone and aggression. Stress, such as pervades our "rat-race" society, has been found to lower testosterone levels. This finding prompts Ramey to ask, "Does this mean that those men who daily do battle with the competitive environment of the high reaches of business and government have chronic undersecretion of testosterone?" (pp. 243-244).

How shall we understand aggressive women? How do the following fit into an explanation in terms of hormones: Joan of Arc as an aggressive leader of the French against the English at Orleans, the Viet Cong women who lead women soldiers into battle, the IRA women guerrillas, and the Israeli women who fought side by side with their male colleagues in the war of 1948? Ramey points out that, although data on the androgen levels of these women are lacking, it is quite likely that they secreted more estrogens than androgens. Why does she hypothesize so? Because society, not hormones, defines human aggressivity and leadership.

The following summary provides an appropriate wrap-up of Ramey's contribution. In all the arguments pro and con on the hormonal determination of human behavior there is no evidence to show males are (statistically) more intelligent than women or psychologically unique in any other way. Certainly, men differ from women biologically, but they also differ in terms of cultural attitudes (such as *machismo*) toward them. Men get elected to the presidency of the United States. Women have become a prime minister of England, premiers of Israel, India, and Ceylon, and a president of Iceland. "Endocrinologists have nothing to contribute to the explanation of these national differences" (Ramey, 1973, p. 244).

THE PROOF OF THE PUDDING

Psychologists are not as free to experiment with humans as they are with chimps, gerbils, and worms. Otherwise, we could test the hypothesis that women can do anything men can do (plus one thing more). However, recent, natural changes in the social scene have provided a setting that permits such a test to a limited degree. The women's movement, the Civil Rights Act of 1964, the Equal Employment Opportunity Act of 1965, and improvement in women's legal rights have provided women with opportunities long denied them. We will examine the partial consequences of this continuing, quiet revolution after a quick survey of the kinds of jobs women have engaged in, and are entering upon, our focus being on the work potential of men and women.

WOMEN IN THE WORK FORCE

Over the past several decades, there has been a trend of greater participation by women in the world's work. Today, it is a truism that women constitute about 50 percent of the civilian labor force.

Just by casually leafing through Stineman's (1979) catalog of occupations, we can get some notion of the wide range of jobs that women have held or are working into. Here is a partial list. Women have been or are now truck drivers, coal miners, butchers, welders, grain elevator managers, race car drivers, cabinet makers, meat packers, printers, mill supervisors, inspectors, "linemen" in telephone and electric power industries, workers in miscellaneous trades (broom, brush, and paper box making) caskets, cork, paint, soap, trunks, pesticide inspectors, photographers, bank officers, newspaper and magazine investigative reporters, newspaper owners and general managers (e.g. Katharine Graham, chairman of the Washington Post Co.; Cathleen Black, publisher of *U.S.A. Today*; and Christie Hefner, who runs Playboy Enterprises), TV reporters, war correspondents and anchor women, and on and on and on.

How about women in top jobs in corporations? Janice Castro (1985) reports that a new class of thousands of ambitious women executives is rising through the ranks in banks, manufacturing companies, retail firms, and service corporations. For example, starting with one women's-wear store in 1971, Verna Gibson worked her way up to head Limited Inc., a major American corporation with 1985 sales of $800 million. She is not alone. There are other highly successful women. Muriel Siebert owns a seat on the New York Stock Exchange, and "about one third of Wall Street's younger professionals are now female" (p. 65). Leanne Lachman is president of the Real Estate Research Corporation. Barbara Proctor has founded the thriving Chicago advertising agency Proctor & Gardner. Madelyn Devine is senior vice-president of Wall Street's Oppenheimer & Co. Susan Fisher, senior vice-president of New York's Manufacturer's and Trader's Trust Co., is quoted as saying, "This bank wouldn't care if I was a purple frog. All that matters is what I can do for the bottom line" (p. 65). We must discontinue Castro's recital of female high achievers with the case of Camron Cooper, Atlantic Richfield treasurer, who "manages $25 billion assets and insists that being a woman has nothing to do with her job. 'I am the treasurer of Atlantic Richfield,' she says, 'not the female treasurer'" (p. 66).

WOMEN IN MEDICINE

A broad panorama of women in medicine is provided by Chaff, Haimbach, Fenichel, and Woodside (1977) *Women in Medicine*, a bibliography of the published literature involving about 2,500 women physicians down through history. The various specialties they engaged in include family practice, social service, surgery, pediatrics, radiology, obstetrics, syphilology, school health care, police surgery, anesthesiology, family planning, public health, psychiatry, disaster medicine, careers in drug industry, pediatric surgery, ophthalmology and eye surgery, neurology, dermatology, and many others. As a phaseout to this brief section, let us note that one of the women of the year 1985 selected by *Ms.* magazine was Dr. Mathilde Krim "for early research on AIDS, for leadership in public fund raising, and for her use of the media to counteract fear and ignorance with knowledge and compassion" (*Ms.*, January, 1986, p. 36).

WOMEN IN SPORTS

Remley (1980) offers biographies of women who achieved excellence in the following sports: golf; gymnastics; horseback riding and racing; motorcycling and auto racing; mountaineering, skiing, and ice skating; swimming, scuba diving, and sailing; tennis; and track and field. We are reminded that women have distinguished themselves in field hockey and lacrosse, martial arts and self-defense, softball, volleyball, and basketball. Among the January 1986 Ms. magazine's ten women of the year excelling in various fields, Lynette Woodard is included as the first woman member of the previously all-male, world-famous Harlem Globetrotters. And we shouldn't overlook the increasing number of women who have been winning gold medals in Olympic competitions.

WOMEN ARTISTS

Although museums and galleries have perpetuated the notion that women have not been artists, Bachmann and Piland (1978) have compiled a historical, contemporary, and feminist bibliography of approximately 160 accomplished artists who did their work between the tenth and twentieth century.

By no means have we exhausted the diversity of job niches that women have fitted themselves into with excellence, but we have just about run out of allotted space. Ireland's (1970) *Index to Women of the World from Ancient to Modern Times: Biographies and Portraits* reminds us that we are completely overlooking the contributions of women in the following areas, women who deserve at least mention: women as pioneers, women in history, women as patriots and military leaders, women in religion, women in the fine arts, women in literature, and women in science and invention. Beyond that, we must not ignore women in government as cabinet members, senators, state governors, mayors, and members of city councils. Nor must we pass over women in law as lawyers and judges in municipal and federal courts and even in the Supreme Court.

WOULD SHAKESPEARE HAVE MADE IT?

Surely, even this sketchy account of women's participation in the world's work should persuade the most obdurate skeptic of the tremendous prospect of human potential, male or female. After all, how many job specifications call for possession of a vagina or penis or for a certain pattern of hormonal secretion?

What does it take if not that? If we were to put that question to Virginia Woolf, her ready response would be, "A room of one's own and a legacy of five-hundred pounds a year." In an essay, *A Room of One's Own* (1929, p.

63), Woolf tells us how an aunt willed her five-hundred pounds a year for life. This windfall gave her an opportunity to travel over the world and observe all sorts and conditions of people, plus leisure, plus a "room of her own." Small wonder that she became a preeminent novelist and essayist of the twentieth century. But the clear implication of her narrative is that her accomplishments as a writer would have been inconceivable had she been born in Elizabethan times, when women were expected to minister to their husbands and rear their children. She also insinuates that because of the role that sixteenth-century women were expected to play, had Shakespeare been born a woman, Shakespeare's plays could never have been written. At that time, confinement of women to the home restricted contact with other people and limited their worldly experience, leaving them bankrupt for something to write about.

Also, had Will Shakespeare been born Wendy Shakespeare, Wendy would have had "no chance of learning grammar and logic, let alone of reading Horace and Vergil" (Woolf, 1929, p. 81). But Will did have those opportunities, and he was allowed to travel to London, to hang around actors and taverns and to meet and observe all sorts of people, to have a "room of his own and five-hundred pounds a year," and so forth. Woolf's (1929, p. 81) argument is supported when she reminds us that "even so late as the nineteenth century . . . Currer Bell, George Eliot and George Sand . . . sought ineffectively to veil themselves by using the name of a man."

What eloquent testimony to the long-lasting denial of developmental opportunities to women! All of which prompts one to ask, as a fitting windup to this section on women, what if (perish the thought!) today's successful women entrepreneurs, stock market consultants, corporation treasurers, physicists, astronomers, astronauts, senators, governors, mayors, and all the rest had been born in the sixteenth century? Good question.

For Further Reading

Chaff, S. L., Haimbach, R., Fenichel, C. & Woodside, N. B. (1977). *Women in medicine: A bibliography of the literature on women physicians.* Metuchen, N.J.: Scarecrow Press.

Ramey, E. R. (1973). Sex hormones and executive ability. *Annals of the New York Academy of Sciences, 208,* 237-245.

THE XYY CHROMOSOME
AND CRIMINALITY

"Seek simplicity," says Whitehead, "and distrust it." Down through the ages, philosophers and scientists were convinced that they had found the essence of the phenomena they were studying, but they erred blindly in trusting their findings. They hoped to discover a few basic elements or even a single, irreducible factor that would explain all of nature, under the assumption of the unity of all things. Thus, fire, earth, air, and water and Democritus's atoms and the void are some of the elements that the Greeks took into account in their naturalistic approach toward an understanding of the universe.

We have come a long way since the Greeks, but the pursuit of the elementary building blocks of the universe continues, as witness contemporary physics. In psychology, the yearning for simplicity has been directed toward the anatomical-physiological level as the appropriate procedure for the understanding of behavioral events. This biological determinism "holds that shared behavioral norms, and the social and economic differences between human groups—primarily races, classes, and sexes—arise from inherited, inborn distinctions, and that society, in this sense, is an accurate reflection of biology" (Gould, 1981, p. 20). The Greek physician Galen (130-200 A.D.) attributed temperament to the proportion of four bodily humors or secretions. Black bile was connected with the melancholic temperament, yellow bile with the choleric, blood bile with the sanguine, and phlegm with the phlegmatic. There have been many other schemes since them.

CRANIOMETRY

Shifting the scene closer to our own time, we come across craniometry, which had earlier beginnings but which flourished under Paul Broca (1824-1880), a Parisian professor of clinical surgery. He sought the key to an understanding of the intellectual level of the various human races by measuring their skulls. His measurements convinced him that the elderly, women, mediocre men, and inferior races had, respectively, smaller brains than mature adults, men, men of talent, and superior races. Therefore, Broca stated that "other things equal, there is a remarkable relationship between the development of intelligence and the volume of the brain" (cited in Gould, 1981, p. 85). Gould (p. 85) points out that the reason Broca was able to reach such conclusions was that he and his colleagues "began with conclusions, peered through their facts, and came back in a circle to the same conclusions." As a skeptic, Gould spent a whole month poring over Broca's data and discovered that Broca's simplistic assumptions determined the outcome of his research.

There are still other quests for simple biological determinants of behavior, such as Cesare Lombroso's excursion into criminal anthropology, which convinced him that criminal behavior was determined by atavistic or "throwback" features belonging to our remote evolutionary kin. W. H. Sheldon's (1954) theory of a causal relationship between body build and personality belongs here, but we move on to twentieth-century criteria: genes and criminal behavior.

THE XYY CHROMOSOME AND CRIMINAL BEHAVIOR

The XY chromosome appears normally in males, but occasionally a male receives an additional Y in the male-determining chromosome. According to a National Institute of Mental Health *Report on the XYY Chromosomal Abnormality* (1970), ever since the 1960s, geneticists and physicians had been studying the behavioral effects of extra chromosomes. They noted that some men with extra chromosomes engaged in violent and aggressive behavior. Consequently, they were set to look for others, and they found them. The report of a murderer in Paris and another in Australia, both with XYY chromosomes, was enough to convince many that XYY chromosomes *caused* men to commit murder.

In the United States, the sensational case of Richard Speck, convicted of murdering eight Chicago nurses, was appealed because it was alleged that he had XYY chromosomes. "Speck's attorney later announced that tests had shown his client's chromosomes to be normal. Nevertheless, news items and professional articles still appear referring to Speck as an XYY type." The NIMH report (1970) concludes:

The demonstration of the XYY Karyotype in an individual does not, in our present state of knowledge permit any definite conclusions to be drawn about the presence of mental disease or defect in that individual. A great deal of further scientific evidence is needed. (P. 5)

LET'S SUPPOSE . . .

Suppose, by some great stretch of the imagination, that some investigator established that "the XYY chromosome *causes* criminality." Would such a relationship really yield understanding, or would we be exchanging one mystery for another by having to clarify how a small bit of flesh, a gene, could *cause* criminality?

If we examine the term *criminality* semantically, we find that people don't go around committing "criminality," for that term covers a multitude of sins. Getting down to specifics, we find that this term embraces such vastly different, concrete actions as hit-and-run, assault and battery, robbery burglary, larceny, embezzlement, murder, arson, rape, extortion, fraud vandalism, and suicide. This diversity of action constitutes another barrier that a genetic theory of criminality would have to hurdle. Would the proponent of such a theory argue that such a gene would only goad its bearer toward *any form of crime*? At this point, the skeptic would deem it appropriate to ask: Are the assumptions that guide our investigation valid ones, or are they leading us into dead ends? At such a time it would be well to recall Whitehead's admonition "Seek simplicity and distrust it."

For Further Reading

Gould, S. (1981). *The mismeasure of man.* New York: W. W. Norton.
National Institute of Mental Health. (1970). *Report on the XYY chromosoma abnormality.* (PHS Publication No. 2103). Washington, D.C.: U.S. Government Printing Office.

YOUTH

I see no hope for the future of our people if they are dependent on the frivolous youth of today, for certainly all youth are reckless beyond words. When I was a boy, we were taught to be discreet and respectful of elders, but the present youth are exceedingly wise and impatient of restraint.

Hesiod (Eighth century B.C)

'Twas ever thus! According to the story in Genesis, the firstborn son of Adam and Eve turned out to be a murderer, in defiance of his parents' teachings. But the rift between generations does not always end in acts of violence and destruction by rebellious youth. Rejection of the establishment can manifest itself in acts of great achievement, as is borne out by the classicists ("dead radicals") such as Beethoven, Mozart, Darwin, and the Renaissance painters, among countless others.

One cannot deny that the relativity revolution in physics has conferred abundant scientific and technological benefits upon us. Prominent revolutionaries in that early-twentieth-century movement were Einstein, Bohr, Heisenberg, and Mach. In a learned work, Feuer (1974) traces the political, social, economic and philosophical conditions that explain the creativity of the participants in that revolution. We focus on Einstein alone.

Feuer argues that in every age young men who resist the established order of things may end up in the Foreign Legion, gangsterism in science, and so on. The important step in that outcome is one's "choice of comrades." During his four years at the Federal Polytechnic School in Zurich, Einstein chose for his comrades socialist exiles and emigrants from Russia, Austria, Germany, Poland, and America. For all of them Zurich provided a climate of freedom that encouraged free thinking in many diverse directions.

Particularly in the first decade of the present century, Zurich was a hotbed of student activists and revolutionaries of different stripes. For Einstein's best friend, the revolt took a political turn that ended with his assassination of the prime minister of Austria, while Einstein's revolutionary thinking was directed against the basic assumptions of classical physics. However, Einstein's rebelliousness did not originate in Zurich. According to Feuer (1974, p. 4), even in his boyhood, Albert resented the rigid school curriculum and its military-style discipline. His high school teacher encouraged him to leave school because of his undesirable influence on other students. In his graduate days, Einstein was on bad terms with his professors. They rated his thesis on relativity "as inadequate" (Feuer, 1974, p. 54) because it did not follow the usual specifications. On top of all else, Einstein had not read the literature of his field. In fact, this may have been the reason he was able to see things in a fresh and different way. His radicalness, supported and nurtured by his dissident colleagues in his revolt against the established order, led him to a world-shaking breakthrough in the science of physics, showing that revolutionaries don't always end up as bomb-throwing terrorists. Intergenerational conflict can also bring great benefits to society.

For Further Reading

Feuer, S. (1974). *Einstein and the generations of science.* New York: Basic Books.

ZEITGEIST

Zeitgeist is a German word that, translated literally, means "the spirit of the times." In a freer sense, the term has come to refer to the intellectual climate of an era or the world view, that is, the pervasive frame of reference or perspective that shapes the way people think about things. For example, the Greco-Roman zeitgeist was a naturalistic one, a perspective in which earthly and heavenly events were viewed as all a part of nature; supernaturals were out. But this naturalism was succeeded by a transcendental perspective that assumed two orders of events, natural and supernatural, or matter and spirit, a notion that was extended to human nature as well. Our contemporary view of humans as a combination of body and soul (or, later, as body and mind) derives from the early centuries of the Christian era.

Later ages stressed one or another aspect of that duality. For example, eighteenth-century materialism saw human nature as a product of organic structure, simply ignoring the spirit aspect of traditional dualism. As such, the theory was an invalid view of behavior because it relied on imaginary attributions to bodily organs. Classical behaviorism saw human activity through materialistic spectacles, while contemporary cognitivism stresses the spiritual side of dualism; neither escapes the age-old intellectual trap. Thus, the zeitgeist of the times determines the way people come to understand and explain their observations.

EPILOGUE

The French have an expression, "Plus ça change plus ç'est la même chose" (The more a thing changes, the more it is the same thing). Psychology has had a long history, one that spans 2,500 years, but the most remarkable feature of that chronicle is that, after Aristotle's naturalistic approach to human behavior, a dualistic paradigm set in that has endured to our own times. According to that venerable paradigm, humans consist of a visible body (matter) and an invisible mind (spirit). The mind is said to live within the organism, more specifically, in the head. Through the years, that dualistic framework has served psychology. At different periods of history, one or the other of the never-to-be-separated twin pair, body-mind, was emphasized or neglected. The overriding pattern is comparable to a Haydnesque theme with variations.

The entry "SOUL": THE TRANSFORMATION OF "SOUL" TO "MIND" AND "MIND" TO "BRAIN" traces that theme with variations. But a finer gradation of changes in the shifting stress of first mind, then body are reflected in the succession of constructs over the years. A bird's-eye view of history must note Saint Augustine's attribution of a transcendental soul to humans, a soul that was the basis of all knowledge, willing and desiring. Gradually, the theology-derived soul was transformed into a somewhat more scientifically palatable mind. In the nineteenth century, expansion of biological knowledge favored the materialistic counterpart of mind, the body, or brain, in explaining human nature, but that didn't solve the problem of the puzzling relationship between the two.

Philosophers who grappled with the body-mind dilemma proposed, but could never prove, a succession of explications of the relationship between the two worlds, the visible and the invisible realms. Here are some of them:

Psychophysical parallelism. Mental and physical processes are parallel and concomitant but without a causal connection between the two.

Interactionism. There is reciprocal causation or interaction between mind and body.

Double-aspect theory. Mind and body, or mental process and physical process, represent two aspects of the same series of events.

Epiphenomenalism. Mental processes are merely a by-product or accompaniment of physical processes, but without causal connection.

Isomorphism. There is a point-for-point correspondence between the conscious content and the brain areas that are activated by a stimulus.

Emergentism. Combinations of elements give rise to something new not predictable from a knowledge of those elements, for example, life. So, when living matter reaches a certain level of complexity, *consciousness* makes its appearance.

Idealism. The ultimate reality of the universe is intelligible only in terms of ideas, not in terms of matter; that is, only ideas exist.

Materialism. Materialism is the only ultimate reality. The body, more specifically the brain, is the *substratum* of psychological functioning, which is, in the final analysis, a product of matter. This is a form of reductionism.

One cannot stress too much that all of the preceding stratagems are derivatives of the dualistic assumption of body-mind. They are all *hypothetical* constructs based on that *assumption* and acted upon as if *established fact.* We are not surprised that such a notion originated during the Dark Ages. The astounding fact is that such a basic idea should have enjoyed such longevity. Consider the fact that physics has profited following its two revolutions and astronomy from its three, while psychology has experienced none but still clings to a basic approach that evolved during the third and fourth centuries A.D.

The reader may remonstrate, "But how about the various schools of psychology? You have had structuralism with its introspection, functionalism, gestalt, psychoanalysis, behaviorism, and existentialism. Are they not revolutionary?" They are not, for each of them is based on the same dualistic paradigm, emphasizing one or another aspect of the duality. Behaviorism attempted to extricate itself from the mind-matter dilemma by denying spirit and choosing materialism. Should skeptical readers doubt that the body-mind postulate is still alive and well even unto today, let them examine the Presidential Addresses in recent issues of the *American Psychologist.*

WHAT'S THE DIFFERENCE?

Clinging to the centuries-old paradigm has had certain drastic consequences. First of all, a largely exclusive preoccupation with the organism as the container of body and mind has led to the improvisation of "prime movers" within the skin of the organism. As pointed out throughout this book, such imaginary constructs are untestable, and until they are verified, they are not serviceable. To reiterate Kuhn's (1961, p. 177) precept, "Merely conceivable theories are not among the options open to the practicing scientist."

Second, because more than one variable is always involved in any event, it is expecting too much of the organism to carry the entire explanatory burden in interpreting psychological events in a self-actional fashion. Such a procedure permits only "merely conceivable theories."

Third, focus on imaginary entities within the organism distracts us from observing the other variables that participate in psychological events.

WHAT'S THE ALTERNATIVE?

The resolution of the problems created by an obsession with the organism lies in an expanded observational framework, one that will recognize the part played by other discriminable variables that enter into psychological events. The comprehensive view called for necessitates a field orientation.

While FIELD THEORY has been discussed at length, a brief summary is in order at this point. Our consideration of field begins with Einstein and Infeld's (1966, p. 245) incomplete formulation of field. Expansion of that notion led to an adoption of Kantor's (1969, pp. 370-371) construct of field as the "entire system of things and conditions operating in any event taken in its available totality. It is only the entire system of factors which will provide proper descriptive and explanatory materials for the handling of events."

In a nutshell, this is the position I have taken in comparing the way field and nonfield theories interpret behavior from the standpoint provided by the various articles that make up the contents of this book. What kind of job the different perspectives result in is left to the judgment of the reader.

In an article, "The Function of Dogma in Scientific Research," Kuhn (1970a) makes the point that the dogmatism observed in the scientific enterprise may have beneficial consequences. Commitments to a certain guiding paradigm and resistance to new facts and ideas keep the researcher's nose to the grindstone, yielding the successes in the hard sciences that are so familiar to us all. And Kuhn believes that not enough attention is paid to the "dependence of research upon a deep commitment to established tools and beliefs" (1970a, p. 371).

Applying Kuhn's thoughts to psychology, one cannot criticize it for not sticking to a two-thousand-year-old paradigm and producing enough data to drown in. Yet we're looking, ever hopefully, for a "breakthrough." Certainly, psychologists need to examine our traditional paradigm and recognize it as *only* a paradigm and not an established fact. More pertinent to the destiny of psychology is Kuhn's (1970a, pp. 370-371) statement: "Almost no one, perhaps no one at all, needs to be told that the vitality of science depends upon the continuation of occasional tradition-shattering innovations." Perhaps a tradition-shattering innovation is what's needed to revitalize psychology.

Kuo (1967, p. xi) is one who, viewing the rapid progress in modern science, believed that "no scientific theory should last for more than two or three decades without being greatly modified or entirely supplanted." One needn't agree with Kuo as to the need for such rapid changes as he proposed;

yet one must ask how the same basic paradigm could serve psychology for two-thousand years?

DA CAPO

It is . . . bewildering that the world order of science is able to live comfortably for years, and sometimes centuries, with beliefs that a new generation discovers to be false. How is it possible that we are able to build higher and higher on the foundations of such beliefs without fear of their sudden collapse? (Maclean, 1970, p. 337)

For Further Reading

Kantor, J. R. (1963). *The scientific evolution of psychology.* Vol. 1. Chicago: Principia Press.

REFERENCES

Achinstein, P. (1965). The problem of theoretical terms. *American Philosophical Quarterly, 11*(3), 103-203.

Amarel, S. (1984). Expert behavior and problem representations. In A. Elithorn & R. Banerji (Eds.), *Artificial and human intelligence* (pp. 1-41). New York: Elsevier Science Publishing Co.

Andrew, A. M. (1983) *Artificial intelligence.* Tunbridge Wells, Kent, England: Abacus Press.

Atkinson, R. L., Atkinson, R. C., & Hilgard, E. R. (1983). *Introduction to psychology* (8th Ed.). New York: Harcourt Brace Jovanovich.

Bachmann, D. G., & Piland, S. (1978). *Women artists: An historical, contemporary, and feminist bibliography.* Metuchen, N.J.: Scarecrow Press.

Baer, D. M. (1970). An age-irrelevant concept of development. *Merrill-Palmer Quarterly, 16*(3), 238-245.

Bakker, C. B. (1975). Why people don't change. *Psychotherapy: Theory, Research and Practice, 12,* 164-172.

Balinsky, B. I. (1975). *An introduction to embryology* (4th Ed.). Philadelphia: W. B. Saunders.

Banks, S. A. (1970). Changing values in psychotherapy. In J. W. Canning (Ed.), *Values in an age of confrontation* (pp. 87-93). Columbus, Ohio: Charles E. Merrill.

Barker, R. G. (1968). *Ecological psychology.* Stanford, Calif.: Stanford University Press.

Bentley, A. F. (1926). *Relativity in man and society.* New York: Putman.

Bentley, A. F. (1935). *Behavior, knowledge, fact.* Chicago: Principia Press.

Bentley, A. F. (1954). The fiction of "retinal image." In *Inquiry into inquiries* (pp. 268-285). (Ed. S. Ratner.) Boston: Beacon Press.

Bergin, A. E., & Strupp, H. H. (1972). *Changing frontiers in the science of psychotherapy.* New York: Aldine-Atherton.

Bernstein, L. (1959). *The joy of music.* New York: Simon and Schuster.

Beveridge, W. I. B. (1951). *The art of scientific investigation.* New York: W. W. Norton.

Bierce, A. (1925). *The devil's dictionary.* New York: Albert & Charles Boni.

Bijou, S. W. (1966). A functional analysis of retarded development. In N. R. Ellis (Ed.), *International Review of Research in Mental Retardation* (pp. 1-19). Vol. 1. New York: Academic Press.

Black, M. (1962). *Models and metaphors.* Ithaca, N.Y.: Cornell University Press.

Blanchard, B. (1958). The case for determinism. In S. Hook (Ed.), *Determinism and freedom in the age of modern science* (pp. 3-15). New York: New York University Press.

Bohm, D., & Welwood, J. (1980). Issues in physics, psychology, and metaphysics: A conversation. *The Journal of Transpersonal Psychology, 12*(1), 25-36.

Bradley, F. H. (1959). *Appearance and reality.* Oxford: Clarendon Press.

Briggs, J. L. (1970). *Never in anger.* Cambridge, Mass.: Harvard University Press.

Broad, C. D. (1952). *Scientific thought.* London: Routledge and Kegan Paul. (Original work published 1923)

Bronfenbrenner, U. (1979). *The ecology of human development: Experiments by nature and design.* Cambridge, Mass.: Harvard University Press.

Bunge, F. M. (Ed.). (1983). *Japan: A country study.* (Department of the Army Publication DA Pam. 550-30). Washington, D.C.: U.S. Government Printing Office.

Bunge, M. (1969). What are physical theories about? In N. R. Rescher (Ed.), *Studies in the philosophy of science. Monograph series,* No. 3., 61-99. Oxford: Basil Blackwell with the cooperation of the University of Pittsburgh.

Burckhardt, J. (1909). *The civilization of the Renaissance in Italy* (S. G. C. Middlemore, Trans.). New York: Macmillan.

Cameron, N. (1947). *Behavior disorders: A biosocial interpretation.* New York: Houghton Mifflin.

Canning, J. W. (Ed.). (1970). *Values in an age of confrontation.* Columbus, Ohio: Charles E. Merrill.

Carlson, N. R. (1984). *Psychology: The science of behavior.* Boston: Allyn and Bacon.

Carraher, R. G., & Chartier, C. (1980). *Electronic flash photography.* Somerville, Mass.: Curtin & London.

Carrel, A. (1931). The new cytology. *Science, 73,* 297-302.

Castro, J. (1985). More and more, she's the boss. *Time,* December 2, 64-66.

Caws, P. (1965). *The philosophy of science.* Princeton, N.J.: Van Nostrand.

Célestine, L. F. (1979). *Mea culpa & the life and work of Semmelweis.* (R. A. Parker, Trans.). New York: Howard Fertig. (Original work published 1937)

Chaff, S. L., Haimbach, R., Fenichel, C., & Woodside, N. B. (1977). *Women in medicine: A bibliography of the literature on women physicians.* Metuchen, N.J.: Scarecrow Press.

Chaplin, J. P. (1975). *Dictionary of psychology* (rev. ed.). New York: Dell Publishing Co.

Chargaff, E. (1976). Triviality in science: A brief meditation on fashions. *Perspectives in Biology and Medicine, 19*(3), 323-329.

Clark, R. W. (1971). *Einstein: The life and times.* New York: Thomas Y. Crowell.

Cleaver, E. (1968). *Soul on ice.* New York: Dell.

Cleaver, E. (1978). *Soul on fire.* Waco, Tex.: World Books.

Comte, A. (1855). *The positive philosophy of Auguste Comte.* (Freely translated and condensed by Harriet Martineau.) New York: G. Blanchard.

Coon, C. S. (1962). *The origin of races.* New York: Alfred A. Knopf.

Cushing, H. (1940). *The medical career and other papers.* Boston: Little, Brown & Co.

DeCasper, A. J., & Fifer, W. P. (1980). Of human bonding: Newborns prefer their mothers' voices. *Science, 208,* 1174-1176.

DeCasper, A. J., & Sigafoos, A. D. (1983). The intrauterine heartbeat: A potent reinforcer for newborns. *Infant Behavior and Development, 6,* 19-25.

Deutsch, A. (1938). *The mentally ill in America.* Garden City, N.Y.: Doubleday, Doran & Co.

Dewey, J. (1896). The reflex arc concept in psychology. *The Psychological Review, 3*, 357-370. Also in *University of Chicago Contributions to Philosophy* (1896), *1*(1), 39-52.

Dewey, J. (1929). *The quest for certainty.* New York: Minton, Balch & Co.

Dewey, J. (1930). Conduct and experience. In C. Murchison (Ed.)., *Psychologies of 1930* (pp. 409-423). Worcester, Mass.: Clark University Press.

Dewey, J. (1938). *Logic: The theory of inquiry.* New York: Henry Holt.

Dewey, J. (1949). *Reconstruction in philosophy.* New York: New American Library. (Original work published 1920)

Dewey, J. (1972). The reflex arc concept in psychology. In John Dewey, *The early works, 1882-1898: Early essays* (pp. 96-109). Carbondale: Southern Illinois University Press.

Dewey, J., & Bentley, A. F. (1949). *Knowing and the known.* Boston: Beacon Press.

Dewey, J., & Bentley, A. F. (1964). *John Dewey and Arthur F. Bentley: A philosophical correspondence, 1932-1951.* (Eds. S. Ratner, J. Altman and J. E. Wheeler). New Brunswick, N.J.: Rutgers University Press.

Dobzhansky, T. (1971). Race equality. In R. H. Osborne (Ed.), *The biological and social meaning of race* (pp. 13-24). San Francisco: Freeman.

Dover, K. J. (1978). *Greek homosexuality.* Cambridge, Mass.: Harvard University Press.

Dreyfus, H. L., & Dreyfus, S. E. (1986). *Mind over machine.* New York: Free Press.

Dugdale, R. L. (1877). *The Jukes.* New York: Putnam.

Durkheim, E. (1893 tr. 1933). *The division of labor in society.* Paris: F. Alcan.

Ebert, J. D. (1965). *Interacting systems in development.* New York: Holt, Rinehart and Winston.

Ehrlich, V. (1965). *Russian formalism* (2nd Ed.). New York: Humanities Press.

Einstein, A. (1954). *Ideas and opinions.* New York: Bonanza Books.

Einstein, A., & Infeld, L. (1966). *The evolution of physics.* New York: Simon and Schuster.

Eissler, K. R. (1961). *Leonardo da Vinci: Psychoanalytic notes on the enigma.* New York: International Universities Press.

Engle, P. (1964). Salt crystals, spider webs, and words. *Saturday Review, 47,* March 14, 10-13.

English, H. B., & English, A. C. (1958). *A comprehensive dictionary of psychological and psychoanalytic terms.* New York: Longmans, Green and Co.

Feuer, L. S. (1974). *Einstein and the generations of science.* New York: Basic Books.

Feyerabend, P. (1975). *Against method.* London: Humanities Press.

Finger, S., & Stein, D. G. (1982). *Brain damage and recovery: Research and clinical perspectives.* New York: Academic Press.

Fraser, J. T. (1975). *Of time, passion, and knowledge: Reflections on the strategy of existence.* New York: George Braziller.

Freud, S. (1933). *New introductory lectures on psycho-analysis.* (W. J. H. Sprott, Trans.). New York: Norton.

Gallup, G. G. (1977). Self-recognition in primates. *American Psychologist, 32*(5), 329-338.

Gardner, M. (1985). Physics: The end of the road? *The New York Review of Books,* 32(10), 31-34.

Gerow, J. R. (1978). Psychology is alive and well. *Contemporary Psychology,* 23, 400-403.

Gesell, A. (1945). *The embryology of behavior.* New York: Harper.

Gibson, J. J. (1979). *The ecological approach to visual perception.* Boston: Houghton Mifflin.

Gleitman, H. (1983). *Basic psychology.* New York: W. W. Norton.

Goddard, H. H. (1935). *The Kallikak family: A study in the heredity of feeble-mindedness.* New York: Macmillan. (Original work published 1912)

Goldstein, K. (1939). *The organism.* New York: American Book Co.

Goodman, N. (1951). *The structure of appearance.* Cambridge, Mass.: Harvard University Press.

Gould, S. (1981). *The mismeasure of man.* New York: W. W. Norton.

Gravetter, F. J., & Wallnau, L. B. (1985). *Statistics for the behavioral sciences.* St. Paul, Minn.: West Publishing Co.

Greenblatt, S. (1980). *Renaissance self-fashioning: From More to Shakespeare.* Chicago: University of Chicago Press.

Grünbaum, A. (1952). Causality and the science of human behavior. *American Psychologist, 7.* 665-676.

Haber, R. N. (1983). The impending demise of the icon: A critique of the concept of iconic storage in visual information processing. *The Behavioral and Brain Sciences, 6,* 1-54.

Hanson, N. R. (1958). *Patterns of discovery.* Cambridge: At the University Press.

Hardin, G. (1957). The threat of clarity. *American Journal of Psychiatry, 114,* 392-396.

Hassett, J. (1984). *Psychology in perspective.* New York: Harper and Row.

Hayakawa, S. I. (1941). *Language in action.* New York: Harcourt, Brace and Company.

Heller, A. (1978). *Renaissance man.* (R. E. Allen, Trans.). London: Routledge & Kegan Paul.

Hendrick, S. (1958). *Facts and theories of psychoanalysis.* (3rd Ed.). New York: Alfred A. Knopf.

Holmes, A. (1965). *Principles of physical geology.* (2nd Ed.). New York: Ronald Press.

Howells, W. W. (1971). The meaning of race. In R. H. Osborne (Ed.), *The biological and social meaning of race* (pp. 3-10). San Francisco: Freeman.

Hudson, L. (1971). Intelligence. *The Listener,* March 18 (Mimeographed).

Hudson, L. (1975). *Human beings: The psychology of human experience.* New York: Doubleday.

Hughes, J. E. (1959). *America the vincible.* Garden City, N.Y.: Doubleday.

Ireland, N. O. (1970). *Index to women of the world from ancient to modern times: Biographies and portraits.* Westwood, Mass.: F. W. Faxon Co.

Jacob, F. (1977). Evolution and tinkering. *Science, 196*(4295), 1162-1166.

Jacob, H. E. (1963). *Felix Mendelssohn and his times.* Englewood Cliffs, N.J.: Prentice-Hall.

James, W. (1918). *The principles of psychology.* Vol. 1. New York: Henry Holt and Company. (Original work published 1890)

Jennings, H. S. (1924). Heredity and environment. *The Scientific Monthly, 19*(15), 225-238.

Kagan, J., Havemann, J., & Segal, J. (1984). *Psychology: An introduction* (5th Ed.). New York: Harcourt Brace Jovanovich.

Kantor, J. R. (1922). The nervous system: Psychological fact or fiction? *Journal of Philosophy, 19,* 38-49.

Kantor, J. R. (1924). *Principles of psychology.* Vol 1. New York: Alfred A. Knopf.

Kantor, J. R. (1933). *A survey of the science of psychology.* Chicago: Principia Press.

Kantor, J. R. (1947). *Problems of physiological psychology.* Chicago: Principia Press.

Kantor, J. R. (1963). *The scientific evolution of psychology.* Vol. 1. Chicago: Principia Press.

Kantor, J. R. (1969). *The scientific evolution of psychology.* Vol. 2. Chicago: Principia Press.

Kantor, J. R. (1978). The principle of specificity in psychology and science in general. *Revista Mexicana de Análisis de la Conducta, 4*(2), 117-132.

Kantor, J. R., & Smith, N. W. (1975). *The science of psychology: An interbehavioral survey.* Chicago: Principia Press.

Kemeny, J. G., & Oppenheim, P. (1970). On reduction. In B. A. Brody (Ed.), *Readings in the philosophy of science* (pp. 307-318). Englewood Cliffs, N.J.: Prentice-Hall.

Keppel, G., & Saufley, W. H., Jr. (1980). *Introduction to design and analysis: A student's handbook.* San Francisco: Freeman.

Kimmel, H. D. (1970). *Experimental principles and design in psychology.* New York: Ronald Press.

King, L. S. (1963). *The growth of medical thought.* Chicago: University of Chicago Press.

Kluckhohn, C. (1960). *Mirror for man.* New York: Fawcett.

Korzybski, A. (1941). *Science and sanity.* Lancaster, Pa.: Science Press Printing Co.

Kraft, V. (1981). *Foundations for a scientific analysis of value.* Dordrecht, Holland: R. Reidel Publishing Co.

Krech, D., Crutchfield, R. S., Livson, N., Wilson, W. A., and Parducci, A. (1982). *Elements of psychology* (4th Ed.). New York: Alfred A. Knopf.

Kuhn, T. S. (1961). The function of measurement in modern science. *Isis, 52,* Part 2, No. 168, 161-193.

Kuhn, T. S. (1970a). The function of dogma in scientific research. In B. A. Brody (Ed.), *Readings in the philosophy of science* (pp. 356-373). Englewood Cliffs, N.J.: Prentice-Hall.

Kuhn, T. S. (1970b). *The structure of scientific revolutions* (2nd Ed.). Chicago: University of Chicago Press.

Kuo, Z. Y. (1967). *The dynamics of behavior development.* New York: Random House.

Lakoff, G., & Johnson, M. (1980). *Metaphors we live by*. Chicago: University of Chicago Press.

Laver, A. B. (1972). Precursors of psychology in ancient Egypt. *Journal of the History of the Behavioral Sciences, 8*, 181-195.

Lawrence, N. (1974). *Alfred North Whitehead: A primer of his philosophy*. New York: Twayne Publishers.

Lee, I. J. (Ed.). (1949). *The language of wisdom and folly*. New York: Harper.

Lichtenstein, P. E. (1980). Theoretical psychology: Where is it headed? *The Psychological Record, 30*, 447-458.

Liddell, H. S. (1956). *Emotional hazards in animals and man*. Springfield, Ill.: C. C. Thomas.

Liley, A. W. (1972). The foetus as a personality. *Australian and New Zealand Journal of Psychiatry, 6*, 99-105.

Lindsley, O. R. (1964). Direct measurement and prosthesis of retarded behavior. *Journal of Education, 141*, 62-81.

Lipowski, Z. J. (1984). What does the word "psychosomatic" really mean? *Psychosomatic Medicine, 46*(2), 153-171.

Loftus, E. (1980). *Memory*. Reading, Mass.: Addison-Wesley Publishing Co.

MacCormac, E. R. (1976). *Metaphor and myth in science and religion*. Durham, N.C.: Duke University Press.

Mackenzie, B. D. (1977). *Behaviorism and the limits of scientific method*. Atlantic Highlands, N.J.: Humanities Press.

Mackintosh, N. J. (1980). A proffering of underpinnings. In A. Montagu (Ed.), *Sociobiology examined* (pp. 336-341). New York: Oxford University Press.

Maclean, P. D. (1970). The triune brain, emotion and scientific bias. In. F. O. Schmitt (Ed.), *The neurosciences: Second study program*. Cambridge, Mass: M. I. T. Press.

Mahoney, M. J. (1975). The sensitive scientist in empirical humanism. *American Psychologist, 30*(8), 864-867.

Manuel, F. E. (1968). *A portrait of Isaac Newton*. Cambridge, Mass.: Harvard University Press.

Mapping the brain's circuits. (1984, August). *A.P.A. Monitor*, p. 39.

Marr, J. (1983). Memory: Models and metaphors. *The Psychological Record, 33*(1), 12-19.

Maxwell, G. (1962). the ontological status of theoretical entities. In H. Feigl & G. Maxwell (Eds.), *Minnesota studies in the philosophy of science*. Minneapolis: University of Minnesota Press.

McConnell, J. V. (1977). *Understanding human behavior* (2nd Ed.). New York: Holt, Rinehart and Winston.

McCurdy, H. G. (1957). The childhood pattern of genius. *Journal of the Elisha Mitchell Scientific Society, 73*, 448-462.

Menninger, K. (1964). Psychiatrists use dangerous words. *Saturday Evening Post*, April 25. (Reprint. No page numbers).

Midgely, M. (1980). Rival fatalisms: The hollowness of the sociobiology debate. In A. Montagu (Ed.), *Sociobiology examined* (pp. 15-38). New York: Oxford University Press.

Minkowski, H. (1964). Space and time. In J. J. C. Smart (Ed.), *Problems of space and time* (pp. 81-88). New York: Macmillan.

Montagu, A. (1956). *The biosocial nature of man.* New York: Grove Press.

Montagu, A. (1965). *The idea of race.* Lincoln: University of Nebraska Press.

Montagu, A. (1980). Introduction. In A. Montagu (Ed.), *Sociobiology examined* (pp. 3-14). New York: Oxford University Press.

Morgan, C. L. (1967). Introduction to comparative psychology. In A. J. Riopelle (Ed.), *Animal problem solving* (pp. 54-61). Baltimore: Penguin Books. (Original work published 1909)

Mullahy, P. (Ed.) (1952). *The contributions of Harry Stack Sullivan.* New York: Hermitage House.

Muller, H. J. (1943). *Science and criticism.* New Haven, Conn.: Yale University Press.

Murray, D. J. (1980). Research on human memory in the nineteenth century. In J. D. Seamon (Ed.), *Human memory: Contemporary readings,* pp. 5-23. New York: Oxford University Press.

Murray, H. A. & Kluckhohn, C. (1948). Outline of a conception of personality. In C. Kluckhohn & H. A. Murray (Eds.), *Personality in nature, society and culture* (pp. 3-32). New York: Alfred A. Knopf.

Myrdal, G. (1944). *An American dilemma: The Negro problem and modern democracy.* New York: Harper and Brothers.

Nalimov, V. V. (1981). *Faces of science.* Philadelphia: ISI Press.

National Institute of Mental Health. (1970). *Report on the XYY chromosomal abnormality.* (PHS Publication No. 2103). Washington, D.C.: U.S. Government Printing Office.

Neisser, U. (1967). *Cognitive psychology.* Englewood Cliffs: Prentice-Hall.

Newton, I. (1946). *Sir Isaac Newton's mathematical principles of natural philosophy and his system of the world.* (A. Motts, tr. [1729]; F. Cajori, reviser). Berkeley, University of California Press. (Original work published 1729)

Observer. (1970). Innate intelligence: Another genetic avatar. *The Psychological Record, 20,* 123-130.

Ornstein, R. E. (1985). *Psychology: The study of human experience.* Orlando, Fla.: Harcourt Brace Jovanovich.

Pavlov, I. (1927). *Conditioned reflexes: An investigation of the physiological activity of the cerebral cortex.* (G. V. Anrep, Trans. and Ed.). London: Oxford University Press.

Penfield, W. (1975). *The mystery of the mind.* Princeton, N.J.: Princeton University Press.

Poincaré, H. (1946). *The foundations of science.* New York: Garrison, (Original work published 1913)

Popplestone, J. A. (1978). Once more, dear friends. *Contemporary Psychology, 23,* 142-151.

Pratt, C. C. (1929). Faculty psychology. *The Psychological Review, 36,* 141-171.

Price, L. (1954). *Dialogues of Alfred North Whitehead as recorded by Lucien Price.* Boston: Little, Brown & Co.

Pronko, N. H. (1969). *Panorama of psychology.* Belmont, Calif.: Brooks/Cole.

Pronko, N. H. (1980). *Psychology from the standpoint of an interbehaviorist.* Monterey, Calif.: Brooks/Cole.

Rachlin, H. A. (1977). A review of M. J. Mahoney's *Cognition and behavior modification. Journal of Applied Behavior Analysis, 10,* 369-374.

Ramey, E. R. (1973). Sex hormones and executive ability. *Annals of the New York Academy of Sciences, 208,* 237-245.

Ranson, S. W. (1942). *The anatomy of the nervous system.* Philadelphia: Saunders.

Rapoport, A. (1953). *Operational philosophy.* New York: Harper.

Ratner, S., Altman, J., & Wheeler, J. E. (Eds.). (1964). *John Dewey and Arthur Bentley: A philosophical correspondence.* New Brunswick, N.J.: Rutgers University Press.

Remley, M. L. (1980). *Women in sport: A guide to information sources.* Detroit: Gale Research Company.

Rokeach, M. (1964). *The three Christs of Ypsilanti.* New York: Alfred A. Knopf.

Rose, S. (1980). "It's only human nature": The sociobiologist's fairyland. In A. Montagu (Ed.), *Sociobiology examined* (pp. 158-197). New York: Oxford University Press.

Rousseau, J. J. (1979). *Émile; or, On Education.* (Introduction, Translation, and notes by Allan Bloom). New York: Basic Books.

Schank, R. C., with Childers, P. G. (1984). *The cognitive computer.* Reading, Mass.: Addison-Wesley Publishing Co.

Schonberg, H. C. (1970). *The lives of the great composers.* New York: W. W. Norton.

Schwartz, J. (1962). The pernicious influence of mathematics on science. In E. Nagel, P. Suppes & A. Tarski, *Logic, methodology and philosophy of science* (pp. 356-360). Stanford, Calif.: Stanford University Press.

Scriven, M. (1970). Explanations, predictions, and laws. In B. A. Brody (Ed.), *Readings in the philosophy of science* (pp. 88-104). Englewood Cliffs, N.J.: Prentice-Hall.

Seamon, J. D. (Ed.). (1980). *Human memory: Contemporary readings.* New York: Oxford University Press.

Secord, P. F., & Jourard, S. M. (1953). The appraisal of body-cathexis: Body-cathexis and the self. *Journal of Consulting Psychology, 17,* 343-347.

Sheldon, W. H. (1954). *Atlas of men: A guide for somatotyping the adult male at all ages.* New York: Harper and Row.

Shute, C. (1941). *The psychology of Aristotle: An analysis of the living being.* New York: Columbia University Press.

Sidman, M. (1960). *Tactics of scientific research.* New York: Basic Books.

Siegler, M. & Osmond, H. (1974). *Models of madness, models of medicine.* New York: Macmillan.

Simons, G. (1983). *Are computers alive?* Boston: Birkhauser.

Skinner, B. F. (1938). *The behavior of organisms.* New York: Appleton-Century-Crofts.

Skinner, B. F. (1953). *Science and human behavior.* New York: Macmillan.

Skinner, B. F. (1959). *Cumulative record.* New York: Appleton-Century-Crofts.

Skinner, B. F. (1971). *Beyond freedom and dignity.* New York: Alfred A. Knopf.

Skinner, B. F. (1978). *Reflections on behaviorism and society.* Englewood Cliffs: Prentice-Hall.

Skorpen, E. (1965). The whole man. *Main Currents in Modern Thought, 22,* 10-16.

Smart, J. J. C. (Ed.). (1964). *Problems of space and time.* New York: Macmillan.

Smith, J. D. (1985). *Minds made feeble: The myth and legacy of the Kallikaks.* Rockville, Md.: Aspen Systems Corporation.

Smith, S. B. (1983). *The great mental calculators: The psychology, methods, and lives of calculating prodigies, past and present.* New York: Columbia University Press.

Spence, M., & DeCasper, A. J. (1982). *Human fetuses perceive maternal speech.* Paper presented at the International Conference on Infant Studies, Austin, Texas.

Stineman, E. (1979). *Women's studies: A recommended core bibliography.* Littleton, Colo.: Libraries Unlimited.

Strother, R. (1955, July 23). The concentrations of Isaac Newton. *Saturday Review, 38,* 7, 25-26.

Suzuki, D. T. (1959). Preface to B. L. Suzuki, *Mahayana Buddhism.* London: Allen & Unwin.

Suzuki, S. (1969). *Nurtured by love.* New York: Exposition Press.

Suzuki, S. (1973). The law of ability and the "mother tongue method" of education. ʳerpts of a talk given to the Japan Institute of Educational Psychology. Aᵥ ailable at the Talent Education Institute, Matsumoto, Japan.

Szasz, T. S. (1957). The problem of psychiatric nosology. *American Journal of Psychiatry, 114,* 405-413.

Szasz, T. S. (1961). *The myth of mental illness.* New York: Hoeber-Harper.

Szasz, T. S. (1966). Mental illness is a myth. *The New York Times Magazine,* June 12, 30, 90-92.

Szasz, T. S. (1984). *The therapeutic state.* Buffalo, N.Y.: Prometheus Books.

Tanner, J. M. (1978). *Foetus into man: Physical growth from conception to maturity.* Cambridge, Mass.: Harvard University Press.

Theobald, D. W. (1968). *An introduction to the philosophy of science.* London: Methuen & Co.

Thomas, M. (1951). Sexual symbolism in industry. *International Journal of Psychoanalysis, 32,* 128-133.

Thomson, G. P. (1966). *J. J. Thomson: Discoverer of the electron.* Garden City, N.Y.: Doubleday.

Titus, H. H., & Smith, M. S. (1974). *Living issues in philosophy* (6th Ed.). New York: Van Nostrand.

Toulmin, S. (1963). *Foresight and understanding: An enquiry into the aims of science.* New York: Harper & Row.

Turbayne, C. M. (1970). *The myth of metaphor* (rev. ed.). Columbia: University of South Carolina Press.

Van Kaam, A. (1970). Assumptions in psychology. In D. P. Schultz (Ed.), *The science of psychology: Critical reflections* (pp. 24-29). New York: Appleton-Century-Crofts.

Walizer, M. H., & Wienir, P. L. (1978). *Research methods and analysis: Searching for relationships.* New York: Harper & Row.

Walker, K. (1955). *The story of medicine.* New York: Oxford University Press.

Wann, T. W. (Ed.). (1964). *Behaviorism and phenomenology.* Chicago: University of Chicago Press.

Warren, H. C. (1934). *Dictionary of psychology.* New York: Houghton Mifflin Company.

Washburn, S. L. (1978). Animal behavior and social anthropology. In M. S. Gregory, A. Silvers & D. Sutch (Eds.), *Sociobiology and human nature* (pp. 53-74). San Francisco: Jossey-Bass.

Washburn, S. L. (1980). Human behavior and the behavior of other animals. In A. Montagu (Ed.), *Sociobiology examined*, pp. 254-281. New York: Oxford University Press.

Weiner, B., Runquist, W., Runquist, P. A., Raven, B. H., Meyer, W. J., Leiman, A., Kutscher, C. L., Kleinmuntz, B. & Haber, R. N. (1977). *Discovering psychology.* Chicago: Science Research Associates.

Weiss, P. A. (1965). A cell is not an island entire of itself. *Perspectives in biology and medicine.* Winter, 1971, 182-205.

Weiss, P. A. (1969). The living system: Determination stratified. *Studium Generale, 22,* 361-400.

Weiss, P. A. (1973). *The science of life.* Mount Kisco, N.Y.: Futura Publishing Co.

Wesman, A. G. (1968). Intelligent testing. *American Psychologist, 23,* 267-274.

Wessells, M. G. (1982). *Cognitive psychology.* New York: Harper & Row.

White, L. A. (1949). *The science of culture.* New York: Grove Press.

Whitehead, A. N. (1944). *Science and the modern world: Lowell Lectures, 1925.* New York: Macmillan. (Original work published 1925)

Whitehead, A. N. (1957). *The concept of nature.* Ann Arbor: University of Michigan Press. (Original work published 1920)

Whitrow, G. (1961). *The natural philosophy of time.* New York: Harper & Row.

Wilson, E. O. (1978). *On human nature.* Cambridge, Mass.: Harvard University Press.

Wohlsetter, A. (1964). Technology, prediction and disorder. *Bulletin of Atomic Scientists, 20,* 11-15.

Wolstenholme, G. E. W., & O'Connor, M. (Eds.). (1969). *Foetal autonomy: A Ciba foundation symposium.* London: J. & A. Churchill.

Woodbridge, F. J. E. (1965). *Nature and mind.* New York: Russell & Russell.

Woodger, J. H. (1929). *Biological principles: A critical study.* London: Kegan Paul, Trench, Trubner & Co.

Woodger, J. H. (1956). *Physics, psychology and medicine.* Cambridge: At the University Press.

Woolf, V. (1929). *A room of one's own.* New York: Harcourt, Brace and World.

World's shortest light pulse. (1985, January 5). *Science News,* 9.

Zimbardo, P. G. (1979). *Psychology and life* (10th Ed.). Glenview, Ill.: Scott, Foresman and Co.

Zimbardo, P. G. (1985). *Psychology and life* (11th Ed.). Glenview, Ill.: Scott, Foresman and Co.

NAME INDEX

SUBJECT INDEX

AI (Artificial Intelligence), 1-4; brain as a model for, 2; defined, 1; evaluation of, 2
Ability, 72-74
Aptitude, 72-74
Aristotle, 8-11; and Greek culture, 7-9; and Medieval culture, 10-11
Assumptions, 12-13, 154-55, 186

Behavior: locus of, 67
Behavior segment, 14-15; and behavior situation, 15; defined, 15
Behaviorism, 87-88
Brain: a classical view of, 16-19; criticism of, 17-19; as model for computers, 121; a modern view of, 20-23; other cultures' views of, 17; as a participating factor, 22-23

Capacity, 72-74
Cause and effect, 24-26, 70
Cause-effect thinking in experimentation, 53
Certainty, the quest for, 160-61
Cognition. *See* Cognitive psychology
Cognitive psychology, 27-29; defined, 27; Skinner's criticism of, 28-29
Contingential behavior, 47-48
Control in science, 5-6
Cultural or Shared Reactions, 30-33

Data, 34-35
Dating, 133
Description as explanation, 55-56
Disease: bodily, 36; mental, 37-38
Dualism, 87
Dynamic view of nature, 40-41

Ecological psychology, 42-43
Ecology, 42

Eldridge Cleaver, Case of, 209
Elementalism, 132
Embryology, psychological aspects of, 45-46
Emergency reactions, 47-48
Environment, 75-78
Epilogue, 245-48
Etc., 133
Event: defined, 50; Whitehead's definition of, 50-51
Explanation: as description, 55-56; Skinner's definition of, 56

Fact, 57
Faculty, 72-74
Fallacy of dogmatic finality, 58
Fallacy of misplaced concreteness, 40, 59-60, 192
Fashions: in geology, 61-62; in medicine, 62; in music, 61; in physics, 62-63
Field theory: in physics, 65; in psychology, 66-67, 70-71
Force, 68
Free will vs. determinism, 69-71

Genius, 72-74
Giftedness, 72-74

Heredity: Jenning's definition of, 75-7o; Weiss's definition of, 76-77
Heredity vs. environment, 75-78
Holism. *See* Reductionism and holism
Human nature, limits of, 106-8; during Renaissance, 106-7; in our time, 107-8
Hyphens, semantic use of, 134

Idiosyncratic action, 79-80
Implicit action, 211-13; field view of,

About the Author

N. H. PRONKO is Professor Emeritus of Psychology at Wichita State University, Kansas. His earlier books include the *Textbook of Abnormal Psychology, Panorama of Psychology,* and *Psychology from the Standpoint of an Interbehaviorist.* He has also contributed numerous articles and papers to such journals as the *Journal of Experimental Psychology,* the *Journal of Psychology,* the *Psychological Bulletin,* and the *Journal of Applied Psychology.*